METHOD, MEANING AND REVELATION

The Meaning and Function of Revelation in
Bernard Lonergan's *Method in Theology*

Neil Ormerod

University Press of America, ® Inc.
Lanham • New York • Oxford

Library of Congress Cataloging-in-Publication Data

Ormerod, Neil.
Method, meaning, and revelation : the meaning and function of revelation in
Bernard Lonergan's Method in theology / Neil Ormerod.
p. cm.
Includes bibliographical references and index.
l. Revelation—History of doctrines—20th century. 2. Lonergan, Bernard J.
F.—Contributions in theology of revelation. 3. Lonergan, Bernard J. F.
Method in theology. I. Title.
BT126.5.076   2000   230'.2'01—dc21   00-041175 CIP

ISBN 0-7618-1752-2 (cloth: alk. ppr.)
ISBN 0-7618-1753-0 (pbk: alk. ppr.)

I would like to dedicate this book to my wife Thea and our four children, John, Chris, Anneliese and Michael, for their patience while I undertook the writing of this thesis.

CONTENT

PREFACE

I still vividly remember my first encounter with the work of Fr Bernard Lonergan s.j. Fr Fred Crowe s.j. was visiting Australia, at the invitation of Fr Peter Beer s.j. He was giving a series of public lectures and gave one at St John's College, Sydney University. I was impressed with what he had to say, so I sought out a copy of *Insight* and started to read it. I remember reading the introduction and thinking to myself, "Either this guy is mad, or I must read this book". Six months later, I had finished *Insight* and begun reading *Method*. All that was over fourteen years ago. I have never looked back, nor regretted the fundamental changes that reading brought about, including a career change from mathematics to theology.

This thesis is the culmination of those long years of interest and research. Throughout all my theological studies and teaching, Lonergan's work has been the source of constant inspiration. Now, I offer this thesis as my contribution to furthering Lonergan studies. I shall leave to others to judge the value and significance of this contribution.

In particular, I hope that my suggestion that Lonergan's work should be seen as a contribution to a tradition of rationality initiated, sustained and prolonged by revelation, will shed new light on the nature of the Lonerganian project. Using the notion of a tradition of rationality, drawn from the writings of Alasdair MacIntyre, I felt able to locate Lonergan's project in a way which overcame various criticisms of either excessive rationalism or subjective fideism. This idea that revelation established such a tradition was itself drawn from my analysis of the carriers and functions of meaning Lonergan identifies in *Method in Theology*.

Anyone who has undertaken a project such as this is aware of their acute dependence on others. I would like especially to thank Fr Tony Kelly c.s.s.r., my supervisor, who has had the difficult task of guiding me through this arduous assignment. Tony has been the source of inspiration, gentle but insistent advice and sound assurance. I have learnt much about writing in general, and thesis writing in particular.

I also thank Fr Frank Fletcher m.s.c., my associate supervisor, particularly for his contribution to the Doran study group we ran at St Paul's National Seminary. Together with Fr Greg Moses and Mr Peter Madden, we worked through Robert Doran's *Theology and the Dialectic of History*. Many of the ideas in this thesis were born and first explored in that study group. I also thank Mr Peter Madden for the gift of his personal Lonergan collection to me, a decision he has probably lived to regret.

I thank, too, my employer at the time of writing this work, St Paul's National Seminary and its rector, Fr Paul Cashen m.s.c. The seminary has been a constant source of encouragement in my studies, providing resources and much needed study leave, for me to complete the project in a reasonable time frame.

Finally, I would like to thank my wife, Thea, and my children, John, Chris, Anneliese and Michael, to whom I dedicate this work. Together we have endured the stresses of my studies among the various crises of family life. I thank my family for its patience and forbearance, as I have worked to complete this task. We have all grown stronger and wiser.

NEIL ORMEROD

ACKNOWLEDGMENTS

The author would like to thank the following for permission to quote from the works listed:

From NATURE OF DOCTRINE by George A. Lindbeck. © 1984 George A. Lindbeck. Used by permission of Westminister John Knox Press.

From the following works by Bernard Lonergan: INSIGHT, METHOD IN THEOLOGY, A SECOND COLLECTION, A THIRD COLLECT-ION, used by permission of the Lonergan Estate.

From THREE RIVAL VERSIONS OF MORAL ENQUIRY by Alasdair MacIntyre © 1990 Alasdair MacIntrye. Used by permission of the publishers, Notre Dame University Press and Gerald Duckworth and Co. Ltd.

CHAPTER ONE:
THE STATE OF THE QUESTION

1.1 Lonergan, Method and Revelation

Bernard Lonergan stands as one of the leading figures in Catholic culture of the twentieth century. His writings cover an enormous range of matters, from mathematical and scientific concerns, to philosophical and theological issues, to his final researches into economics. Throughout this vast array of intellectual endeavour the one constant has been a concern for method. How, then, does Lonergan understand the place of method in theology and other disciplines? As Lonergan conceived it, method is not "a set of rules that, even when followed blindly by anyone, none the less yield satisfactory results."[1] Rather, it is "a normative pattern of recurrent and related operations, yielding cumulative and progressive results."[2]

In this brief overview I shall attempt to indicate the central place which method, both in theology and more broadly, has had in Lonergan's intellectual development. This concern with method began in his earliest years of serious study. His very first published article, entitled "The form of mathematical inference" (1928), dealt with Euclidean method in geometry, and already it prefigures his interest in "insight into phantasm."[3] At this stage he had even toyed with the idea of studying a course in methodology, but was refused permission by his superior.[4]

In the introduction to his first major theological work, *Gratia Operans*, Lonergan bemoaned the lack of any methodical approach for the resolution of theological disputations. Faced with the interminable disputes between Banezian and Molinist interpretations of Thomas Aquinas, he writes:

> Unless a writer can assign a *method* that of itself tends to greater objectivity than those hitherto employed, his undertaking may well be regarded as superfluous.[5] [emphasis added]

There follows perhaps his first attempt to develop a method for settling issues in "speculative theology", based on an *a priori* scheme of development in speculative thought.

The next major advance in his project of developing an adequate method in theology was his study of human understanding, first in an historical study of the thought of Thomas Aquinas on the Trinitarian processions, published as *Verbum: Word and Idea in Aquinas*, and then in his major opus, *Insight: A Study of Human Understanding*. A concern for cognitional questions did not begin with his study of Aquinas, but, after "spending years reaching up to the mind of Aquinas"[6], it certainly came to an appropriate term. Understanding, or, more correctly, an understanding of understanding, becomes central to the whole methodological enterprise. As Lonergan writes:

> Thoroughly understand what it is to understand, and not only will you understand the broad lines of all there is to be understood but also you will possess a fixed base, an invariant pattern, opening upon all further developments of understanding.[7]

From the time of its inception he had always thought of *Insight* as preparatory to a further study on theological method. Twice in the epilogue he speaks of his work as a contribution to method in theology and he spells out, for several pages, the nature of that contribution.[8] Further, he indicates in the first chapter of *Method in Theology* that, unless one has engaged in the slow "process of self-appropriation" by struggling with "some such book as *Insight*", one will find "not merely this chapter but the whole book about as illuminating as a blind man finds a lecture on color."[9]

After completing *Insight*, Lonergan spent several years from 1953-1965, lecturing at the Gregorian University in Rome. Apart from undergraduate courses in Christology and Trinity he ran a number of graduate seminars on theological method.[10] Fred Crowe, the renowned Lonergan scholar, has described this period as one of "experiments in method", where Lonergan attempted various "solutions" to the problem of theological method.[11] The key problem which he sought to solve was that of finding a place for historical studies in theology. As he stated in an essay written just after the end of this period:

> [Theology] has become largely an empirical science ... It has be-come empirical in the sense that Scripture and Tradition now supply not premises, but data. The data has to be viewed in its historical perspective ... this shift ... has come to stay.[12]

In fact, this on-going attempt to find a place for history in theo-logical method highlights another life-long interest of Lonergan, that of developing a philosophy of history. The origins of this interest pre-date his years "reaching up to the mind of Aquinas."

The key breakthrough occurred in 1965, when he first established the eight-fold structure which was to form the basis of the theological method. The mature fruits of this life-long labour were published in 1972 as *Method in Theology*, a work whose significance can be meas-ured in terms of the many doctoral theses, learned articles, books and theological projects it has launched.

Finally, his concern with method did not stop with the publication of *Method in Theology*. In the post-*Method* era we see a number of significant essays which extend and apply his methodological ap-proach. Especially noteworthy are his essays "Healing and Creating in History" and "Christology Today: Methodological Reflections", both published in the collection of essays, *A Third Collection*.[13]

This brief overview is perhaps enough to establish the central place which method in general, and, specifically, method in theology, has had in Lonergan's intellectual life.

1.2 The Problem: Revelation and Lonergan's Method

I want now to contrast this central place of theological method with the place given in Lonergan's works to the notion of revelation. Why should we expect there to be a connection between the two issues of method and revelation?

I would suggest that there must be some correlation between method in theology and revelation since theology is, at least in some sense, reflection on revelation. Because of this correlation there must be some form of "structural isomorphism" between the object under study and the method for studying it.[14]

On the other hand, it is a perceived lack of such a correlation that has been the basis of significant criticism levelled against Lonergan's method from figures such as Karl Rahner and Tony Kelly.[15] Rahner has complained that Lonergan's proposal was not a method for theology but a method appropriate to any of the human sciences.[16] For his part, Kelly has expressed concerns about the lack of a Christological focus to Lonergan's method. "How does this theological method take faith in Christ into its inner vitality?", Kelly asks.[17] There seems to be no place for the content of revelation, and specifically Christian revelation, to act as a shaping principle in Lonergan's conception of the doing of theology.

Further, one can admit that, while method has been a central concern for Lonergan, there has not been as obvious a concern with the notion of revelation. As another of Lonergan's critics, J.P. Mackey has noted, "This is not a subject to which he himself has devoted much specific attention."[18] Mackey saw this lack as a difficulty. Even Fred Crowe has conceded that "Lonergan did not speak much about revelation", while noting however that:

> it is clearly at the basis of his theology that God once in a while said something doctrinal, not only about creation but about the divine being too.[19]

As Crowe has expressed it, Lonergan clearly assumes that God does communicate something to humanity, that it is true, in the cognitive sense, and that the truth of that communication is mediated in the doctrines of the Church. Mackey, too, has noted that "special divine revelation is often tacitly assumed to be a source of truth" in Lonergan's writings.[20] Nonetheless, consulting the indices of Lonergan's various works uncovers scant references to entries on revelation – a page here or there, but certainly not a sustained interest in the topic.

What is more, in *Method* Lonergan lists a number of questions which "are not methodological but theological." Among these he cites "questions on revelation."[21] Revelation thus appears to be a categorical question, whereas his methodological approach is transcendental. In his method this transcendental basis establishes the critical foundation within which revelation is to be understood. The question then arises:

How can a methodology which is based on a transcendental analysis of human consciousness hope to incorporate the concrete particularity of Jesus Christ, the Nazarene rabbi? For Lonergan, such questions are not simply methodological; they are theological in the strict sense. For his critics, the very real concern is that this particularity of revelation will be absorbed by the generalised transcendental method Lonergan has employed.

To put the matter more sharply, can there be such a clear distinction between reflections on theological method and the content of theology? If the former is an heuristic anticipation of the later, then clearly, options in the former are, in a sense, already theological. As Avery Dulles comments:

> Granted one's views on authority will necessarily depend on one's theory of revelation, Christology, and church, I am convinced that method in theology cannot be adequately treated without some attention to these questions. In theology as in other sciences, method and content are dialectically interdependent.[22]

The same point was made more forcefully by Donald Keefe, a strong critic of Lonergan's whole project:

> Theological method is such only in this concrete posture of conversion to the historical revelation in the historical Church; it can no more prescind from the concreteness and particularity of this conversion than it can from conversion itself ... [method] must begin and end with the concreteness of the Christian conversion to the explicitly Christian faith; a dehistoricized method of theology is immediately and irredeemably autonomous, incapable of that reflection upon the historical faith which Lonergan's method intends.[23]

Even in terms of his own project in *Method*, the distinction between methodology and content is not as clear as Lonergan seeks to maintain. One could argue that the whole project of *Method* is itself a significant contribution to the functional specialty he calls foundations. He has indicated that one task of foundations is the development of general and special categories for doing theology.[24] Much of the early chapters of *Method* are engaged in developing general categories, on the good, on meaning, and on religion. Already in these chapters, Lonergan is making theological options within the specialty of foundations.

While some have criticised Lonergan for not attending sufficiently to the content of revelation in shaping his methodology, there are those who have criticised his whole methodological project for incorporating various theological, in fact dogmatic, *a priori*.[25] For example, Lonergan himself has noted the influence of Bernard Leeming's course on Christology in his acceptance of a real distinction between "essence" and "existence."[26] This distinction was later to become the distinction between understanding and judgment in *Insight*. He also regularly cites Romans 5:5 and I Tim 2:4 in his "transcendental" account of religious experience. Yet these citations are clearly particular accounts drawn from Christian sources. Doran has also drawn attention to critics who felt that the central place given to conversion, in the later writings of Lonergan, was a retreat from his previous hard-headed intellectualism, so evident in *Insight*, and represented a capitulation to soft-headed religious sentiment and conservative dogmatic *a priori*.[27] He writes:

> ... some of Lonergan's most devoted students were not prepared for his talk of conversion, of falling in love with God, of religious fidelity and attunement, at the time when be began to disclose the contents of what would become *Method in Theology*. Some of these students have perhaps not recovered from their surprise, indeed their disappointment, at what seemed to them to be a capitulation of a rigorous critical intellectualism to the softheadedness of religious piety, or even an invasion into foundational thinking of a doctrinal commitment that, in their view, was to be either justified or repudiated on strictly cognitional-theoretic, critical grounds.[28]

Thus, there are critics claiming that the content of Christian revelation has not had sufficient input in structuring Lonergan's method, and there are those who have claimed that it has had too much. Neither claim can be addressed without resort to a clearer understanding of the nature of revelation than is available from commonsense notions, and so it is time to turn our attention to the larger theological context provided by various theologies of revelation.

1.3 The Larger Theological Context

Now while theological method has attracted some interest among theologians, there has been far more significant interest in theological literature on the whole question of revelation. This interest has been part of the whole review of what has in the past been called fundamental theology, and is now sometimes referred to as foundational theology.[29] Thus, at this stage, I would like to consider the significant contributions to the topic of revelation from some leading theologians. I shall also relate them, in a preliminary way, to issues raised by Lonergan's writings, particularly *Method in Theology*.

1.3.1 Dulles' *Models of Revelation*

One of the more standard references in theological circles to the question of revelation is Avery Dulles' book, *Models of Revelation*.[30] In this work Dulles presents five different models of revelation, as found in modern theological literature, and then goes on to develop his own model of symbolic mediation. Here, the term *model* refers more to "ideal types", built around a paradigmatic example which illustrates the type.[31] Dulles does not claim that any particular theological author exactly fits into any particular model, though he does maintain their general usefulness in clarifying questions on revelation. I will briefly describe and comment upon each model presented by Dulles and show how each model relates to aspects of Lonergan's approach.[32]

Revelation as Doctrine

In Dulles' first model the paradigmatic examples of revelation are the Bible and/or Church teaching. Revelation is conceived in terms of "clear propositional statements attributed to God."[33] Such propositions are to be found in the Bible (especially for evangelical Christians), and in the pronouncements of the Church magisterium (for Catholics). They are direct verbal communication from God (or at least should be treated as such).[34] Aspects of this position are reflected in Vatican I, which speaks of the written and unwritten traditions of the New Testament coming "from the mouth of Christ himself" or by "dictation from the Holy Spirit" (DS 3006). Within this model the infallibility and inerrancy of either Scripture or Church teaching is a central issue.

Without this there can be no guarantee that the originally revealed word will be faithfully transmitted.

This model makes a sharp distinction between natural and supernatural revelation. Natural revelation is either possible but inadequate (the Catholic position) or simply impossible (the evangelical position). Both claim the need for a special supernatural revelation as necessary for salvation.

In general, there has been a wholesale rejection of this model within contemporary theology. The reasons for this rejection are twofold.

Firstly, it fails to come to grips with the question of meaning. Propositions are fixed, but, as cultures change, the meaning given to propositions will vary. How can we ensure that meanings are preserved within changing cultures if we have canonized past formalized propositions? Modern hermeneutical studies raise profound questions about the relationships between meaning, authorial intention and expression in the process of communication. Inasmuch as this model fails to address such questions of meaning, one would have to say that it is hermeneutically naive.

Secondly, it simply does not do justice to modern historical and scriptural studies. The fierce battles which took place as the early Church struggled to reach the doctrinal definition of the great Church Councils were not simply a matter of making explicit what as implicit. Far more often they were raging conflicts about the central meanings of Christian faith. The a-historical approach which this model uses simply does not stand up to historical scrutiny.

There are certainly those who would place Lonergan's work within this paradigm.[35] All his writings give evidence of a strong commitment to the place of dogmas and the authority of Scripture within theology. In his writings he has defended the dogmatic definition of the Assumption[36], and, most emphatically, the definitions of Nicea and Chalcedon.[37] Further, Church dogmas find their place in the normative phase of *Method*, in the functional specialty of doctrines.[38]

On the other hand, Lonergan's approach can hardly be labelled hermeneutically naive. He has written extensively on the problems of historical consciousness, particularly as it relates to questions of meaning.[39] Some would go so far as to argue that his life work was a matter of bringing historical consciousness into the heart of theology.[40] Thus, while his work has some points of contact with Dulles' propositional model, it can not be contained within it. Something more is needed. Perhaps the question of history provides a clue.

Revelation as History

In Dulles' second model revelation is conceived in terms of God's mighty deeds, especially those recorded in the Bible. The paradigmatic examples here are the Exodus, and the Resurrection of Jesus. Dulles considers two forms of this model. The first is the salvation history model, supported by authors such as Oscar Cullman[41] and Jean Daniélou.[42] This model sees God as acting within a certain sphere of history, which is designated salvation history, as reported in the Bible. It is the task of the prophet to alert people to the presence of God acting in history, and so of distinguishing salvation history from a mere secular history. This model has largely fallen from favour because of its rigid distinction between the secular and divine spheres of history.

The second form of this model is found in the early writings of Wolfhart Pannenberg.[43] Rejecting the separation between secular and salvation history, Pannenberg sees revelation in terms of universal history. Thus all human history is salvation history. Not only is revelation historical, but all history is revelatory.

Pannenberg spells out his position in terms of seven theses on revelation. While it is not necessary to delve into all these theses here, I will refer to one which has caused considerable controversy. In his third thesis, Pannenberg states:

> In distinction from special manifestations of the deity, the historical revelation is open to anyone who has eyes to see. It has a universal character.[44]

On the one hand, he rejects the notion of special manifestations of God which can directly communicate some type of special knowledge, as the propositional model seems to imply. On the other hand, he conceives revelation as historical events which are verifiable, using strict historical techniques, by anyone "who has the eyes to see." Indeed, Pannenberg goes on to state that,

> Nothing must mute the fact that all truth lies right before the eyes, and that its appropriation is a natural consequence of the facts. There is no need for any additional perfection of man as though he

could not focus on the 'supernatural' truth with his normal equipment for knowing.[45]

Pannenberg is trying to rule out any need for faith in arriving at the "facts" of revelation, in order to insure its universal accessibility.[46]
Pannenberg's emphasis on universal history is a clear advance on both the propositional model and the salvation history model. Also, he gives a definitive place for the person of Jesus within his model. However, his emphasis on historical method does seem to ground faith in the products of scholarly research. Further, there is an implicit empiricism in his phrase, "anyone who has the eyes to see." Just how open to universal validation is the work of historical scholarship? Not everyone has the required expertise, though they may have "eyes to see."

As with Dulles' propositional model, there are connections that can be made here with the work of Lonergan. From his earliest writings Lonergan displayed an interest in history and in the development of methodological categories for understanding history.[47] Further, as his thought develops, Lonergan begins to speak of revelation as an entry of divine meaning into human history.[48] His writings, particularly *Insight*, also provide a framework for rendering intelligible a universally efficacious divine providence. Such a framework would allow us to see history as replete with divine action. Indeed, Crowe has picked up this theme in his book, *Theology of the Christian Word*.[49] Because of these connections I shall develop a more extensive comparison between Pannenberg and Lonergan, focusing on the question of history, in Chapter 5 of this thesis.

However, once again, Lonergan's approach cannot be contained within the model that Dulles elucidates here. While Lonergan is interested in the categories of history, and develops them to a high degree, his method is basically transcendental. It reflects a "turn to the subject", to human interiority. As his thought developed, we see him becoming more interested in the categories of religious experience; and so, we should turn in this direction to further enlighten our understanding of Lonergan's approach to revelation.

Revelation as Inner Experience

In this third model Dulles conceives of revelation in terms of mystical experience, that is, a "privileged interior experience of grace or communion with God."[50] Here the paradigmatic example of revelation is the mystic in his/her cell. As with the previous model, nothing "objective" is said to be revealed, certainly no revealed doctrines. What the mystic experiences is God, and God cannot be reduced to any mere doctrine or definition. Any expression which arises out of the experience is secondary. It is meant simply to be a means into the original experience. Thus, George Tyrrell speaks of doctrines as a "protective husk round the kernel of apostolic revelation", while Evelyn Underhill claims that since the expression is inadequate, "the degree of its inadequacy is of secondary importance."[51]

Historically, this model was important in the Modernist movement within Catholicism at the turn of the nineteenth century. It sought to ground religious faith in personal experience and offered many people the opportunity for real mystical experiences. It shifted religious authority away from ecclesial institution and towards the individual.

The main weakness of this model is that, in practice, it is prone to elitism. While, in theory, anyone can be the subject of mystical experience, few are, at least regularly. Most of us are left with so called secondary formulations. Such secondary formulations may often reflect diametrically opposed positions within different religious traditions. For example, Christian mystical experience is interpreted in theistic terms, that is, as experience of God, while Buddhist mystical experience may well be interpreted in non-theistic or a-theistic terms. Again, Christians tend to interpret their experience in Trinitarian terms, while Jews and Moslems remain strictly monotheistic. The danger here is that revelation becomes an individualistic and privatized phenomenon. In this way the model fails to come to grips with the social dimension of revelation. It does not advert to the fact that revelation establishes a community held together by common meanings and values.

We must also ask how this model deals with the person of Jesus. Is Jesus' own mystical experience simply one among many, perhaps quantitively different, but qualitatively the same? Or does Jesus represent something totally new in the area of religious experience? In this regard, it is significant to note that this model blurs the distinction between natural and supernatural revelation, seeing them merely as a matter of degree.[52]

Now it is clear that, in Lonergan's writings, the question of religious experience becomes increasingly important. He has drawn attention to his own failure in *Insight* to raise the question of religious experience in his account of the existence of God, an oversight he sought to correct in *Method in Theology*.[53] In *Method* he speaks of religious experience as "being in love in an unrestricted fashion"[54], and of faith as "knowledge born of religious love."[55] He draws on the researches of Friedrich Heiler to find common elements in a variety of world religions.[56] As we shall see later, the Protestant theologian George Lindbeck locates Lonergan's work within what he calls an "experiential expressivist model" of religion.[57]

Still, Lonergan's work cannot be contained within the "inner experience" model. Not only must we account for the previous elements of dogma and history, but we must note that, even in his dealing with religious experience, Lonergan does not present us with a simplistic appeal to "experience." His account of religious experience is immediately followed by observations on the dialectical nature of religious development.[58] Religious development and expression admit of a variety of dialectical distortions arising from human bias, from unauthenticity. If we are to appreciate Lonergan's contribution we must allow for a more dialectical approach to the question of revelation.

Revelation as Dialectic Presence

The fourth model that Dulles considers is that of revelation as dialectic presence. Of those he develops, this model is the most difficult to understand. The main examples he gives are the leading Protestant theologian, Karl Barth[59], and his Catholic counterpart, Hans Urs von Balthasar.[60] In this model "God encounters the human subject when it pleases him by means of a word in which faith recognizes him to be present." This word "simultaneously reveals and conceals the divine presence", since, even in revelation, God remains transcendent and wholly other.[61] The paradigmatic example of revelation for this theology is the simultaneous revelation and concealment of God in the crucifixion of Jesus.

The main strength of the model is that it is explicitly Trinitarian. This is particularly clear in the theology of Barth.[62] In revelation God speaks God's Word, which cannot be distinguished from God himself - God's Word is God. Further, the Spirit enables us to receive God's Word as God's Word, without reducing it to a merely human word.

Both Barth and von Balthasar have uncompromising positions when it comes to accepting God's revelation. For Barth, it is very important that we do not place ourselves in the position of judging God, since it is God who judges us. All we can do is accept God's revelation in faith. For von Balthasar, the radical unexpectedness of revelation "demands belief without allowing a moment's pause for reflection."[63]

However, there was also a negative side to this position. As an extreme stance, its end result is fideism, a faith without any ground other than the divine authority, without any reference to human reason. One must simply accept the claim to divine authority without question. It is of no matter that what is being believed may be absurd. Barth will claim, "Faith ... grips reason by the throat and strangles the beast"![64] Matthew Lamb notes that "a charge of theological fideism would be a compliment to Barth."[65] However, for von Balthasar, who operates within a Catholic framework, fideism is a real risk and it is not clear how he avoids it.

Now, as I have already indicated above, Lonergan subjects his exposition of religious experience to a dialectical critique. His accounts of dramatic, individual, group and general bias make it clear that he is aware of the depths of human sinfulness, and the distortions which afflict our grasp of the divine.[66] He also draws attention to the mysterious quality of religious experience which is "conscious without being known"[67], so that, in some sense, revelation both reveals and conceals. It is for these reasons that the functional specialty of dialectic plays an important, if not pivotal, role in Lonergan's theological method.

Still Lonergan's approach cannot be reduced to this single aspect of dialectic. Not only are there connections with the previous models that Dulles considers. There are further elements which do not quite fit in the models thus far. Dulles' next model helps to further fill out the picture.

Revelation as New Awareness

In this fifth model, revelation is conceived in terms of a change in the subjectivity of the human person, brought about by grace (or, equivalently in this model, by faith) which enables him/her to see things in a new light. Again, in this model nothing "objective" is revealed; there is no revealed truth. All that occurs is a new conscious state, which enables people to grasp what is already there to be grasped, if they had not been blinded by their own bias and sin. The paradigmatic example for this model is the prophet, who, in the light of his/her transformed consciousness, sees the suffering of the poor as the result of social injustice. The fact of suffering is always there to be seen, but it is only in the light of consciousness-transforming grace that the real meaning is grasped. Typical of this model is the position of Gregory Baum:

> The Christian message is not information about the divine, to be intellectually assimilated. It is rather salvational truth; it raises man's consciousness; it constitutes a new awareness in man through which he sees the world in a new light and commits himself to a new kind of action.[68]

Further, for Baum, traditional faith assertions can validly be translated into "sentences dealing with human possibilities promised to man and changes of consciousness offered to him."[69] Dulles places a number of contemporary theologians in this category. Perhaps the best know are Baum[70], Leslie Dewart[71] and Gabriel Moran.[72] He also notes common elements with the positions of Karl Rahner[73] and Paul Tillich.[74]

The strength of this model is that, of all the models, it takes seriously the Kantian question of the role of the subject in the constitution of knowledge. The subject does not passively receive any communication, secular or divine. It is, rather, the coming together of subject and object, a process in which the subject plays an active role in uncovering meaning. The model also shifts attention away from questions of cognitive content, towards questions of existential praxis.

However, the weakness of this model is that it underplays the "objective" side of revelation. It denies that there is any objective revelation, either in the form of revealed truths (as in the first model), or divine historical interventions (as in the second), or God in mystical experience (as in the third). While this may be appealing to some, it does come up against traditional beliefs about the nature of Jesus, of Scripture, and of Church dogmas. In particular, is Jesus simply the subject of a fully transformed human consciousness, or is he, in some sense, the definitive self-revelation of God?

As with the previous models, we can see points of contact between this account of revelation and Lonergan's writings, particularly with his emerging emphasis on conversion.[75] In *Method*, conversion, as a radical transformation of consciousness, becomes the pivotal point in his method, standing as it does between the positive and the normative phases of theology.[76] For Lonergan, the converted theologian is the foundation of theology, since the authenticity born of conversion is the only true guarantee of objectivity.[77]

However, as I have noted with each of the previous models, the model of new awareness provides us with only one aspect of Lonergan's approach. A thorough understanding must synthesise each of these elements which Dulles' models have brought to light if it is to encompass to totality of Lonergan's work. Perhaps we should now turn our attention to Dulles' own proposed synthesis to see if it can assist us.

The model of symbolic mediation.

Apart from the first, each of these models is an attempt to move beyond the obvious inadequacies of the previously prevalent "propositional model" of revelation. Yet each in its turn has its own significant difficulties, as we have suggested above. Dulles seeks to overcome these by developing what is, in fact, a further model, that of symbolic mediation. Dulles sees this model as providing a "dialectic retrieval" of the positive values of the other models, so that this new model will "sublate" the others.[78] He considers this as a more fruitful approach than either adopting one, eclectically picking bits and pieces from each, or providing a false harmonisation.

Dulles' starting point for the model of symbolic mediation is that,

> ... revelation never occurs in a purely interior experience or an unmediated encounter with God. It is always mediated through symbol – that is to say, through an externally perceived sign that works mysteriously on the human consciousness so as to suggest more than it can clearly describe or define. Revelatory symbols are those which express and mediate God's self-communication.[79]

Dulles draws on the work of a number of authors in the area of symbol, in particular Paul Ricoeur[80], Michael Polanyi[81] and Mircea Eliade[82], to give his account of the role of symbols significant depth. In particular, he notes that, according to these authors, symbols share a number of significant features with revelation. Firstly, they give a participatory, self-involving type of knowledge. Secondly, they have a transforming, healing effect upon the person. Thirdly, they have a powerful influence on our praxis. Finally, they put us in touch with realms of awareness not normally accessible to discursive, rational thought. It is easy to see how each of these features has a significant advantage over a purely cognitive understanding of revelation.[83]

Dulles then proceeds to indicate how this model incorporates the strengths of the previous models while overcoming some of their perceived weaknesses.

Concerning the first, Dulles sees symbols as giving existential depth to the purely cognitive meaning found in the propositional model. At the same time, doctrines provide an interpretive key to understanding revelatory symbols. "Christian doctrine sets necessary limits to the kinds of significance that can be found in the Christian symbol", so that doctrines enrich the meaning of symbols.[84] Further, given that "the symbol gives rise to thought" (cf. Paul Ricoeur), symbols are never without cognitive significance.

Concerning the historical model, Dulles observes a "profound affinity" between it and the symbolic approach. However, he affirms that the symbolic model provides important qualifications to the historical model. For the historical model, "revelation can be certainly know by rational inference from the nature of the events themselves."[85] On the other hand, the symbolic approach "denies that the deeds of God can count as revelation unless they are symbols of his presence."[86] The symbolic approach preserves the concreteness of the historical model. However,

> it does not demand that the events be of such a nature that their revelatory meaning can be strictly proved by academic research, but only that the religious inquirer be capable of discerning in them a divinely intended significance.[87]

This is not a dissimilar position to that of the salvation history model with its account of the role of the prophetic interpreter.

The symbolic model challenges the assumption of the inner experience model that there can be a directed unmediated experience of God in this life. Indeed, Dulles notes that some great Christian mystics have been very cautious in speaking about such an unmediated perception of God. He argues that the inner experience model "complements and enriches the symbolic approach", though he goes on:

> ... the experience of grace cannot be rightly interpreted ... without the help of symbols derived from the world known through sensory experience. Apart from such symbolic concretizations, the rarefied ecstasies of the mystic would not be sufficiently articulate to merit the name of revelation.[88]

The dialectic model shows some hostility to the notion of symbolic revelation. Dulles indicates that Barth was "fearful that the category of symbol, applied to revelation, might compromise the divine transcendence", and that a symbolic model might reduce Christ to "one symbol among many others."[89] Dulles acknowledges this as a real difficulty and tries to deal with it at a later stage of his work.[90]

Concluding his analysis, Dulles identifies a close connection between the notion of symbolic revelation and the new awareness model. He states:

> Since symbol ... invites participation, a revelation imparted through symbol ... tends to elicit a higher degree of spiritual activity. The plasticity of symbol gives it a power to speak to people of different sociocultural situations and to assure that relevance is not lost ... the symbolic mode of communication is favorable to interfaith dialogue.[91]

However, he also acknowledges that the symbolic model may not overcome the weaknesses of the new awareness model, such as "subjectivism, relativism and a reductionist humanism."

Again, we can make connections between the model which Dulles has developed and Lonergan's overall project. In *Method*, Lonergan gave a significant role to symbols in what he called the "internal communication" between heart, mind and body.[92] Further, because of their relationship to our affective responses to value, symbols take on an existential and religious significance.[93] In his post-*Method* writings on religious experience, Lonergan even spoke of "man, the symbolic animal."[94] Is Dulles' model of symbolic mediation a suitable synthesis with which to consider Lonergan's work?

Critique of Dulles' model of symbolic mediation

The dangers that Dulles alludes to, of "subjectivism, relativism and a reductionist humanism", are substantial and it is not at all clear that he can overcome them. Even Paul Ricoeur, one of the leading authors in the area of symbols and myth, has warned against the "Don Juans of myth" who take a cavalier attitude to the interpretation of symbols and myths. Ricoeur has commented that symbols not only give rise to thought, "they are also the birth of idols. That is why the critique of idols remains the condition of the conquest of symbols."[95] While Dulles tries to maintain that Christian symbols are not infinitely pliable, the question remains open as to just how pliable they are.

Dulles sought to overcome this pliability by giving doctrine a role in interpreting revelatory symbols. However, this explains nothing. Where did these doctrines come from, except out of the process of symbolic mediation? And which doctrines does one take? Why favour the Council of Trent over Luther, or Nicea over Arius? Dulles is not equipped to address such questions, so that the problems of relativism and subjectivism remain.

The major difficulty is that Dulles' dialectic retrieval is not critical. Dulles' criteria for evaluating his various models – internal coherence, plausibility, adequacy to experience, practical fruitfulness, theoretical fruitfulness and value for dialogue[96] – never rise above a commonsense framework. His dialectic retrieval, though it invokes Lonergan's name, is simply an extension of this commonsense approach. **Lacking is any critical principle, such as the self-appropriation of the subject (as in Lonergan's work), which could ground the positions and reverse the counter-positions which underpin Lonergan's notion of dialectic.** We have known since the days of Socrates that commonsense will never solve the problems of relativism and subjectivism, and Dulles has provided no reason for thinking that he will either.

Any understanding of how revelation can be related to Lonergan's theological method will have to go beyond the type of synthesis posed by Dulles' model of symbolic mediation. While Lonergan's writings acknowledge the role of the symbolic in religious experience, the symbolic alone will not be an adequate means of encompassing his approach. He was too profoundly aware of the problems of "subjectivism, relativism and a reductionist humanism" for the symbolic approach alone to be the key synthesising element.

The writings of Avery Dulles have provided a rich tapestry to draw from in the theology of revelation, and, in that tapestry, we have found may threads which connect with the thought of Bernard Lonergan. We have also seen some of the limitations of those approaches, often drawing on principles taken from Lonergan's work. I would now like to turn to three other theologians, two Catholics, namely Karl Rahner and Edward Schillebeeckx, and a Protestant, George Lindbeck, each of whom has contributed to the theology of revelation in a significant manner. Since these three do not fall simply into Dulles' models, it is of value to consider their contributions in some detail.

1.3.2 Karl Rahner and Divine Self-communication

It is perhaps natural to turn to Karl Rahner to seek some type of dialogue partner with Bernard Lonergan. Both are often placed together under the heading of "transcendental Thomism", though both are creative and independent thinkers. Further, Rahner has been critical of Lonergan's theological method, as I noted earlier in this chapter, so that an exposition of Rahner's own approach will assist us in the task of this thesis.

Perhaps the single most powerful concept that summarises Rahner's theology of revelation is "divine self-communication." It could be argued that this is the central concept for the whole of Rahner's theology. Beginning with his seminal work, *Hearers of the Word,*[97] his anthropology is based on an understanding of the human person as the potential recipient of a divine self-communication, where God reveals not something about God's self, but rather, God communicates God's very self to the recipient. Rahner's concept of divine self-communication has even found its way into official Church teaching, where *Verbum Dei*, the Constitution on Divine Revelation from the Second Vatican Council, speaks of God revealing Godself.[98]

For Rahner, revelation as self-communication has two poles which require our attention. There is the objective pole, whereby God speaks God's Word to us. God's Word is not simply information about God, but is rather God's own self, communicated to us. For Rahner, the "full and unsurpassable event of the historical objectification of God's self-communication to the world" is the incarnation of the Word in the humanity of Jesus Christ.[99] This definitive revelation by God brings revelation to a climax, and also, in a sense, brings it to a close. There is nothing more to come: "It is because the definitive Reality which resolves history proper is already here that Revelation is 'closed'."[100]

The first thing that can be said about the divine self-communication is that it occurs as the result of a free and gracious decision by God. As such, it meets the human within the history of human freedom, and so has the character of an historical event:

> [God's] Word and Act are free in the further sense that they are freely directed to men already in existence, and so are essentially Event and History ... What happens in saving history is ... the free, incalculable, ever new Event of God's activity.[101]

Rahner's emphasis of the historical event character of revelation connects with Dulles' model of revelation as history.

The concept of divine self-communication is able to reconcile both the salvation history variant of Cullman and the universal history variant of Pannenberg. On the one hand, "the history of salvation and revelation is coexistent with the history of the world"[102], while, on the other, there is a real "categorical and special history of revelation." Such a revelation can know itself to be willed by God, and can be assured of the legitimacy of this knowledge in ways which are offered by its history. "There we have the history of revelation in the sense which is usually associated with this word."[103]

While this self-communication of God cannot be reduced to information about God, this is not to say that it does not contain, as an intrinsic part of that self-communication, the transmission of true statements about God's saving actions. For Rahner, doctrines play an essential role in the process of revelation. Indeed, he claims that "we must not overlook the fact that this revelation, which closes and discloses the infinite, has the human word as a constitutive element of its essence."[104] Thus, his theology contains a propositional understanding of revelation without reducing it to propositions.

However, these elements, which reflect the objective pole of revelation, should not be seen as rendering superfluous the subjective pole. Apart from the historical, categorical mode of revelation, in the Word, there is also the transcendental mode of revelation, in the Spirit. This mode of revelation effects a permanent transformation of human subjectivity, what Rahner calls the "supernatural existential." Such a permanent offer of grace constitutes the human subject as a potential "hearer of the Word":

The *a posteriori* proposition of verbal revelation which comes in history can be heard only within the horizon of a divinizing and divinized *a priori* subjectivity. Only then can it be heard in the way that it must be heard if what is heard is seriously to be called the 'Word of God'.[105]

The supernatural existential also grounds the reality of a universal revelation, particularly through the activity of human conscience. This aspect of Rahner's theology reflects Dulles' new awareness model.

Further, Rahner's theology of revelation is, like Barth's, thoroughly Trinitarian. In identifying the historical and transcendental aspects of revelation with the activity of the Word and Spirit, he integrates his theologies of Trinity and revelation in an intrinsic manner. He claims that "if there occurs a self-communication of God to historical man, who is still becoming, it can occur only in this unifying duality of history and transcendence which man is."[106] For Rahner, a self-communicating, self-revealing God must be Trinitarian. He also speaks of revelation as both "revealing and concealing" God, a notion also drawn from Barth's dialectic approach to revelation.

Finally, Rahner has written on the theology of symbol.[107] Here he affirms:

The principle that God's salvific action on man, from its first foundation to its completion, always takes place in such a way that God himself is the reality of salvation, because it is given to man and grasped by him *in the symbol* ... .[108] [emphasis added]

Given his identification of the reality of salvation with the reality of revelation, he here asserts the central role of symbols in revelation. So again, Rahner's account of revelation reflects elements of Dulles' symbolic model of revelation.

In many ways Rahner's account of revelation has given us a more adequate account of the totality of revelation than does Dulles' model of symbolic mediation. It can certainly provide us with a more significant dialogue partner than what has gone before, in terms of matching the richness to be found in Lonergan's work. However, it is not without its own difficulties.

Critique of Rahner's theology of revelation

As is clear from the above discussion, it is not possible to separate out Rahner's theology of revelation from the rest of his theology. Its intrinsic connection with his theology of Trinity, with his central categories of transcendence and history, and with his core concept of the existential supernatural, means that any critique of his theology of revelation will also be a critique of his whole theological project, and vice versa.

Criticisms of Rahner's theological project have come from a number of quarters. The notion of "quasi-formal causality", which provides the metaphysical underpinning of his notion of divine self-communication, has been subject to severe criticism from neo-Thomists, particularly those drawing on the writings of Lonergan.[109] Walter Kasper has been very critical of his assertion that there is one divine subject in the Trinity, rather than three, claiming that his position could "easily be misunderstood as modalist."[110] To Hans urs von Balthasar, "Rahner has been the great theological opponent who makes faith inadmissibly easy, who adapts to the needs of contemporaries, and trivializes the seriousness of God's history with humanity."[111] Further, Rahner's student, Johann Baptist Metz, has levelled a number of criticisms of his theological project. In particular, Metz has been critical of Rahner's dependence on the transcendental-idealist turn to the subject of German philosophy, embodied in Hegel and Kant.[112]

There is perhaps a common thread to these last two criticisms which directly relate to Rahner's theology of revelation. It is the transcendental-idealist turn which threatens to "trivialize the seriousness of God's history with humanity." There is a formalism to his understanding of revelation which could easily reduce history to historicity. Apart from references to the life, death and resurrection of Jesus, there is little contact made with the messy details of the actual human history of revelation. By sufficiently abstracting from such details there is a danger of missing the point, of winning the race without ever having to run in the event.[113]

Thus, while Rahner was concerned that the content of revelation, the Christ-event, has not sufficiently entered into Lonergan's theological method, his critics point to a similar abstraction in his own approach. This is a serious issue which we shall have to keep in mind in dealing with Lonergan's own "transcendental" method. This brief excursus into Rahner's writings will be filled out with a fuller comparison with Lonergan at a later stage of this thesis, in Chapter 5.

1.3.3 Edward Schillebeeckx on revelation

Another leading Catholic theologian who has contributed to the on-going debate concerning the nature of revelation is Edward Schillebeeckx. In his series of profound Christological works, *Jesus, an Experiment in Christology*[114], *Christ, the Christian Experience in the Modern World*[115], and *Church, the Human story of God*[116] (henceforth referred to as *Jesus, Christ,* and *Church*), Schillebeeckx devotes considerable attention to the question of the relationship between human experience and divine revelation. Indeed, the initial chapters in both *Christ* and *Church* deal specifically with this question.

In reading his work, we are aware of entering a different framework to that of Rahner and Lonergan. It is surprising how little contact there is between Schillebeeckx and these two great thinkers. In the relevant material in *Christ* neither Rahner nor Lonergan rate a mention, while, in *Church*, Lonergan is relegated to a bibliography entry and Rahner to a few scant references.

Schillebeeckx's starting point in *Christ* is an analysis of human experience. Here, what is most significant is the interpenetration of experience and interpretation:

> We experience in the act of interpreting, without being able to draw
> a neat distinction between the element of experience and the element
> of interpretation.[117]

This place given to interpretation in human experience raises important questions about the nature of objectivity. Our real experiences are neither "purely objective nor purely subjective",[118] rather objectivity is a function of our enriched subjectivity. Thus, "a man with a musical ear will hear more in a symphony than someone with little feeling for music."[119] From this, he concludes that "man is a constructive, rational being: a *projecting* existence."[120] However, such human projects constantly come up against "the permanent resistance of reality to our rational inventions."[121] Schillebeeckx is influenced here by the falsificationism of Karl Popper. These three basic principles, one cognitional (experience always interpreted), one epistemological (objectivity not divorced from subjectivity) and one metaphysical (reality resists rational inventions), provide the foundations of his analysis of revelation.

The resistance of reality to our expectations gives new experiences an authority to which we must attend. "[T]he authority of (new) experiences is itself defined by the surprising nature of reality which continually proves different from what we think."[122] However, such authority is not immediate but requires a discerning of spirits which "is an essential part of what we call the authority of experiences."[123] Here, Schillebeeckx is attempting to break down the opposition between "the authority of a revelation handed down in tradition and the authority of new experiences." Such an opposition is, "at the least, pre-critical and naive."[124]

As Schillebeeckx has stated, his concern is not to present a complete theology of revelation. Rather, he wishes to "demonstrate the basis of revelation in experience",[125] against a view of revelation, fostered at Vatican I and reinforced in attacks against Modernism, which excluded appeals to human experience as purely subjective:

> Only in historical human experience and human practice does revelation shine out as God's action: by virtue of its transcendence this cannot be added to the efforts of historical man to create meaning. God's saving action cannot be added to human action, but it cannot be reduced to man's liberating action either.[126]

Further,

> The very fact that revelation comes to us in human language ... shows that revelation is essentially concerned with human experience. However, language is the deposit of a common *experience*. Revelation is experience expressed in the world; it is God's saving action as experienced and communicated *by men*.[127]

Hence, he understands revelation as occurring in a dialectic unity between the world (reality), thought (interpreted experience) and language. Of these, the weakest element is language.[128] This does not mean that he wishes to reject outright a propositional understanding of revelation. Rather it "must be kept in right relation to the experience with which this propositional language is associated."[129]

Schillebeeckx indicates two directions in which the transcendence that lies in human experience is necessarily expressed. These are in a mystical and in an ethical direction. The mystic is not in contact with some other world above this world. Rather,

> the very existence of man and the world is a symbol or a manifestation of the divine, but always in such a way that there is a necessary identity between revelation and concealment of the divine.[130]

God is revealed in symbols which both reveal and conceal God. All our talk, all our symbols are inadequate, though "creeds and liturgies are ... a necessary (and dangerous) form of anamnesis."[131] Religious statements about God are not just "facts" about God:

> Any religious statement about the God who reveals himself is in fact a statement about man and his world, but understood in such a way that any religious statement about man and the world is also in fact a statement about God. Theology is not anthropology, but a theological statement is *at the same time* an anthropological statement.[132]

The other direction in which revelation finds valid expression is that of ethics. Without reducing religion to ethics, he maintains an intrinsic connection between the two. Indeed, he claims that this connection is maintained in almost all religions. Moreover, he gives priority to this ethical expression over the mystical:

> Both seem to me to be indispensable, but in view of the experiential structure of revelation, the symbolic religious talk of God owes its density of reality to the *mediation* of *ethical existence*.[133]

It was his hope that the book *Christ* "will point the way towards a meaningful solution" to the problem of the relationship between faith and ethics.[134]

In this account, we see Schillebeeckx approaching approximations to a number of Dulles' models of revelation. He gives a place to doctrinal statements (propositional model), though keeping them relative to other concerns. He acknowledges the role of mystical experience (inner experience model) and his emphasis on orthopraxis is in keeping with the new awareness model. Revelation both reveals and conceals (dialectic model) through its use of symbols (symbolic mediation model). Perhaps the weakest point of contact is with the historical model. While he is emphatic that revelation is within human and hence historical experience, there is not the emphasis that history itself is revelatory. This dimension of revelation finds fuller expression in his later work, *Church*.

In *Church*, Schillebeeckx has taken the opportunity to expand on his position in *Christ* by responding to criticism and "radicalizing" his previous account. The foundational principles enunciated in *Christ* remain but are given more concrete context. In particular, the "resistance of reality" to our human projects becomes more focussed on experiences of suffering and negativity. Our indignation, our "No!", to such experiences are basic pre-religious experiences which lead to ethical and religious reflection. The fundamental question which arises for Christians is whether we side with the oppressed or the oppressors, in the face of suffering and negativity.[135] Revelation always presupposes some history of human liberation, "an event that already has relevance for [men and women] and liberates them, without direct reference to God."[136] However "believers see the face of God in the history of human liberation."[137] Thus "only the human meaning of a historical process can become the material of 'supernatural' or religious meaning, of revelation."[138] The influences of both liberation and political theology are clear in this position.

However, Schillebeeckx does not simply identify a universal saving history with a history of revelation. Such a saving history is independent of our awareness of "the gracious structure of salvation."[139] It is only when salvation history becomes "a conscious and literate experience of faith" that we can speak of a history of revelation.[140]

Another aspect of the "resistance of reality" is seen in Schillebeeckx's new emphasis on conversion. The disintegration that resistance produces leads to a new integration so that "any 'experience of revelation' includes conversion, amendment of life, reorientation."[141] Revelation always includes a subjective pole, that is, conversion, faith, a new praxis, as well as an objective pole, something which 'shows itself objectively in ... experience ... in a veiled form ... in such a way that it can be affirmed or denied."[142] He concludes: "there can be no revelation without faith and no faith without revelation."[143] In other words, "experiencing-and-understanding revelation is also a constitutive element in the process of revelation itself."[144]

Reflection on these two poles of revelation leads to a deeper appreciation of the role of culture in the process of revelation. How do we maintain and identify Christian identity in the plurality of cultural forms which constitute our human situation? As in *Christ*, Schillebeeckx is trying to avoid "the Scylla of fundamentalism and the Charybris of modernism"[145], or what we have previously identified as authoritarianism and relativism. He rejects the notion of some abstract substance of faith, "stripped down and free of any culture."[146] The power of the Gospel is transcendent, universal and, in a sense, "transcultural." However, the offer of salvation is always "acclimatized in a particular culture, while that offer can never be found in an unhistorical and supra-cultural form."[147]

He concludes his analysis of revelation with some comments on the role of dogmas. What is important is the relationship between the saving message and the socio-cultural context to which that message is addressed. He even expresses this in the form of a mathematical ratio.[148] Thus, Christian identity is not grounded in a constancy of understanding, as expressed in dogmas, but in a constancy of the relationship between message and context. He rejects the notion of a development of dogma as a

> permanent explication of a substance of faith which was always already implicit, an explication from the implicit to the explicit; from the Bible in roughly a straight line to the present day.

In their cultural and historical forms, dogmas,

> can become irrelevant and indeed meaningless for later generations if they are simply repeated as they stand, because earlier generations expressed their deepest convictions about Christian faith within another semantic field, in another system of communication and through a different perspective on reality.[149]

Something more than a linear, genetic development of doctrines is needed. Christian identity is "already given *in* the specific action of believers",[150] in orthopraxis rather than orthodoxy.

Schillebeeckx has certainly produced an impressive and challenging account of revelation in these works. What is significant in this brief comparison with Lonergan is his starting point, that is, human experience. Both Lonergan and Schillebeeckx take as their starting point a critical appropriation of human experience, an anthropological "turn to the subject." However this turn, most clearly exemplified in the philosophy of Emmanuel Kant, is not without its danger, and it is to these that I turn in considering the weaknesses of Schillebeeckx's project.

Critique of Schillebeeckx on revelation

It is clear that the "socio-cultural" factors conditioning Schille-beeckx's account of revelation include his repeated conflicts with magisterial authorities and the authoritarian manner of their interventions. While rejecting their "fundamentalism", however, he also wants to avoid the subjectivism and relativism of "modernism", which he finds unsatisfactory. Correctly he wants to stress the role of the subject in the process of revelation – no revelation without faith, without experience-and-understanding – but his turn to the subject inevitably comes up against the Kantian problem of relativism and subjectivism.

Indeed, the influence of Kant on Schillebeeckx is clear, not only by direct reference but also in the philosophers of science on whom Schillebeeckx has drawn.[151] At one stage he rejects Kant's position as leading to a "modern close-knit subjectivity"[152], but it is not at all clear that he can overcome the problem. If we consider his foundational principles, that experience is always interpreted, that objectivity cannot be divorced from subjectivity and that reality resists rational inventions, we can analyse some of the difficulty. If reality always resists our rational inventions and projects, as he sometimes (over)states, then this indicates the intrinsic unintelligibility of reality. All our meanings are simply models and interpretations which are projected onto reality. This is very close to the Kantian distinction between the "thing in itself" and the "object for me", as Schillebeeckx himself concedes.[153] Once the split is made between cognitional activity and metaphysical reality, objectivity becomes a major problem, since the interpretative activities of the subject are no longer commensurate with reality. In the end, he invokes the notion of a "discernment of spirits", a notion which he never fully explicates, in order to save some notion of objectivity.

Schillebeeckx's work highlights the Kantian problematic present in much of contemporary theology and culture. One solution is to repudiate the turn to the subject initiated by Kant, to see it as inevitably flawed. The other solution is a more radical insertion into human subjectivity, in search of cognitional activities which could ground objectivity. Whereas Schillebeeckx speaks of experience-and-understanding, Lonergan, for example, speaks of experience, understanding and *judgment*.[154]   Judgment becomes *the* cognitional activity which involves a cognitional self-transcendence of the subject, so that cognitional activity relates to metaphysical reality. Thus, Lonergan's account extends Schillebeeckx's cognitional position to include judgment. It then transposes Schillebeeckx's epistemological principle so that genuine objectivity is seen as the fruit of authentic subjectivity. Finally, his account reverses Schillebeeckx's third principle so that reality is seen as intrinsically intelligible.[155]

This same Kantian problem is also present in Schillebeeckx's dealing with the question of dogmas. On the one hand, he wishes to maintain the "irrevocable and irreversible" nature of dogmas. On the other hand, they can become "irrelevant and meaningless" with subsequent changes in culture.[156] However, if reality is known through objective judgments on the meaning of experience, as Lonergan holds, then doctrines may have more to do with judgments than with interpretations.[157] The assertion of the permanent significance of doctrines is, then, not an assertion of the normativity of a given culture (what Lonergan calls classicism). Nor is it the assertion of some supra-cultural, unhistorical plane of existence accessed in some mysterious manner. Rather, it points to the possibility that every culture contains elements which are potentially transcultural in their significance, and that these elements ground the possibility of universally valid judgments.[158]

Thus, it remain unclear whether Schillebeeckx has broken free from the close-knit subjectivity which he recognises as the danger in adopting the "turn to the subject." The references to Lonergan above give some indication as to how he has sought to avoid these dangers. Yet, as with Rahner, we can see here the pitfalls into which Lonergan's own project may fall. It raises questions which we must seriously address to Lonergan's overall project.[159]

1.3.4 George Lindbeck: *The Nature of Doctrine, Religion and Theology in a Post-Liberal Age.*

In the book, *The Nature of Doctrine: Religion and Theology in a Post-Liberal Age*, George Lindbeck develops a new and startlingly different way of approaching questions of religion and claims to divine revelation.[160] Further, with this work, we see a theologian entering into critical dialogue with Lonergan's writings, particularly *Method in Theology*. This initial account of Lindbeck's stance will be filled out in a more detailed comparison with Lonergan's work in Chapter 5 on this thesis.

Though revelation is not a key concept in Lindbeck's *The Nature of Doctrine*, his discussion of religion and doctrine clearly embraces a view of revelation and its role for both religion and doctrinal formulations. Throughout his work, he compares and contrasts a cognitional, propositional understanding of religion and doctrines (similar to Dulles' propositional model), and an experiential-expressivist model (with elements of Dulles' inner experience and new awareness models) with his own preferred account, that of a cultural linguistic understanding of religion and doctrine. Given the lack of plausibility he attaches to the cognitional, propositional approach, the main dialogue is between the experiential-expressivist approach, which he sees as the present dominant approach, and the cultural-linguistic approach.

Lindbeck characterises the experiential-expressivist approach as beginning with religious experience and then seeing religion and doctrines as organised expressions of this common, basic experience.[161] He identifies Rahner and Lonergan as key proponents of this approach. Further he makes special reference to Lonergan's treatment of religious experience in *Method in Theology*, which draws on the work of Friedrich Heiler. Lindbeck rejects this treatment on the grounds of its dependence on the notion of some type of unthematized, pre-linguistic conscious experience. He alludes to the arguments of Wittgenstein which reject the notion of "private language", but himself adopts the concept of Ockham's razor to argue that the notion of such experience is unnecessary to explain the phenomena of religion.[162] Rather than religious experience giving rise to religion, in the cultural-linguistic approach, religion, as an organised cultural and linguistic system, shapes and gives rise to religious experience. Initiation into a religion then becomes the adoption of a praxis, through which one is led to certain structured experiences which one has learnt to identify as religious. For Lindbeck, the normative praxis of the religion is found through the stories it tells, through its narratives.[163]

Such an approach is radically different from the experiential-expressive approach. Yet it does have some similarities with the cognitive-propositional approach, as Lindbeck notes.[164] Both assume a givenness about religion/doctrine/revelation. It is a givenness to which one must conform in one's adoption of a certain religious faith. However, the cultural-linguistic approach steps back from the ontological claims of the cognitive approach. Rather than doctrines being truth claims with some ontological reference in God, they become linguistic and grammatical rules with only an intrasystemic significance. Different religions have different doctrines, but this need have no more significance than different road rules applying in different countries. Religions are different in the same way that cultures and languages are different. They are basically incommensurable.[165]

Despite this bracketing of ontological questions, Lindbeck argues that Christians should take seriously Christian claims to being unsurpassable, and to the exclusive nature of salvation offered in Christ. He rejects Rahner's notion of "anonymous Christians", and understands the salvation of non-Christians as being determined by a post-mortem encounter with the Risen Christ.[166] He finds this more satisfactory than claims to some unverifiable notion of unthematized, transcendental revelation.

Lindbeck's approach clearly represents a serious critique of the basis of Lonergan's whole approach, that is, the transcendental "turn to the subject." I shall postpone a fuller dialogue between Lindbeck and Lonergan to a later stage in this work. At this stage it is suff/cient to note that the issues raised by Lindbeck will need to be addressed, while at the same time to raise some critical questions of his approach as well.

Critique of Lindbeck

As a theory of religion, and hence implicitly of revelation, Lindbeck's use of cultural-linguistic model has certain advantages over other approaches. Over the cognitive approach, it stresses the praxis nature of religious faith. However, in congruence with the cognitive approach, it stresses the formative role of a religious tradition. In fact, it gives a much more nuanced analysis of the role of tradition than is available within the cognitive account. Nonetheless, it suffers from the same difficulties as the cognitive account: how does religion come about in the first place? If it is religion, as a cultural linguistic system, which shapes and gives rise to religious experience, what shapes and gives rise to religion itself? Is it simply a given, with no prior explanation possible? Just as the cognitive approach must give an account of the origins of doctrines, without falling over into a naive, ahistorical "direct speech from God", so too, Lindbeck needs to be able to give an account of the origins of religions and, in particular, the emergence of new religious belief out of an existing religious framework, for example, Christianity's emergence out of Judaism. As one reviewer has commented:

> To be sure, religious traditions do change. They change because anomalies appear in religious praxis ... Pragmatic anomalies, in turn, result from "the interaction of a cultural linguistic system with changing situations." But that only pushes the question one step back: why do "situations" change? Are they somehow independent of the reality that has already been socially constructed? If they are, presumably they would go unnoticed ... if not, presumably there is no call for adjusting the interpretive system as it stands.[167]

Another concern with his account is the incommensurability of differing religions. His claim is that, just as different cultures cannot be compared, neither can different religions. Here, the mention of cultures is illuminating. Has Lindbeck assumed a general cultural relativism with no grounds for evaluating cultures (and hence religions), except the norms within some particular culture? Alternatively, one cold ask whether there are genuine, transcultural norms which allow a study of cultures (and religions) which are truly empirical, critical *and normative*? If no such position is possible, then the only alternatives seem to be either religious relativism and indifferentism, which he deplores,[168] or an authoritarian dogmatic fideism. The shift to a cultural-linguistic account of religions does not solve the problems we have already encountered in discussing revelation. It merely transposes them.

Despite these criticisms Lindbeck has added something significant to the question of revelation, that is, the role of tradition and culture in revelation. This is something that we shall have to keep in mind in dealing with Lonergan's theological method.

1.4 This Thesis

How, then, can we develop an understanding of the relationship between Lonergan's theological method and the theology of revelation? The purpose of this thesis is to argue that Lonergan's theological method, as expounded in *Method in Theology*, contains elements of a theology of revelation which is more comprehensive and integrated than the theologies of revelation currently available in the theological literature. On the basis of this understanding of revelation, it is possible to address those critics who either see Lonergan as tending to a rationalist exclusion of revelation in his theological method and or those who see him as having capitulated to soft-headed religious fervour and dogmatism.

In order to achieve this the thesis shall move through four stages.

First of all I shall use a genetic method to analyse Lonergan's writings, seeking clues in them for a development in Lonergan's understanding of the nature of revelation.[169] Thus, in the second and third chapters, I shall be concerned to move from some of his early writings, through to *Method in Theology* and beyond, to trace developing themes which relate to the issue of revelation. This will include an effort to trace the few explicit references to revelation which occur in these works. In this process, earlier stages are linked to later stages in the general unfolding of Lonergan's own development as an original and creative thinker.

Secondly, there is the question of "what is going forward" in this material. Thus, these two chapters lead then to the fourth chapter. There I attempt to develop a synthesis which makes explicit a theology of revelation which correlates with Lonergan's understanding of theological method. It claims to present "what is moving forward" in his thinking with regard to the question of revelation, even though this forward movement may not be clear to Lonergan himself.

Thirdly, this approach shall lead to the use of a dialectical method to compare and contrast the understanding of revelation developed in the fourth chapter with those present in other writings, and to respond to various criticism which have been levelled at Lonergan's project. This will be the aim of the fifth and sixth chapters.

Finally, I shall seek to develop aspects of the synthesis outlined in chapter four, by way of illustration of the position developed there. This is primarily a constructive task, picking up clues in Lonergan's writings but also going beyond them, seeing themes which are relatively underdeveloped and extending them in the light of the approaches of others and their criticisms of his position. I would hope that this material in particular is a positive contribution to extending his approach by attending to issues raised by a theology of revelation.

1.5 Conclusion

In this chapter I have raised the question of the place of method in Lonergan's overall project and its relationship to a theology of revelation. I have indicated how various criticisms have been made with regard to his handling of the question of revelation, and have considered the broader context of the theologies of revelation to highlight questions raised by his approach. In light of the methodology outlined above, I shall now review, in the next chapter, Lonergan's writings in their historical development, up to the time of *Method in Theology*.

---

1. B. Lonergan, *Method in Theology* (London: Darton, Longman & Todd, 1972), 5-6.
2. Lonergan, *Method*, 4.
3. Cf. F. Crowe, *Lonergan* (London: Geoffrey Chapman, 1992) 14.
4. Crowe, *Lonergan*, 13-4.
5. "Introduction to dissertation *Gratia Operans*" by B. Lonergan, edited by F. Crowe, published in *Method: Journal of Lonergan Studies*, 3/2 (1985), 10.
6. B. Lonergan, *Insight: A Study of Human Understanding* (London: Darton, Longman & Todd, 1957), 748.
7. Lonergan, *Insight*, xxviii.
8 Cf. *Insight*, 733ff.
9. Lonergan, *Method*, 7.
10. These courses were entitled *De intellectu et methodo* (1959), *De methodo theologiae* (1962). For a detailed study of their significance in Lonergan's struggles towards developing a method in theology, see, C. Boly, *The Road to Lonergan's Method in Theology: The Ordering of Theological Ideas* (Lanham: UPA, 1991), Chapters 5, 6.
11. Cf. Crowe, *Lonergan*, 80ff.
12. B. Lonergan, "Theology in its New Context", *Second Collection*, W. Ryan and B. Tyrell (eds) (Philadelphia: Westminster Press), 1974, 58-9.
13. B. Lonergan, *A Third Collection: Papers by Bernard Lonergan, s.j.*, F. Crowe (ed.) (Mahwah: Paulist Press, 1985).
14. A "structural isomorphism" means a direct correspondence between the structures of two objects. Thus every structural element in revelation has its corresponding element in theological method and vice versa. Lonergan uses this same notion to critically establish his metaphysics, by noting the structural isomorphism between the knowing and the known, cf. *Insight*, 486: "There exists a necessary isomorphism between our knowing and its proportionate known".
15. See A. Kelly, "Is Lonergan's *Method* Adequate to Christian Mystery", *Thomist*, 39/3 (1975), 437-470. For a discussion of and response to Kelly's concerns, see T. Renyolds, "Method Divorced from Content in Theology: An Assessment of Lonergan's *Method in Theology*", *The Thomist*, 55/2 (1991), 245-269. I shall present a detailed analysis of these articles in Chapter 6.
16. K. Rahner, "Kritische Bemerkungen zu B.J.F. Lonergan's Aufsatz: 'Functional Specialties in Theology'", *Gregorianum*, 51/3 (1970), 537-540.

17. Kelly, "Is *Method* Adequate?", 440.
18. Cf. J.P. Mackey, "Divine Revelation and Lonergan's Transcendental Method in Theology", *Irish Theological Quarterly*, January, XL/1 (1973), 10. Mackey is quite severe in his treatment of *Method*, but overall he has not paid sufficent attention to the details of the book, nor to the intervening literature by Lonergan, where the development in Lonergan's thinking becomes clearer. I shall consider his position in more detail in Chapter 6.
19. F. Crowe, "Rethinking God-with-us: Categories from Lonergan", *Science et Esprit*, XLI/2 (1989), 170.
20. Crowe, "Rethinking".
21. Lonergan, *Method*, 119. Indeed this lack of reference is reflected in the secondary literature on Lonergan. One computer search covering religious periodicals, multi-author works and book reviews from 1975-93 revealed 248 works on Lonergan, only one of which, a minor essay by George Worgul, could be cross-matched with the topic of revelation. Similarly, various collections of essays on Lonergan's thought, such as the various *Lonergan Workshops* edited by Fred Lawrence, show little interest in the area of a theology of revelation. I note the following exceptions: C. Hefling, "On Reading *Road to Nicea*", *Religion and Culture: Essays in Honor of Bernard Lonergan, s.j.*, T. Fallon & Riley (eds) (Albany; SUNY, 1987) 149-166; Q. Quesnell, "Beliefs and Authenticity", *Creativity and Method*, M. Lamb (ed) (Marquette University Press, Milwaukee, 1981), 173-183.
22. A. Dulles, review of *Method in Theology*, *Theological Studies*, 33/3 (1972), 555.
23. D. Keefe, "A Methodological Critique of Lonergan's Theological Method", *The Thomist*, 50/1 (1986), 44. I shall consider Keefe comments in more detail in Chapter 6.
24. Cf. Lonergan, *Method*, 282ff.
25. For example, Keefe criticises Lonergan for his *a priori* adherence to the grace-nature distinction, "A Methodological Critique", 28-65, esp. 54. For a response to Keefe on Lonerganian lines, see T. Tekippe, "Response to Donald Keefe on Lonergan", *The Thomist*, 52/1 (1988), 88-95.
26. See, for example, R. Liddy, *Transforming Light: Intellectual Conversion in the Early Lonergan* (Collegeville; Glazier, 1993), 114ff.
27. Doran does not identify to whom he refers, but it is likely that one such critic would be David Tracy whose theological project entails a public intellectual defence of Christian faith not built on a doctrinal stance.
28. R. Doran, *Theology and the Dialectics of History* (Toronto: University of Toronto Press, 1990), 166.
29. On the significance of the shift in name from fundamental to foundational theology see F. Fiorenza, *Foundational Theology* (New York: Crossroad, 1985), 285ff.
30. A. Dulles, *Models of Revelation* (Dublin: Gill & Macmillan, 1983).

31. Dulles is not using the term *model* in Lonergan's technical sense of a set of terms and relations.

32. Dulles himself makes only one significant reference to Lonergan's work (plus one minor footnote). He invokes Lonergan's notion of "dialectical retrieval". I shall comment upon this later in this chapter.

33. Dulles, *Models*, 27.

34. Dulles, *Models*, 36-45.

35. See, for example, J. O'Leary, "The Hermeneutics of Dogmatism", *Irish Theological Quarterly*, 47 (1980), 96-118. For a response see C. Heffling, "On Reading *The Way to Nicea*".

36. Cf. B. Lonergan, "The Assumption and Theology", *Collection: Papers by Bernard Lonergan*, F. Crowe (ed.) (New York: Herder & Herder, 1967), 68-83.

37. See, for example, B. Lonergan, "The Origins of Christian Realism", *A Second Collection*, 239-262.

38. Cf. Lonergan, *Method*, Chapter 12.

39. See, for example, B. Lonergan, "The Transition from a Classicist World-View to Historical-Mindedness", *Second Collection*, 1-10.

40. See Crowe, *Lonergan*, 84: "Lonergan towards the end of his life saw his whole work as one of introducing history into theology".

41. Cf. O. Cullman, *Christ and Time* (Philadelphia: Westminster Press, 1950, rev. ed., 1964). Also, his book *Salvation in History* (New York: Harper & Row, 1967).

42. Cf. J. Daniélou, *The Lord of History* (Chicago: Regency, 1958).

43. See, for example, W. Pannenberg, "Redemptive Event and History", in his *Basic Questions in Theology*, vol.1 (Philadelphia: Fortress, 1970) and his contributions to Pannenberg et al., *Revelation as History* (New York: MacMillan, 1968).

44. W. Pannenberg, "Dogmatic Theses on the Doctrine of Revelation", in *Revelation as History* , 135.

45. Pannenberg, "Dogmatic Theses", 136

46. One consequence of his approach was his belief in the historically verifiable nature of the resurrection, not in terms of an old-fashioned *a priori* apologetic, but in strict critical historical terms. This suggestion has not been well received.

47. I shall outline this in the next chapter.

48. Cf. F. Crowe, *Lonergan*, 97.

49. F. Crowe, *Theology of the Christian Word* (NY: Paulist Press, 1978), 116-123.

50. Dulles, *Models,* 27

51. Both are cited in Dulles, *Models*, 73-4.

52. Dulles, *Models*, 70.

53. Cf. B. Lonergan, "Insight Revisited", *Second Collection*, 277.

54. Lonergan, *Method*, 105.

55. Lonergan, *Method*, 115.

56. Lonergan, *Method*, 108ff.

57. G. Lindbeck, *The Nature of Doctrine: Religion and Theology in a Postliberal Age* (Philadelphia: Westminster Press, 1984), 30ff.

58. Lonergan, *Method*, 110ff.

59. See, for example, K. Barth, *Church Dogmatics* Vol.1 Part 1 (Edinburgh: T. & T. Clarke, 1975), 339ff.

60. See, for example, H. urs von Balthasar, *Love Alone: The Way of Revelation* (London: Burns & Oates, 1968), *A Theology of History* (London: Sheed & Ward, 1963), *The Glory of the Lord: A Theological Aesthetics* Vol.1, *Seeing the Form* (Edinburgh: T. & T. Clarke, 1985).

61. Dulles, *Models*, 28.

62. In deliberate contrast to Friedrich Schleiermacher, whose theology of Trinity is an awkward conclusion to his main work, *The Christian Faith* (Edinburgh: T. & T. Clarke, 1928), Barth begins his *Church Dogmatics* with a discussion of the self-revelation of a Trinitarian God.

63. Cf. Doran, *Theology,* 419.

64. K. Barth, *Epistle to the Romans* (London: OUP, 1933), 143.

65. M. Lamb, *Solidarity with Victims* (New York: Crossroad, 1982), 74.

66. Cf. Lonergan, *Insight*, 191ff, 218-238.

67. Lonergan, *Method*, 106.

68. Dulles, *Models*, 101. It should be noted that this represents an early phase in Baum's writings and is not necessarily congruent with his present position on these matters.

69. Dulles, *Models*, 104.

70. G. Baum, *Faith and Doctrine* (New York: Newman, 1969).

71. L. Dewart, *The Future of Belief: Theism in a World Come of Age* (New York: Herder & Herder, 1966).

72. G. Moran *Theology of Revelation* (New York: Herder & Herder, 1966), and *The Present Revelation* (New York: Herder & Herder, 1972).

73. For references to Rahner's work, see the section of Rahner below. Given the similarities between Rahner and Lonergan it seems incongruous that Dulles does not mention Lonergan at this point of his discussion.

74. For Tillich, see his *Systematic Theology* (Chicago: University of Chicago Press, 1951), vol.1.

75. The category of conversion begins to take on importance in Lonergan's essay, "Theology in its New Context", *Second Collection*, 55-67. Though Crowe, *Lonergan*, notes that *Insight* is about "the need for a radical intellectual conversion". He finds it "remarkable that *Insight* from beginning to end is an exercise in radical intellectual conversion, yet never says so", 68.

76. Cf. Lonergan, *Method*, 267ff.

77. Cf. *Method*, 292.

78. Dulles, *Models*, 127. Dulles draws the terms "dialectic" and "sublation" from Lonergan, though it is not clear that he really understands their use in Lonergan's sense. This is the only significant reference to Lonergan's writings in Dulles' *Models*.

79. *Models*, 131.

80. Cf. Ricoeur, *The Symbolism of Evil* (Boston: Beacon, 1969).

81. Cf. M. Polanyi and H. Prosch, *Meaning* (Chicago: University of Chicago Press, 1975).

82. Cf. M. Eliade, *Patterns of Comparative Religion* (New York: Sheed & Ward, 1958).

83. Dulles, *Models*, 136ff.

84. Dulles, *Models*, 143.

85. Dulles clearly has Pannenberg's account in mind rather than the earlier "salvation history" model.

86. Dulles, *Models*, 145.

87. Dulles, *Models*, 146.

88. Dulles, *Models*, 149.

89. Dulles, *Models*, 151.

90. While Barth appears hostile to this model the same need not be said of von Balthasar. His insistence on the aesthetic dimension of faith and theology provide a clear opening for the symbolic. Indeed Robert Doran speaks of von Balthasar's theology as "a statement in aesthetic terms of Christian doctrine, and a massive collection of materials that can be employed in the communication of Christian constitutive meaning to people of a cultivated aesthetic an symbolic sensitivity". (Doran, *Theology*, 641.) Thus, it would seem that his theology is not as hostile as Barth's to a symbolic mediation of revelation. As one would expect from such a paradoxical model it is hard to make generalisation.

91. Dulles, *Models*, 153.

92. Lonergan, *Method*, 64ff.

93. See, for example, Lonergan's discussion of mystery in *Insight*, 533.

94. Cf. B. Lonergan, "Religious Knowledge", *A Third Collection*, 133.

95. Quoted in John Polkinghorne, *Reason and Reality* (London: SPCK, 1991), 32 (direct source not given).

96. Cf. Dulles, *Models*, 16ff.

97. K. Rahner, *Hearers of the Word* (London, Sheed and Ward, 1969).

98. *Dei Verbum* in A. Flannery, *Vatican Council II: The Conciliar and Post Conciliar Document* (Northport: Costello Publishing Co., 1984), 750. Indeed recently Gerald O'Collins has shown that the concept of divine self-communication has become part of the standard vocabulary of Pope John Paul II, cf. "The Pope's theology", *The Tablet*, 27 June, 1992, 801.

99. K. Rahner, *Foundations of Christian Faith: An Introduction to the Idea of Christianity* (New York: Crossroad, 1982), 157.

100. K. Rahner, "The Development of Dogma", *Theological Investigations* (London: Darton, Longman and Todd, 1961), Vol.1, 49.
101. K. Rahner, "Theos in the New Testament", *Theological Investigations*, Vol.1, 87.
102. Rahner, *Foundations*, 153.
103. Rahner, *Foundations*, 155.
104.   K. Rahner, "Considerations on the Development of Dogma", *Theological Investigations* (London: Darton, Longman and Todd, 1966), Vol.4, 10.
105. Rahner, *Foundations*, 150.
106. K. Rahner, *The Trinity* (London: Burns & Oates, 1979), 92.
107.   K. Rahner, "The Theology of Symbol", *Theological Investigations*, Vol.4, 221ff.
108. Rahner, "Theology of Symbol", 245.
109. Cf. G. Mansini, "Quasi-Formal Causality an 'Change in the Other': A Note on Karl Rahner's Christology", *The Thomist*, 52/2 (1988), 293-306.
110. W. Kasper, *The God of Jesus Christ* (London: SCM, 1983), 288.
111. Cf. H. Vorgrimler, *Understanding Karl Rahner* (NY: Crossroad, 1985), 124.
112. Cf. J.B. Metz, *Faith in History and Society* (London: Burns & Oates, 1980), esp. 154ff. Also M. Lamb, *Solidarity with Victims* (NY: Crossroad, 1982), 122ff.
113. Metz, *Faith*, 161ff.
114. E. Schillebeeckx, *Jesus, an experiment in Christology* (London: Collins, 1979).
115. E. Schillebeeckx, *Christ, the Christian Experience in the Modern World* (London: SCM, 1980).
116. E. Schillebeeckx, *Church, the Human Story of God* (NY: Crossroad, 1990).
117. Schillebeeckx, *Christ*, 33.
118. Schillebeeckx, *Christ*, 33
119. Schillebeeckx, *Christ*, 33
120. Schillebeeckx, *Christ*, 34.
121. Schillebeeckx, *Christ*, 35.
122. Schillebeeckx, *Christ*, 37
123. Schillebeeckx, *Christ*, 38.
124. Schillebeeckx, *Christ*, 43.
125. Schillebeeckx, *Christ*, 45.
126. Schillebeeckx, *Christ*, 48.
127. Schillebeeckx, *Christ*, 46.
128. Schillebeeckx, *Christ*, 50.
129. Schillebeeckx, *Christ*, 54.
130. Schillebeeckx, *Christ*, 55.

131. Schillebeeckx, *Christ*, 55
132. Schillebeeckx, *Christ*, 56.
133. Schillebeeckx, *Christ*, 61.
134. Schillebeeckx, *Christ*, 61.
135. E. Schillebeeckx, *Church the Human Story of God* (New York: Crossroad, 1990), 5.
136. Schillebeeckx, *Church*, 7.
137. Schillebeeckx, *Church*, 7.
138. Schillebeeckx, *Church*, 8.
139. Schillebeeckx, *Church*, 10
140. Schillebeeckx, *Church*, 12.
141. Schillebeeckx, *Church*, 22. Cf. also 29.
142. Schillebeeckx, *Church*, 23.
143. Schillebeeckx, *Church*, 28.
144. Schillebeeckx, *Church*, 40.
145. Schillebeeckx, *Church*, 36.
146. Schillebeeckx, *Church*, 36.
147. Schillebeeckx, *Church*, 36.
148. Schillebeeckx, *Church*, 41-2.
149. Schillebeeckx, *Church*, 43.
150. Schillebeeckx, *Church*, 35.
151. Cf. Schillebeeckx, *Christ*, 56. Also see E. Schillebeeckx, *Interim Report on the books Jesus and Christ* (London: SCM, 1980) 17, and *Church* 31.
152. Schillebeeckx, *Church*, 47.
153. Cf. Schillebeeckx, *Christ*, 56: "since Kant this problem has been discussed in terms of the difference between the 'thing in itself' and the 'object for me' - a distinction which is unavoidable".
154. This is of course not to say that Schillebeeckx's notion of experience is the same as Lonergan's. Indeed, they do differ, but I have argued elsewhere on the inherent difficulties in Schillebeeckx's notion of experience, cf. N. Ormerod, "Schillebeeckx's Philosophical prolegomenon: A Dialectic Analysis", *Australian Lonergan Workshop* (Lanham: UPA, 1993), W. Danaher (ed.), 69-78.
155. In Lonergan's terms, this is a process of expanding positions and reversing counter-positions.
156. Schillebeeckx, *Church*, 43.
157. Cf. Lonergan, *Method* Chap.12.
158. See my paper on "The Transcultural Significance of the Council of Chalcedon", *Australasian Catholic Record*, LXX/3 (1993), 322-332, where I explicate these ideas with regard to the definition of Chalcedon.
159. Indeed, Pannenberg has expressed concern that Lonergan's approach falls into subjectivism. I shall refer to this again in Chapter 5 and 6.

160. G. Lindbeck, *The Nature of Doctrine, Religion and Theology in a Post-Liberal Age* (Philadelphia: Westminster Press, 1984).
161. Lindbeck, *Nature of Doctrine*, 31ff.
162. Lindbeck, *Nature of Doctrine*, 38.
163. Lindbeck, *Nature of Doctrine*, 40.
164. Lindbeck, *Nature of Doctrine*, 57.
165. Lindbeck, *Nature of Doctrine*, 63ff.
166. Lindbeck, *Nature of Doctrine*, 57ff.
167. C. Hefling, "Turning Liberalism Inside-Out", *Method, Journal of Lonergan Studies*, 3/2 (1985), 65-66.
168. Lindbeck, *Nature of Doctrine*, 128-130.
169. In *Insight*, Lonergan specifies four basic methods for handling all possible data. These are classical method, which provides a direct correlation between two sets of data; statistical method which provides a statistical correlation between two sets of data; genetic method which sees two sets of data as related through a process of genetic development; and, finally, dialectic method which sees two sets of data as related by linked but opposed principles: "... one begins by noting that understanding leads to the formulation of systems, and that systems may be supposed either to be constant over time or to change over time. Again, besides the direct understanding that posits systems, there is the inverse understanding that rests on the opposite assumption of defective intelligibility. Accordingly, the anticipation of a constant system to be discovered grounds classical method; the anticipation of an intelligibly related sequence of systems grounds genetic method; the anticipation that data will not conform to system grounds statistic method; and the anticipation that the relations between successive stages of changing system will not be directly intelligible grounds dialectic method. But data must either conform or not conform to system, and successive systems must be either related or not related in a directly intelligible manner. Accordingly, taken together, the four methods are relevant to any field of data ..." (*Insight*, 485). While the first two are particularly important in the physical sciences and the third in the biological sciences, it is the third and fourth of these methods which are of particular importance in dealing with the human sciences and questions of meaning. Thus it will be these two methods which will be most commonly used in this thesis.

CHAPTER TWO:
OVERVIEW OF LONERGAN'S
DEVELOPING THOUGHT PRIOR
TO *METHOD*

In the previous chapter I outlined the questions which can be raised concerning the relationship between Lonergan's theological method and the theology of revelation. In this chapter I shall give an overview of the development of Lonergan's thinking, up to the time of the publication of *Method in Theology*. While not attempting a completely comprehensive analysis, I hope to indicate the genesis of developing themes and issues, with particular attention to the question of revelation, culminating in the achievement of *Method*.

2.1 Developing Thought Prior To *Insight*

2.1.1 Earliest writings

Few of Lonergan's earliest writings are available to a general audience. They are only to be found in specialised research centres. Studies by Frederick Crowe[1] and Richard Liddy[2] have done much to illuminate the tone and direction of these writings which predate his doctoral studies in Rome. Some were published in in-house journals, or survive as talks given to student groups. Already Lonergan was developing a "respect for intelligence", was concerned with the general question of method and was reading works on and by Plato,

Augustine and Newman. Early writings dealt with inference, syllo-
gism and judgment in the sciences. They reveal the initial seeds of
what will be a life-long concern with cognitional theory. This concern
will, of course, flower in his studies on St Thomas in the *Verbum*
articles and his major work, *Insight*.

However, there is another emerging interest during this period
which runs as a current throughout his later writings, namely, an interest in history. As early as 1935 Lonergan was seeking to develop a
philosophy of history, one which would, in his own words, "throw
Hegel and Marx, despite the enormity of their influence on this very
account, into the shade."[3] Central to his account of history was an
analogy draw from Newton's account of planetary motion. It consists
of a series of three approximations.[4] In the first approximation, the
ideal line of history, people "always do what is intelligent and reasonable" and there results pure progress. In the second, one grasps the
presence of the unintelligible, unintelligent surd in human affairs,
whereby people are unintelligent and unreasonable in their decisions,
and there results decline. In the third, there is renaissance or redemption, which, through the assistance of God's grace, moves humanity
closer to the ideal line of history, of pure progress.[5]

This initial interest in history foreshadows Lonergan's concern to
integrate history into the very fabric of theology. As indicated in the
discussion of the previous chapter on Dulles' model of "revelation as
history", this concern has implications for the question of revelation

2.1.2 Thomistic Writings: *Grace and Freedom* and *Verbum*.

The next major phase in his work involved a more direct engagement with doctrinal themes. He spoke of this time as his years of
"reaching up to the mind of Aquinas."[6] The fruits of this labour were
the two works which were later published in book form as *Grace and
Freedom: Operative Grace in the Thought of St. Thomas Aquinas*[7] and
Verbum: Word and Idea in Aquinas.[8] They represent Lonergan's retrieval of an authentic Thomism through a study of Aquinas in the
areas of grace and the Trinitarian processions. Interestingly, he saw
his task as basically an historical one, as an exercise in historical
method to resolve theological issues.[9] This is not to say that his investigation did not involve serious philosophical and theological issues.
Rather, the systematic use of historical method allowed for a clearing
away of false trails built on inadequate historical approaches.

As I noted in the beginning of Chapter One, it is in the introduction to his thesis *Gratia Operans* that Lonergan first raises the pressing issue of theological method. Bemoaning the inability of the Banezians and Molinists to resolve their conflict about the interpretation of Aquinas on grace, he states:

> Unless a writer can assign a method that of itself tends to greater objectivity than those hitherto employed, his undertaking may well be regarded as superfluous.[10]

He finds such a method in a "theory of the history of theological speculation." Lonergan proposes an "*a priori* scheme that is capable of synthesizing any possible set of historical data irrespective of their time and place",[11] drawn "solely from a consideration of the nature of human speculation on a given subject."[12]

At this stage, he restricts his concern to development in speculative thought. As far as his study is concerned he has no interest in the questions of dogmatic development and their implications:

> Dogmatic truths are one thing; their speculative correlation and unification quite another ... the two are quite disparate, so that no specialized inquiry can possibly deal with both at the same time. Hence when we speak of speculative development, we do not mean the development of dogma: as far as our argument goes there need be no dogmatic development whatever from St Paul to the Council of Trent; and the reason why there is no such need, is that speculative development and dogmatic development are quite different ...[13]

Of course, Lonergan does not say that there is no dogmatic development between Paul and Trent. Merely that it falls outside the scope of the type of theological method he employs in his thesis. It has been bracketed from the study. From this point of view, revelation is simply given; it is a fact on the horizon which needs no further explanation.

It is beyond the scope of this present work to go over the details of the method Lonergan is here employing. While it prefigures what he will later call the development of a "universal viewpoint", the precise details are mainly of historical interest.[14] What is of present interest is the achievement of the work itself. Not only does he retrieve the thought of Aquinas on operative grace, he also locates Aquinas' position within an overarching framework of divine transcendence and a universally efficacious providence. While the theme of operative grace will come to flower in *Method* with his mature understanding of religious experience and conversion, the positions on divine transcendence and providence find their fulfilment in Chapter 19 of *Insight*. This study clearly gave a permanent direction to Lonergan's developing thought. Its significance is also evident in view of the understanding he gained of history, and how history may be viewed within an account of revelation.

Lonergan adopts much the same approach in his study on the Trinitarian processions, *Verbum: Word and Idea in Aquinas*, as he did in *Grace and Freedom* . Again, his method here is basically historical, though, as in his previous work, it is history presented with more than a touch of philosophical acumen.[15] However, there is a shift of focus between these two works. While *Grace and Freedom* remains a basically objective, metaphysical account of grace, freedom and divine providence, *Verbum* represents a more serious "turn to the subject."[16] In *Verbum*, Lonergan is exploring the interiority which grounds the metaphysical world of theory. Thus, while the questions may be framed in metaphysical terms, the answers are to be found through a detailed examination of conscious acts of understanding, judging and deciding. He argues that it is only in this way that the meaning of Aquinas' texts can be properly understood:

> ... to follow Aquinas here, one must practice introspective rational psychology; without that, one no more can know the created image of the Blessed Trinity, as Aquinas conceived it, than a blind man can know colors.[17]

Once more, this is not the place of this thesis to review all the gains made in *Verbum*. This work represents a major rejection of a static conceptualism, and the development of a dynamic intellectualism, in the context of understanding the Trinitarian procession. In its own way it lays the ground-rules of the game which is played out in *Insight*. It is the recovery of the old, the *vetera*, which he brings into intense dialogue with the new, the *nova*, with science, with commonsense, with history and politics in his major philosophical work, *Insight*. Methodologically, its significance lies in its appeal to the data of interiority, of consciousness, to settle the problems of interpretation which had beset Thomistic studies on the Trinity.

We must concede that there is no special interest in the issue of revelation in this work. The doctrine of the Trinity is simply given. Lonergan is neither interested in its origin, nor in its relationship to the "economic Trinity", nor in the question of the development of dogma, nor in any related issue. While he is interested in questions of historical development, the context of that interest remains one of speculative development, not dogmatic development.

Still, the *Verbum* studies do indirectly raise some interesting questions about the nature of revelation. In particular, one can ask: What are the profound philosophical issues that Lonergan was dealing with here, doing in a work whose ostensible purpose is a study of the Trinitarian processions? This is more a question of considering his performance than of attending to the subject matter of the work. At this stage I simply observe that the close connection between Church dogma and Lonergan's philosophical stance requires further attention.

I shall move on now to two essays Lonergan published between *Verbum* and *Insight*. These essays appeared in the work, *Collection*, and impinge in a significant manner on the concerns of this thesis.

2.1.3 "The Assumption and Theology" [1948][18]

This essay is significant for understanding Lonergan's notion of revelation at this stage of his thinking, not because of any explicit reflection on the nature of revelation, so much as it provides a performative illustration of a notion of revelation operative in his thinking at this time.

The issue at stake is whether the Assumption is a proper object for dogmatic definition; and if so, why?[19] Such questions can only be answered in terms of some notion of revelation, however implicit such a notion may be.

As to whether the Assumption could be defined, Lonergan states that "the answer undoubtedly is affirmative."[20] The basis for this certainty was the firm conviction of the Church indicated by a tradition going back to the Middle Ages, and evidenced by a large number of petitions from bishops and others requesting that such a definition be made. He concludes:

> Were the Assumption not truth but error, then one would have to admit what no Catholic can admit, namely, that God has not promised preservation from error to the Church.[21]

This rather summary treatment of the question of fact obviously assumes a whole series of beliefs concerning the nature of revelation and the role of the Church as a bearer of revelation under the guidance and guarantee of the Holy Spirit. It, in turn, leads on to a fuller discussion of reasons why the Assumption can be defined.

Lonergan does not hold that there is any explicit revelation of the Assumption, either in Scripture or Tradition. Rather, it is "implicit." What does he mean by this? Firstly, he gives a Scriptural account (mainly from Paul, and especially from Romans) of "man's fall through Adam and his redemption through Christ." Adam sinned; and so sin and death entered the world. Christ died for the remission of sin, and rose to give us grace. In Christ's victory, death is swallowed up, and in the end the dead will rise immortal. "Such is the general perspective presented explicitly to our faith by holy scripture."[22]

Lonergan then proceeds to address this general perspective with a series of questions. Where does Mary stand in this picture? As Christ rose, was she too assumed? Or does she still wait, with sinners? He reflects on Mary's privileges – full of grace, free from sin, ever virgin, Mother of God. Can all this be granted, yet the Assumption denied? Can she be freed from sin, but not from death? Would not the Assumption be a grace, for the one full of grace? He concludes, "Such then is the implication of the assumption in the teaching of scripture."[23]

But such an implication is not a matter of conceptualist deduction. Rather is it a progressive, dynamic, developing "understanding of man illumined by faith and moved by the grace of the Holy Spirit", confirmed by the judgment of the Church.[24] Inasmuch as there may be a problem for theology is this matter, "one has to get beyond conceptualism and give a central role in thought to the act of understanding."[25]

From this we see that Lonergan accepts a process of doctrinal "development", conceived in terms of a movement from "implicit" to "explicit", coming about as a result of a dynamic process of questions and answers, illumined by faith and the Holy Spirit. Still, that process is not given any concrete historical setting apart from very general references to the Middle Ages and beyond. Nor is such a process part of the question of settling the matter of dogmatic fact – "Can the assumption be defined?." Rather, it is a theological inquiry into why it could be defined. It is concerned, not with the *An sit?*, but with the *Quid Sit?*. The answer to the question *An sit?* is found by reference to the authority of the one revealing, handed on through the Church.

2.1.4 "Theology and Understanding" [1954][26]

Ostensibly, this particular essay is a review of the work *Theologie als Glaubensverständnis* by Fr. Johannes Beumer. Beumer proposes a ideal for theology based on understanding rather than certitude, a position consonant with that of Lonergan. Yet Lonergan uses this essay as an opportunity to further explore issues of theological method and the relationship between the classical ideals of theology as understanding, and the emerging positive, **historical** theology. Again, we see that the issue at stake is the integration of historical studies into theology. Our concern is with the implications of this for an understanding of revelation.

While Beumer proposes an ideal for theology similar to that of Lonergan's, Lonergan takes issue with Beumer's preference for Scheeben over Aquinas as representative of the ideal in question. While Beumer distinguishes between an understanding of the truths of faith (*Glaubensverständnis*) and a science of the truths of faith (*Glaubenswissenschaft*), Lonergan prefers to distinguish between the *causa cognoscendi* and the *causa essendi*, between the *prior quoad nos* and the *prior quoad se*, between the *ordo inventionis* and the *ordo doctrinae*.[27] These two ways he finds amply illustrated in the two major works of Aquinas, the *Summa Contra Gentiles* and the *Summa Theologiae*, particularly in their respective treatments of Trinitarian doctrine. The *via inventionis* begins with the revealed affirmation of three persons in one God, and concludes with the psychological analogy. The *via doctrinae* begins with one God and the processions of knowing and loving, and concludes with three distinct, yet consubstantial, persons.[28]

In this Trinitarian context, Lonergan's discussion prescinds from any historical issues. He considers merely the systematic ordering of understanding within a systematic theology. He is not concerned with the historical genesis of understanding, as he was in the introduction to his thesis, *Gratia Operans*. Nor is he concerned with the historical origins of what is being understood, the dogmas of revelation. These are simply given and are apparently non-problematic:

> From revelation comes the premises of the *ordo inventionis* and on the truth of the premises rests the truth not only of their conclusions but also the subsequent development of the *ordo doctrinae* ... Indeed one may add that the deductions of the *ordo inventionis* are all the

more secure if not only the initial premises are revealed but also the conclusions are confirmed by revelation and, inversely, the more extensive such confirmation, the greater the section of revealed truth that is unified in the *ordo doctrinae*.[29]

Where then does Lonergan place the emerging historical studies in theology?

In the final section of the review, Lonergan takes up this issue of the relationship between speculative and positive theology. He recalls that Vatican I spoke not only of an understanding of the mysteries of faith, but also individual and collective progress in that understanding. This progress is uncovered in historical studies. Yet, while it is one thing to undertake the duty of such uncovering, "it is another to discover the methodological principles on which the duty can be performed" satisfactorily.[30] Given the "flood tide of scholarly research" into every aspect of the Church's past, into the Bible, the fathers, heretics, Councils and so on, how can the diverse results of scholarship be encompassed within the unity of a speculative system?

Here, Lonergan distinguishes two types of historical questions: those settled by reference to the methods of exact positive research, and are thus subject to the vicissitudes of developing opinion; and those settled, not by a more exact application of positive research, but by reference to "the empiricist, naturalist, existentialist, idealist, relativist, or realist philosophy which individual scholars implicitly or explicitly invoke" in their use or interpretation of that method. The first type of questions, he claims "are not very relevant to theology"; while the second type are "extremely relevant to theology", because they are not subject to the vicissitudes of new historical opinions.[31]

To address these questions adequately, historical method needs "higher level controls" to provide an *a priori*, in much the same way as differential equations provide an *a priori* for the physical sciences. In discussing the more general question of the relations between speculative theology and the empirical human sciences, of which history is only one, Lonergan makes clear that these "higher level controls are to be provided by theology." For the data of the human condition are not simply intelligible. They "suffer from the effects of original sin and of personal sin" which require the grace of healing and forgiveness. Thus, the "only correct general form" for understanding in the human sciences is to be provided by theology.[32]

Here we find two themes merging in Lonergan's thought. In *Gratia Operans* he also searches for an *a priori*. But there it is provided by reflection on the general process of the emergence of systematic thought. In the present essay, the *a priori* is found in a theological view of history which incorporates sin and grace. He re-introduces his earlier interest in a philosophy of history into his theological method. This historical *a priori* provides elements of the upper blade for historical studies. Further, it anticipates the functional speciality of dialectics in his later work, *Method in Theology*. Finally, because this *a priori* is based on revelation, which is historically non-problematic for Lonergan at this stage, dogmatic concerns basically determine the outcome of positive historical studies.

At the time of the publication of "Theology and Understanding", Lonergan was already in the throes of writing his major work, *Insight*. We will not be surprised then to see some of the same issues emerge in that more thorough context.

2.2 *Insight: A Study of Human Understanding*

Even Lonergan's most severe critics recognise his work *Insight: A Study of Human Understanding* to be an outstanding contribution to philosophy. For Lonergan himself, it was "a long book on methods generally to underpin ... [a] book on method in theology."[33] He employs his cognitional theory to discuss issues in science, depth psychology, the history of philosophy, ethics, metaphysics and theology. The book is written "from a moving view point." Its horizon expands from an initial phenomenology of the experience of insight; to the role of insight in science and common sense; to the biases which inhibit insight; to the role of judgment in knowledge; to the basic self-affirmation of the knower; to a critical metaphysics ground in cognitional theory; to an ethics; and, finally, to general and special transcendent knowledge. In these latter chapters we gain most understanding of how Lonergan views the question of revelation.

In these brief comments I shall focus on key issues which relate to the interests of this thesis.

2.2.1 Position on knowing, being and reality

The key to *Insight* is the position on knowing, developed in its first eleven chapters. Given the claim of revelation to be, in some sense, a form of knowing, it is not difficult to see that some account of knowing can play an important part in any theology of revelation.

The basis of *Insight's* account of knowing is the identification within human consciousness of a "detached, disinterested desire to know": the eros of the mind. Here, consciousness is not self-knowledge or self-awareness, but simply self-presence. It is a presence immanent in various acts which we call conscious. Consciousness is not something we add to these acts. It is constitutive of the acts themselves.[34] A key element in human consciousness is our desire to know, as evidenced from the child's relentless questioning, to the vast array of books which continue to fill our libraries. Our desire to know is unrestricted in its object; we can ask questions about anything.

Examining this unrestricted desire to know, Lonergan identifies human knowing as a three-fold activity: experience, understanding and judgment. Experience deals with data. Data include both the data of our sensing, perceiving, imagining, feeling, and the data of consciousness itself. Understanding arises from questioning, which leads to insight. Central here is this act of insight. It dissolves the tension of inquiry in the clear grasp of possibility. It involves the movement from not understanding to quite clear and distinct understanding. Through it, the data are organised into an intelligible whole.[35] Insight then generates hypothesis, formulation, concepts. Yet, despite its brilliance, insight is not enough. Even the most brilliant hypothesis can be wrong. Insight does not of itself satisfy our desire to know. It must contend with the 'Yes' or 'No' of judgment. Judgment demands sufficient reason. The weighing of evidence is needed before the knower can make a truthful judgment. For Lonergan, the immanent term of judgment occurs when the subject grasps in reflective insight that there are no further relevant question to ask. When the conditions to be fulfilled, are in fact fulfilled, a virtually unconditioned affirmation occurs.[36]

Lonergan correlates this three-fold activity with three distinct levels of human consciousness. The activity of experiencing corresponds to empirical consciousness, constituted by conscious acts of seeing, hearing, touching, tasting, feeling, perceiving, imagining, speaking, moving. The activity of understanding corresponds to the intellectual level of consciousness, which is constituted by conscious acts of inquiry, questioning, insight, forming hypotheses, working out the presuppositions and implications of our insight. The activity of judging corresponds to rational consciousness. This is constituted by acts of marshalling and weighing the evidence, so as to ground a possible, probable or certain judgment.

This account of knowing constitutes the basic elements of Lonergan's cognitional theory. From it flows an epistemology and a metaphysics. In this context, he addresses the questions of the objectivity of knowledge and the relationship of knowledge to being: the object of the detached, disinterested and unrestricted desire to know is being itself. Being is what is known in our intelligent grasp and reasonable affirmation. It is the object of our desire to know. Since we head towards this object, not only consciously, but also intelligently and reasonably, he speaks of consciousness as containing a *notion* of being. Thus, our conscious questioning is a heuristic anticipation of being.

Lonergan summarises his achievement in *Insight* in three basic positions:

(1) The real is the concrete universe of being and not a subdivision of the 'already our there now'.

(2) The subject itself becomes known when it affirms itself intelligently and reasonably; and is not yet known in any state prior to questioning, insight and judgment.

(3) Objectivity is conceived as a consequence of intelligent inquiry and critical reflection. Hence, it is not a property of vital anticipation, extroversion, and satisfaction, of "taking a good look."[37]

Thus (1) represents the breakthrough into a critical realism: reality is identified with being. And being is known through intelligent inquiry and reasonable affirmation. Consequently, reality is not "what is seen", but what can be known to be. In (2) the supposed epistemological gap between knower and known is overcome. The knower is known in the same way that any other object can be known – through intelligent inquiry and reasonable affirmation. Epistemology is, then, not a question of bridging a gap between subject and object. It is more one of building a moat, of learning to make the appropriate distinction, through judgments, between subject and object.[38] Finally, in (3) Lonergan specifies objectivity in terms of the authentic operations of intelligence and reason. It is not a matter of "taking a good look and seeing what is there and not seeing what is not there." Lonergan refers to stances which are opposed to his three basic positions as counter-positions.

Clearly, I have already relied upon these positions in the previous chapter, in analysing the various models of revelation presented by Avery Dulles and the theology of revelation presented by Edward Schillebeeckx.

2.2.2 Bias and moral impotence

Despite the overwhelming significance Lonergan gives to our detached, disinterested desire to know, he was certainly not unaware of the various forces which restrict that desire in the attainment of its object. He specifies a number of biases which operate to subvert our pure desire to know, and so undermine our ability to live an intelligent and reasonable life. The problems created by bias make revelation a moral necessity.[39]

First, there is a *dramatic bias* manifest in the censorship of the images needed for the insights which could reshape our living. This repression of images leads to a splitting off of associated affects to become attached to incongruous objects. This process suggests the genesis of neurosis and other psychic disturbances. Here, Lonergan uses the insights of Freud, even if somewhat tailored to his own ends.[40]

Then there is the question of *individual bias*. This involves the interference, by our psychic spontaneity[41], with the development of intelligence. Such spontaneity is centred on the self, while intelligence seeks to decentre the self within the realm of being. Egoism is not just spontaneous, self-regarding appetite. It is an incomplete development of intelligence. It leads to the suppression, not of images, as in dramatic bias, but of the intelligent questions which would generalise one's concerns to others.

A third kind of distortion is termed *group bias*. It comes into play when our spontaneous intersubjectivity encompasses our identification with a given social group. It too interferes with the proper development of intelligence, and promotes the suppression of further relevant questions. Group spontaneity does not regard all changes proposed by practical intelligence in the same cold light of reason. It is willing to sacrifice the general good of the society for its own limited perspective. When group bias dominates social living it leads to "the short cycle of decline." One dominant group is overthrown by another, more creative, group. This new group begins by initiating changes demanded by practical intelligence, but eventually becomes simply dominant; and so is itself overthrown by another. The notion of the short cycle of decline is an important element in Lonergan's developing philosophy of history.[42]

Fourthly, Lonergan speaks of *general bias*, arising from the omnicompetent pretensions of common sense. For Lonergan, common sense,

> is concerned with the concrete and the particular. It entertains no aspirations about reaching abstract and universal laws. It is easily led to rationalize its limitations by engendering a conviction that other forms of human knowledge are useless or doubtfully valid.[43]

General bias, of its nature, leads to a neglect of the long term, theoretical questions which go beyond the horizon of common sense. Instead, it concentrates on the immediate short term questions which common sense feels competent to handle. General bias leads to what Lonergan calls "the longer cycle of decline", "characterized by the neglect of ideas to which all groups are rendered indifferent by the general bias of common sense."[44] The result is a accumulation of less and less intelligent solutions to the problems of human living. The implementation of these solutions creates a cumulative deterioration of the social situation and a greater distortion of human intelligence in its struggle to make sense of what is less and less intelligible in society. This cumulative deterioration is termed "the social surd." Lonergan finds ample evidence of this longer cycle of decline in the history of the twentieth century.[45] Clearly, this notion of a long cycle of decline is also a key element in Lonergan's developing philosophy of history, and it is especially significant for understanding the function of revelation.

The cumulative effect of these biases leads to the moral impotence of the human subject. If moral action demands a universal willingness to match the unrestricted nature of our desire to know, moral impotence arises from the incomplete intellectual and volitional development of the subject, brought about by the biases concerned. There results a gap between the effective willingness of the subject and the universal willingness which is demanded to match our unrestricted desire to know.

Moral impotence implies that, once affected by bias, the subject, of itself, is unable to sustain its own cognitional development. It requires the assistance of a higher integration of human living. Revelation, then, helps supply this higher integration.

2.2.3 General and special transcendent knowledge

The final two chapters of *Insight* are of special importance for this thesis. Here Lonergan spells out the relationship between human knowing with its proportionate object, that is, proportionate being, and the transcendent object of that knowing, that is, transcendent being. Following traditional Thomistic lines, he argues from the radical contingency of proportionate being to the necessity of a transcendent cause of existence, which we call God. God is conceived as an unrestricted act of understanding, who understands everything about everything. Indeed, divine intelligence is the ground for the complete intelligibility of being.

Hence, Lonergan formulates his basic argument for the existence of God in the following terms: "If the real is completely intelligible, God exists. But the real is completely intelligible. Therefore God exists."[46] The complete intelligibility of reality requires an intelligent ground. This ground must be an unrestricted act of understanding, to be the cause of all intelligibility. On the other hand, the notion of being, which is a constitutive element of human consciousness, commits us to the complete intelligibility of reality. We can deny such a commitment only if we are willing to be unintelligent and unreasonable. However, in Chapter 11 of *Insight*, "Self-Affirmation of the Knower", Lonergan invites such a commitment from the reader through invoking the very crucial judgment, "I am a knower." By this he means,

> I am a knower, if I am a concrete and intelligible unity-identity-whole, characterized by acts of sensing perceiving, imagining, inquiring, understanding, formulating, reflecting, grasping the unconditioned, and judging.[47]

Such a judgment is not only empirical. It is also normative. As an immanent law, it demands a personal commitment. This affirmation plays a central role in Lonergan's argument for the existence of God.[48]

The affirmation of transcendent being has a number of consequences, which are spelt out in great detail in *Insight*. Most significant for the direction of this thesis are those pages where Lonergan spelt out a doctrine of a causally efficacious divine providence: "From the viewpoint of unrestricted understanding, the non-systematic vanishes to yield place to a fully determinate and absolutely efficacious plan and intention."[49] Providence encompasses the whole of human and, indeed, cosmic history.

There remains, however, the problem of evil, which, in turn, promotes a discussion of faith and revelation. What is of significance for this thesis is that, in his handling of the questions of faith and revelation, Lonergan firmly correlates the notion of what might be called supernatural revelation (what he calls special transcendent knowledge) with the divinely ordained solution to the problem of evil. The problem of evil is a given. Revelation, as special transcendent knowledge, comes as a solution to the problem, as it is found in human history. Already, we see that, for Lonergan, revelation has an *historical significance*. It offers a solution to the historical problem of evil.

For Lonergan, evil has two components: physical evil and moral evil. Physical evil, such as suffering, arises from the evolutionary nature of the world. Moral evil arises from basic sin which originates from a human refusal to be intelligent and reasonable. This refusal introduces an unintelligible surd into human living. Clearly, the fact of such an unintelligible surd raises serious problems for a philosophy which argues from the intelligibility of reality. Lonergan seeks to resolve the problem in the following manner:

> Nonetheless, there is the problem of evil, for besides man there also is God ... Because God is omniscient, he knows man's plight. Because he is omnipotent, he can remedy it. Because he is good, he wills to do so. The fact of evil is not the whole story.[50]

Thus, in Chapter 20, he outlines what he calls the "heuristic structure" of the divinely ordained solution to the problem of evil. This solution "consist[s] in the introduction of new conjugate forms [i.e. habits] in man's intellect, will, and sensitivity."[51] He describes these habits in the traditional terminology of faith, hope and charity. His specification of the divinely originated solution to the problem of evil remains heuristic, since it can only be further categorised by an appeal to the concrete events of human history.

Such an appeal moves beyond the transcendental method that Lonergan is developing. We can see here the problem alluded to by

the critics mentioned in Chapter One of this thesis, that is, the problem
of the interface between transcendental method and historical contingency. Transcendental method anticipates what can only be resolved
through historically contingent data.

In the context of revelation, a significant section of Lonergan's
discussion of the problem of evil deals with faith. In what he acknowledges as an "excessively long parenthesis", he analyses the
notion of belief. Concerned to establish the reasonableness of believing, he places it in the general context of the collaborative advance in
human knowledge:

> The general context of belief, then, is a sustained collaboration of
> many instances of rational self-consciousness in the attainment and
> the dissemination of knowledge. The alternative to the collaboration
> is a primitive ignorance.[52]

Belief is, then, our reasonable willingness to assent to knowledge
communicated to us by another, without immanently generated
knowledge of our own on the matter.

This intellectualist understanding of belief is maintained in the
discussion of religious faith. Faith is "the requisite conjugate form that
the solution [to the problem of evil] brings to man's intellect."[53] In
very Scholastic terms,

> the act of faith will be an assent of intellect to truths transmitted
> through the collaboration [of human beings with God] and it will be
> motivated by man's reliance on the truthfulness of God.[54]

Given such an understanding of faith, it is quite consistent to then
speak of revelation in almost propositional terms as "a permanent
deposit confided to the Church and by the Church to be preserved and
defended."[55]

2.2.4 The Epilogue to *Insight*

In the Epilogue of *Insight*, Lonergan turns his attention to the
overarching motivation for his labours, that is, questions of theological
method. He notes the relevance of his present work, particularly the
chapters on general and special transcendent knowledge, for apolo-
getics, which, as an exercise in *intellectus quaerens fidem*, arrives at a

symbiosis of faith and reason. Assessing the contribution of *Insight* to theological method, particular his notion of positions and counter-positions, he claims to lay bare the roots of the revolts of both pietists and modernists against dogma, and of various metaphysical disputes.[56] He argues that the metaphysics developed in *Insight* is transcultural. It can ground a universal viewpoint needed as an upper blade for interpreting the past and the present as the cumulative product of the dialectic interplay of positions and counter-positions in history.

In such a context, Lonergan addresses the issue of the development of doctrine. With Vatican I he affirms both revelation, as "a permanent deposit confided to the Church and by the Church to be preserved and defended", and the "advance in human understanding, knowledge and wisdom, by which the same doctrine with the same meaning was to be apprehended ever more fully."[57] Armed with a "theologically transformed" universal viewpoint, the theologian, facing the mass of historical data, can come to appreciate how "in a pre-eminent and unique manner the dogmatic decision is ... the true interpretation of Scriptural texts, patristic teaching and traditional utterances."[58]

But these same historical data need to be considered as a "cumulative, historical development, first of the chosen people and, then, of the Catholic Church, both in themselves and in their role in the unfolding of all human history."[59] For Lonergan, this "historical aspect of development" should be undertaken in a treatise on the Mystical Body, and requires for its formal element a theory of history using the categories of progress, decline and supernatural recovery.

His writings up to this point yield evidence of a continuing struggle to find the proper place for history within theology. While the products of historical study are subsumed under the theologically transformed universal viewpoint, this viewpoint allows theologians to see dogmas as valid, true interpretations of divine revelation. On the other hand, history itself, in its manifold movements of progress and decline, is subsumed with the theological treatise on the Mystical Body of Christ.

2.3 The Period Between *Insight* and *Method*[60]

Lonergan completed *Insight* in 1953, after he had learnt of his appointment to Rome to teach theology at the Gregorian University, though it was not published until 1957. This appointment initiated a

period of teaching and researching under academic conditions he described as "hopelessly antiquated."[61] It also meant exposure to a large
student body who collectively had "read everything", forcing the
lecturer to expand his own horizons considerably.[62]

Crowe has described this period as one of "experiments in
method."[63] Apart from his undergraduate courses in Trinity and Incarnation, in which Lonergan brought his own methodological reflections
and approaches into the restrictive confines of the Roman thesis style
of teaching, he taught graduate courses in the area of methodology.
The emerging themes of this era are those of meaning and historical
consciousness.

2.3.1 Graduate Courses on Method, 1959, 1962.[64]

In 1959 Lonergan gave the first of a series of post-graduate seminars in the topic of theological method. While he treats some of the
issues in his directly theological works, these seminars communicate
his more detailed reflections on the issue of method.

The first of these seminars has been printed under the title, *De
Intellectu et Methodo*, gathered from notes collected and transcribed
by students at the seminar. In these notes we see Lonergan struggling
with the same issues present in the earlier paper, "Theology and Understanding", that is, the issues that arise from the introduction of
historical studies into the heart of theology. While the issues are the
same, this time Lonergan arrived at a different solution.

He begins by noting the way in which theological systems
emerge. One begins with questions. These questions must be ordered
in a logical and coherent manner, as must their answers. The answers
must bear some relation to reality, so that there is a movement beyond
logic into metaphysics. Finally, the same totality can be ordered in
different ways, either from what is first for us (*priora quoad nos*) to
what is first in itself (*priora quoad se*), or vice versa, from articles of
faith to proper theological principles and then back again. Such a
totality is a theological system.[65]

Though the activity of analysis and synthesis operates within a
theological system, there is another process which must be understood:
that of moving from one system to another. New problems, new
questions may not be solvable within a particular system. These
problems may call for a new ordering and the development of new
principles. How, then, can one justify the movement from one system

to another? The introduction of historical studies forces theology to face this issue. Lonergan addresses the problem of historical studies under three headings, (1) the problem of foundations, (2) the problem of historicity, and (3) the problem of the chasm:

> The foundational problem occurs within any system when a new kind of problem appears on the scene whose solutions does not seem available within the system.[66]

In Lonergan's view, the whole history of theology and philosophy can be understood as a series of systems and transitions from one system to another. How does one then determine whether these transitions are justified? They cannot be simply a matter of logical deduction. If they were, then the supposed new system would be contained logically within the first.[67]

Positive historical studies highlight the problem in a special way. Such studies uncover the multiple transitions that occur in human thought within the dynamics of history. Hence, the problem of historicity arises because of the emergence of positive studies calling attention to these transitions from one system to another. Lonergan addresses the problem directly as he asks:

> Why is the introduction of positive studies a problem for speculative theology? To answer this question we need only consider one point. If St Paul conceived the divine missions in the same way as St Thomas did, then the two theological processes mutually correspond, their respective notions are equivalent, and so development of positive studies is absolutely equivalent to the development of theology. But because St Paul and St Thomas do not conceive the divine missions in the same way, because the divine missions are not conceived in the same way systematically and historically, then there is no possibility of using some kind of logical deduction by which to move from one ordering of ideas to another.[68]

Historicity thus appears to undermine both the foundations of systematic speculation and any continuity between various conceptions of dogma:

> For these dogmas are not only conceived in diverse ways in different times, but absolutely one thing seems to be conceived by biblical writers, another by the Fathers, another by medieval theologians.[69]

In what, then, does the continuity of faith consist? If the biblical writers, the Fathers and the medieval theologians have such absolutely different conceptions of the content of faith, in what sense do they hold to the same faith? This is the problem of historicity.

Finally, there is the problem of the chasm, or gulf, which arises between the horizon of the simple faithful and that of the systematic theologian:

> The more theology becomes systematic, and the more it gathers questions, responses, orderings of responses, to that degree does it move further away from a scriptural way of speaking in general, and not just from the immediate, concrete needs of humanity. Therefore, there is a reaction against systematization.[70]

Significantly for his later development, Lonergan understood the solution to the problem of foundations in terms of wisdom. Wisdom is "a principle of ordering and of judging, making judgments about everything." Wisdom can judge the validity of moving from one system to another.[71] This appeal to wisdom prefigures his later emphasis on conversion as the foundation for theology.

More to the point, he attempts to solve the problem of the chasm. He argues that theologians must (i) become more familiar with the different orders of analysis and synthesis; (ii) and attend to the experience of communicating through preaching in a popular vein both what must be believed and the understanding of the faith. In this way they can bridge the chasm between intellectual and sensitive life.[72]

This "solution" to the problem of the chasm allows Lonergan to attack the problem of historicity. According to his cognitional theory, understanding bridges the gap between sensitive and intellectual consciousness, between image and concept. Historically, concepts appear in such variety because they are dependent on the intelligence and intention of the person who generates them. As understanding develops, there will be an evolution of the concepts used to express understanding. Thus, Lonergan's dynamic intellectualism, as opposed to static conceptualism, lies at the heart of his proposed solution to the problem of historicity.

Lonergan envisages a solution to these problems by bringing together historical and speculative theology. "Historical theology is speculative theology as it develops (*in fieri*), while speculative theology is historical theology as it exists in its term (*in facto esse*)."[73] He argues strongly that only a theologian can properly undertake positive studies. For only the theologian properly understands what the process of development is, by relating it to his or her own process of "internal evolution." The task of historical theology is to discover the internal intelligibility of a transition from one situation to another.[74]

On this reading, there must be a close connection between histori- cal and speculative theology. Without speculative theology, historical theology loses its proper method. Without historical theology, specu- lative theology is separated from its proper origins, namely, historical revelation. These origins can then become falsified "through anachro- nism that projects later categories onto earlier stages."[75] While speculative theologians may refer to the teaching of the Church magisterium, this will only tell them what to believe, but it will not help in their understanding of the faith.[76]

What we see in *De intellectu et methodo* is Lonergan's attempt to unify historical and speculative theology, while bracketing dogmatic issues from consideration. Historical theology helps speculative the- ology to keep in touch with its proper origins, that is, historically revealed data. But one does not get the sense yet that history has entered fully into the process of revelation itself. He acknowledges dogmatic development, but is very wary about accepting a position of "transformational evolution" of dogmas, as asserted by "rationalists and modernists."[77] By diagnosing the problem posed by historical studies in terms of the relationship between speculative and historical theology, Lonergan effectively allows dogmatic theology to control the overall process. Still, by seeking a foundation to the solution of the relationship between the two in wisdom, Lonergan is moving towards the solution adopted in *Method*, where converted subjectivity is foundational for theology.

This bracketing of the question of dogmatic development is over- come in the later graduate course, *De methodo theologiae*. There Lonergan moves away from his concern to integrate historical studies with the analytic and synthetic processes, and addresses the "concerns and questions that flow from the account of the development of dogma."[78] To meet these concerns and questions he shifts focus from the object of theology – God, revelation and so on – to the subject who theologises. The subject operates in worlds of community, theory and interiority. This subject, inhabiting an horizon which is either authen- tic or unauthentic, is called to greater intellectual, moral and religious conversion.[79]

How, then, does Lonergan account for dogmatic development at this stage of his "experiments in method"? He begins by reflecting on the human good, value and meaning. Meaning is a formal element of the human good. For "without meaning, there is no human cooperation expect in the most elementary forms."[80] Such meaning develops as human activity, constituted by meaning, develops and expands. Thus, to understand human activity is to understand developing meanings. Awareness of such developments in meaning is what Lonergan calls "historical consciousness." By focusing on meaning and historical consciousness, he opens up a new perspective on the dynamics of revelation itself:

> What is revelation? It is a new meaning added into human life. By bringing new meaning into this process of the human good, one transforms something that is formally constitutive of that human good.[81]

In this way, dogmatic development is identified as a process of moving from implicit to explicit meanings. Lonergan finds this procedure illustrated in the works of Landgraf on the doctrine of grace, and the works of Lottin on the question of human freedom. One and the same reality can be transposed from a commonsense mode of apprehension to a theoretic mode of explicit meaning.[82]

These new revealed meanings are to be found in the sources of revelation, particularly the Scriptures. Thus, while the dogmatic theologian asks questions out of a contemporary dogmatic context, the answers are to be found by attending to the Scriptures as true, and "finding in them precise elements that settle one way or another the questions arising from the dogmatic-theological context."[83] This context is itself the product of a gradual accumulation over centuries of development in both dogma and theology.

According to Boly, in *De methodo theologiae*, Lonergan,

> makes what seems like a quantum leap in his methodological thinking when he turns his attention to the subject, who in differentiated operations dwells in a dogmatic-theological context that makes possible a *de facto* notion of theology that empowers an historical consideration of theology.[84]

Lonergan no longer brackets questions of dogmatic development. Further, in turning to the subject, he was able to develop resources which can make sense of that development, as implying a move from implicit to explicit meanings in an historical context of developing meanings. Nonetheless, while he speaks of revelation in terms of the entry of new meanings into human history, the way he makes reference to dogmatic theologians appealing to Scripture still has an a-historical dimension. It is as if one could attend to "the Scriptures as true", but apart from a context of "the experiences, thoughts, or sensibility that lie behind the words of scripture."[85] What is lacking still is a full explication of the role of the positive phase of theology, which Lonergan later develops in *Method*.

2.3.2 *De Deo Trino, The Way to Nicea*, 1961, 1964.

In 1964 Lonergan published his Latin lectures on the Trinity, *De Deo Trino* in two parts, one dogmatic, the other systematic. Both volumes were revised editions of earlier works. The revision is noticeable mainly in the shift in method that was achieved as a result of the "experiments" undertaken up to this point.

I shall focus attention on the *Pars Dogmatica* since it contains the most significant methodological material. Here, I shall draw on the analyses of Craig Boly and Charles Hefling.[86]

The key methodological issue raised by the introduction of the *Pars Dogmatica* is that of dogmatic development: How are we to understand the relationship between dogmatic theology and positive historical studies? To answer this one must turn from abstract considerations about the movement from implicit revelation to explicit dogma, to the *concrete historical context* in which those implication were drawn:

> Quibus in omnibus, etsi eadam generice semper quaeratur vel connexio vel consequentia vel implicatio, secundum quam dogmata implicite revelata esse dicuntur, ipsa tamen haec implicatio non abstracte tantummodo consideranda est sed etiam concrete, et quidem organice, genetice, dialectice.[87]

These concrete considerations, which seek organic, genetic and dialectic developments in the historical data, distinguish it from Lonergan's consideration of the doctrine of the Assumption, for example.

The process of question and answer used in his earlier paper on the Assumption is now placed in an historical context:

> Non enim evolvuntur doctrinae ut nuda quaedam propositionum series quasi seorsim exsistat, sed ideo efformatae atque perfectae sunt ut quaestionibus respondeant, difficultates amoveant, problemata resolvant. Quod si hae quaestiones, difficultates, problemata neque exacte neque plene cognoscuntur nisi in concreto illo atque historico rerum cursu ubi sunt ortae, sequitur et ipsam doctrinam iis correspondentem sub adiunctis sui loci et temporis investigandam esse atque addiscendam.[88]

Dogmatic statements cannot be abstracted from their historical context.

Nonetheless, he still maintains the distinction between the methods of positive and dogmatic theology. While the questions for positive method arise spontaneously from the evidence under consideration, questions for dogmatic method arise because of apparently different meanings in various sources. Positive theology is endlessly divided into fields of specialisation, seeking what is particular within strict disciplinary boundaries. Dogmatic theology seeks what is common, not particular. Positive theology seeks to elucidate the obscure, in matters that are doubtful or uncertain. Dogmatic theology seeks foundations for dogma, by determining what is clear, ordinary and certain. Positive method uses only the categories present in the documents studied, while dogmatic method uses theoretical language (e.g. metaphysics), to render explicit what is implicit in its sources. If positive theology seeks the intelligibility in the particular, dogmatic theology seeks a particular process of universalisation in the evolution of dogma. Finally, positive method is happy to leave some questions unanswered and some problems unsolved. But in dogmatic theology, faith is most certain right now, since the object of faith has been drawn from the sources with the assistance of the Holy Spirit.[89]

Thus, positive and dogmatic methods are different, even though both deal with historical material. Yet Lonergan sees great danger in confusing the methods. For example, using positive methods to seek dogmatic answers, or vice versa, compounds the problems of each. Confusion destroys both, but methodological distinction enriches both.[90]

In a perceptive article entitled, "On Reading *The Way to Nicea*", Charles Hefling identifies a basic tension present in Lonergan's handling of the relationship between history and dogma in *De Deo Trino*:

> ... the *pars Dogmatica* of *De Deo Trino* arrives at one doctrine by two routes. Part one presents the Son's consubstantiality with the Father as the result of a historical process; part two recapitulates that process in Lonergan's own argument for the first thesis. This raises an interesting question: why does *De Deo Trino* go over the same ground twice?[91]

Hefling observes that, at the time of writing *De Deo Trino*, Lonergan "was not yet ready to turn historical scholarship loose on Christian texts, unsupervised by dogmatic theology ... his aim was to include the study of history *within* dogmatics."[92] Hefling notes a structural similarity between *De Deo Trino* and the account of the relationship between historical studies and dogmatics given in the epilogue of *Insight*. Thus, a tension is apparent between such a procedure and Lonergan's own developing methodological reflections, as recounted in the previous section of this thesis. This hesitation in applying his own research can perhaps be accounted for by the strictures he experienced in meeting the demands of a Roman curriculum.

Whatever the case, Hefling has identified an unresolved methodological question at the heart of these "experiments in method":

> ... it is because in 1964 he had not yet fully resolved the methodological question of where judgments of truth stand in relation to historical scholarship: does the doctrinal belief that there has been a divine revelation, a disclosure of meaning that is cognitively true, precede or follow investigation into what the early Christian community was doing as it hammered out its doctrines?[93]

To answer this unresolved methodological question, Lonergan needed to disengage historical scholarship from dogmatics. This demand eventually led to the eight functional specialties of *Method*. But to achieve this, Lonergan needed to reflect more on questions of meaning and historical consciousness.

I shall now turn attention to a selection of essays published between *Insight* and *Method*. These essays reflect the developing themes of meaning and historical consciousness which had begun to emerge in his Latin works.

2.3.3 "Dimensions of Meaning" [1965][94]

The essay, "Dimensions of Meaning", marks a significant new phase in Lonergan's thinking. We find here themes which will be more fully developed in *Method in Theology*. Indeed, as Crowe notes, this essay was originally intended as "a section of a projected book on the method of theology", though recast as an occasional address.[95] The key considerations deal with meaning, the control of meaning, and the crisis of culture that arises when there is a breakdown in this control.

Lonergan begins by distinguishing between the child's world of immediacy and the world mediated by meaning. The child enters the latter world through the use of language. This immeasurably larger world is more than the sum of everyone's world of immediacy. It goes beyond mere experience to what is understood and affirmed as true. In this world, meaning has a constitutive role. By creating or changing meaning, we create new realities, both social and cultural. Once the constitutive role of meaning is recognised, the control of such meaning becomes a crucial issue.[96]

By appealing to Socrates, Lonergan distinguishes the primary spontaneous manner in which we use language, from the secondary reflexive manner by which we attempt to say what we mean. The Athenians all knew what courage was – contrasted with its opposite in cowardice. But at a reflexive level, they could not define it. For Lonergan, the distinction is necessary if we are to break the power of myth and magic over human life:

> Just as the earth, left to itself, can put forth creepers and shrubs, bushes and trees with such excessive abundance that there results an impenetrable jungle, so too the human mind, led by imagination and affect and uncontrolled by any reflexive technique, luxuriates in a world of myth with its glories to be achieved and its evils banished by the charms of magic.[97]

The breakthrough occasioned by the Greek mediation of meaning allowed for a more developed control of meaning. In turn, it allowed for significant social and cultural advance. However, this control of meaning, and the classical culture it helped create, is now "dead and almost forgotten." It has been replaced by a modern culture which is still to find an effective means of controlling meaning. One key difference between these two cultures is their respective understandings of the nature of science. In classical culture, science was "true certain knowledge of causal necessity." In contrast, the modern view of science emphasises understanding rather than truth. It is content with probability, rather than seeking unattainable certainty. It proceeds by way of hypothesis rather than by deduction. It correlates empirical data rather than argue from Aristotle's four causes. In short, empirically verified intelligibility supplants the classical ideals of certainty and necessity.[98]

When we turn to the realm of religion we find no immunity to the problems created by this collapse in the classical control of meaning. In particular, it causes problems for the definitions of faith, namely, doctrines:

> [Doctrines] exist, but they no longer enjoy the splendid isolation that compels their acceptance. We know their histories, the moment of their births, the course of their development, their interweaving, their moments of high synthesis, their periods of stagnation, decline, dissolution ... But such endlessly erudite and subtle penetration generates detachment, relativism, scepticism. The spiritual atmosphere becomes too thin to support the life of man.[99]

Neither can we turn to authorities. Because they, too, are historical entities, the complex problems of meaning remain.

On this basis, Lonergan saw the crisis of the Church at that time as more one of culture than of faith. It has been caused by a breakdown in the classical mediation of meaning:

> There has been no new revelation from on high to replace the revelation given through Jesus Christ. There has been written no new Bible and there has been founded no new Church to link us with him. But Catholic philosophy and Catholic theology are matters, not merely of revelation and faith, but also of culture. The breakdown of classical culture and ... the manifest comprehensiveness and exclusiveness of modern culture confront Catholic philosophy and Catholic theology with the gravest problems ...[100]

Something is needed to replace the classic control of meaning. In *Method* Lonergan will identify this replacement with an emerging third stage of meaning, grounded in the interiority of the knowing, loving subject.

The whole question of meaning raises questions which are pertinent to the nature of revelation and its working in human history. While Lonergan states that "there has been no new revelation", the shift from classical culture to modern culture entails a new understanding of the nature of revelation itself. Already, Lonergan has noted the pressure that historical method is placing on the traditional sources for theology, namely, Scripture and doctrine. As meaning and historical consciousness become more central themes we can observe a corresponding shift in Lonergan's explicit language about revelation.

2.3.4 "The Transition from a Classicist World View to Historical Mindedness" [1966][101]

The problems of meaning and historical consciousness are taken up again in this essay. As the title indicates, it is concerned with the transition from what Lonergan calls the "classicist world view" to a world view characterised by "historical consciousness." The differences between these two are not immediately theological, but relate to a basic horizon, a total mentality, a culture.

Here there is a key contrast. On the one hand, there is a purely abstract consideration of human nature. It prescinds from all the ways in which humans differ, in culture, mentality, social ordering and so on. This abstract notion is allied to the eternal, the immutable, the universal in a world of stable natures and essences. On the other hand, there is the empirical reality of human being. Considered concretely, it entails humanity's varying histories and cultures, its varieties of common sense, myths and legends. Such human reality is embedded in the temporal, the spatial, the changing, the developing, and the particular. While the classicist, abstract view of humanity has dominated the Church's view of the world, the new, historical, concrete view has now emerged to shape modern consciousness. This shift has particular relevance for the Church and theology, since,

> On this view intentionality, meaning, is a constitutive component of human living; moreover this component is not fixed, static, immutable, but shifting, developing, going astray, capable of redemption; on this view there is in the historicity which results from human nature, an exigence for changing forms, structures, methods; and it

is on this level and through this medium of changing meaning that divine revelation has entered the world and that the Church's witness is given to it.[102]

From such a perception of historicity, Lonergan argues that only a transcendental method, based on a concrete apprehension of the conscious and intentional operation of the subject, is capable of providing foundations adequate to this concrete study of humanity, in a way which precludes the danger of pure relativism. Moreover, given the concrete, historical nature of the good, "the immediate carrier of human aspiration is the more concrete apprehension of the human good through ... theories of history" such as Marxism, or the liberal doctrine of progress. Lonergan then refers to his own historical reflections in *Insight* and *De Verbo Incarnato*, where he developed the categories of progress, decline and redemption.[103]

2.3.5 "Theology in its New Context" [1968][104]

In the essay, "Theology in its New Context", we can detect a major shift in Lonergan's thinking about theological method. It is closely linked to the emergence of eight distinct "processes" (in the terminology of *Method*, eight functional specialties) in theological method. Previously Lonergan was struggling with the relationship between historical studies and the dogmatic and systematic issues of theology. His concern was to keep historical studies under the guidance of dogmatic end-points. It was as though one did history always knowing what answer one should get! By letting go of this concern, he now allows historical studies to take their own proper place within theology. The essay, "Theology in it New Context", marks the full integration of historical consciousness into theology. It registers a shift from viewing theology as "scientific" in an Aristotelian sense (that is, certain knowledge of things through causes), to understanding it as "scientific" in the modern sense – that is, as thoroughly empirical.
Locating the historical origins of this shift in terms of the birth of modern science and the Enlightenment, Lonergan states:

> First, then, theology was a deductive, and it has become largely an empirical science. It was a deductive science in the sense that its theses were conclusions to be proven from the premises provided by Scripture and Tradition. **It has become an empirical science in the**

sense that Scripture and Tradition now supply not premises, but data. The data has to be viewed in its historical perspective. It has to be interpreted in the light of contemporary techniques and procedures ... Secondly, this shift from a deductivist to an empirical approach has come to stay.[105] [emphasis added]

Central to any empirical approach is the study of human living in its historical concreteness. What distinguishes a concern for historical concreteness from the classicist construct of an ahistorical human nature is the attention given to the constitutive role of meaning in human living. Such meanings are those by which we think out possibilities for living, and make choices between them. In this context, Lonergan can now speak of revelation as the entry of a new meaning, God's meaning, into human living. Thus,

> divine revelation is God's entry and his taking part in man's making of man. It is God's claim to have a say in the aims and purposes, the direction and development of human lives, human societies, human cultures, human history.[106]

Hence, theology not only reflects on revelation, it also mediates God's meaning into the whole range of human affairs. Revelation is, then, not only a particular theological theme. It is a dynamic reality pervading the whole of theological method.

These shifts require a new foundation for theology. God's entry into human living is not found in Scripture or Tradition, since these are themselves the product of this entry. Further, in the mediation of God's meaning into human affairs, Scripture and Tradition do supply not premises, but data, to which the subject may, or may not, attend. The new foundation for theology is not to be found "out there", in some already constituted reality, but in the constituting subject, specifically, in the converted subject:

> Now theology, and especially the empirical theology of today, is reflection on religion. It follows that theology will be reflection on conversion. But conversion is fundamental to religion. It follows that reflection on conversion can supply theology with its foundation and, indeed, with a foundation that is concrete, dynamic, personal, communal, and historical.[107]

At this stage, we draw attention to the remarkable synthesis that Lonergan has achieved in this essay. By bringing together the questions of historical consciousness and the dimensions of meaning, particularly constitutive meaning, he has been able to bring about a more complete "turn to the subject." With this shift, the concrete, dynamic, personal, communal and historical reality of conversion become foundational for theology. Indeed, this is the first major essay where the term "conversion" takes such a central place in Lonergan's thought. At the same time, we note various terminological correlations. Theology is variously described as reflection on revelation, on religion, and on conversion. Similarly, where revelation is spoken of as the entry of God's meaning into human living, conversion is identified in terms of "new meanings":

> The convert apprehends differently, values differently, relates differently because he has become different. The new apprehension is not so much a new statement or a new set of statements, but rather new meanings that attach to almost any statement.[108]

I shall return to these observations when I deal more directly with the issue of revelation.

2.3.6 "The Subject" [1968][109]

In this essay, our author is concerned with the turn to the subject which is so significant for modern philosophy. Lonergan attempts to analyse some of the difficulties inherent in this turn by drawing attention to the ways in which the subject is neglected, truncated and rendered totally immanent with no possibility of real self-transcendence.

Most of these are well-worked issues for Lonergan by this stage. However, a new theme is emerging – the existential subject: the subject who not only knows, but also does: "one that deliberates, evaluates, chooses acts."[110] The existential subject not only affects the world, but through its decision, it affects itself; it becomes self-constituting, through the responsible exercise of freedom. This notion of the existential subject was overlooked by an older Scholasticism with its faculty psychology of intellect and will. The existential subject is the subject at the fourth level of consciousness:

rational consciousness is sublated by rational self-consciousness, when we deliberate, evaluate, decide, act. Then there emerges human consciousness at its fullest. Then the existential subject exists and his character, his personal essence, is at stake.[111]

From his recognition of the existential subject, Lonergan develops a notion of the good, distinct from the notion of being which was the primary consideration of *Insight*. Particular goods satisfy particular appetites. The good of order, found in institutions and economic systems, supplies the steady stream of particular goods. But, beyond these, there is the good of value: "by appealing to value or values ... we satisfy some appetites and do not satisfy others, ... we approve of some systems ... and disapprove of others."[112] Value is a transcendental notion, like being, which intends, but does not of itself know, particular values. Value is intended in questions for deliberation, of what is worthwhile. Values are not just particular goods or the good of order. More importantly there is the ethical reality of the good human being, the moral existential subject.

This essay signals a significant shift in Lonergan's thinking. He is moving beyond the intellectualism of *Insight*, towards the existentialism which fully flowered in *Method*.

2.3.7 "The Response of the Jesuit as Priest and Apostle in the Modern World" [1970][113]

The essay now under consideration marked a further development which deepens both the notion of the existential subject and the meaning of revelation. Under the influence of Max Scheler and Dietrich von Hildebrand, Lonergan begins to identify a more significant role for feelings in his treatment of the existential subject.[114] Feelings are now spoken of as providing the "mass and momentum" of our living. Here, Lonergan relates feelings to values: "Beyond the pleasures we enjoy and the pains we dread, there are the values to which we respond with the whole of our being."[115] Now, the world is not simply a world mediated by meaning, "it also is a world motivated and regulated not by self-seeking but by values."[116]

Regarding the process of revelation, Lonergan reflects on the twofold missions of the Spirit and Word in human history. In a section headed "The Spirit", Lonergan speaks of what will later be called "religious conversion", as an experience of "being in love" with God.[117]

This experience is at the topmost, existential level of consciousness. It produces a dynamic state of being in love which is the source of all subsequent decisions and choices. Using the text of Romans 5:5, Lonergan identifies this kind of love with the inner activity of the Holy Spirit.

However, in a section headed "The Word", Lonergan gives two reasons why the activity of the Spirit is not the complete account of divine activity in the world. Firstly, being in love is not just a state of mind and heart. It places us in an interpersonal and ongoing context of mutual presence and community. In this way, human love mirrors the Trinity: "What is true of the love of intimacy, also is true of the love of God. Though God is one, he is not solitary. The one God is three persons: Father, Son and Spirit."[118]

The second reason is the anonymity of the gift of the Spirit:

> What removes this obscurity and anonymity is the fact that the Father has spoken to us of old through the prophets and in this final age through the Son ... His communication is two-fold; it is both by linguistic meaning and by incarnate meaning. By linguistic meaning he rebuked those that gave scandal ... But all such linguistic meaning is endlessly reinforced by the incarnate meaning to be contemplated in the life and ministry and, above all, in the suffering, death, and resurrection of Christ.[119]

As previously noted, revelation is God's entry into the world of human meaning. Here, this entry is specified in terms of both linguistic, and, more importantly, incarnate meaning. Lonergan will give a fuller account of these and other carriers of meaning in the material of *Method in Theology*.

2.4 Summary of Lonergan's developing position on revelation prior to *Method*

In this chapter I have traced the development of Lonergan's thought from his earliest writings up to the time of *Method in Theology*, with a focus on theological method and revelation. While much of the reflection on method is explicit, as Lonergan struggles to explicate a method proper to theology, references to revelation are more peripheral and implicit. However, as Lonergan's thought on method develops, there is a corresponding development in his understanding of revelation.[120] I would now like to summarise the evidence for such a development.

Perhaps the clearest, if implicit, stance on revelation in his earliest writings is found in the essay "The Assumption and Theology." Here, Lonergan is investigating whether the Assumption of Mary is a proper object for dogmatic definition. By modern standards, his handling of the question is remarkable. The question is simply settled by reference to the firm conviction of the Church, as indicated by a tradition going back to the Middle Ages and then current petitions before the Pope. To admit anything but an affirmative answer would be "to admit what no Catholic can admit", namely, that the Church had not been pre-served from error. The question of fact is thus to be settled simply by reference to the appropriate authorities.

At this stage, Lonergan is operating out of an accepted Catholic dogmatic and Scholastic mentality of the day. There is no critical in-vestigation of historical developments, no dialectic analysis of alternatives, no reference to conversion. It is, as Crowe has noted of an earlier age, an horizon of "simple possession of the truth",[121] but with no critical reflection as to how that truth came to be "possessed." While it is true Lonergan engages in a dynamic process of questions and answers which seeks to settle the reasons why the Assumption is definable, this in no way relates to the more fundamental question of fact, nor to any historical process. It is simply a matter of settling, for the present believer, how such a definition can be intelligible.

The same dogmatic mentality can be seen to operate in the later essay, "Theology and Understanding", and even in the Epilogue of *Insight*. In both these, Lonergan is struggling to find a place for his-torical studies in theology. As John McDermott notes:

> In treating theology as a science [*Insight*] started with the given of divine revelation, which is then communicated and applied to di-verse audiences before the speculative theologians seek "a universal formulation of the truths of faith" and historical theologians uncover the doctrinal identity in the diverse formulations of the preceding three steps.[122]

Yet, how are these historical studies to be properly controlled? Lonergan's answer is that, basically, the theologically informed hori-zon of the historical investigator ensures that he or she arrives at the correct answer, in conformity with the "permanent deposit confided to the Church." Rather than historical studies entering in a vital way into the process of determining the content of this permanent deposit confided to the Church, they become part of a theological thesis on the Mystical Body, as an historically integrated ecclesiology.

Cracks begin to appear in this classical mind-set as Lonergan struggles with the category of meaning, particularly in its historical constitution, in the essays "Dimensions of Meaning" and "The Transition from a Classicist world View to Historical Consciousness." One could argue that the Catholic dogmatism, that Lonergan was so firmly wedded to in his writings in the forties and fifties, begins to appear as the dying remnants of a classicist world view. The more an historical mindedness penetrates his thinking, the more the "simple possession of the truth" becomes an untenable classicist assumption. In the latter essay, Lonergan begins to speak of revelation in terms of the category of meaning. Indeed, it is through the "medium of changing meaning that divine revelation has entered the world."[123] This interconnection of revelation, meaning and history marks a significant achievement.

This shift becomes explicit in the major essay, "Theology in its New Context." Here, Lonergan contrasts an earlier deductive approach to theology with an emerging empirical demand. In the earlier deductive approach, "the premises were provided by Scripture and Tradition." In the empirical stance, "Scripture and tradition now supply not premises, but data." Further, this data "has to be viewed in its historical perspective."

This makes explicit the shift in understanding with regard to revelation. Data here have a technical meaning. In the terminology of *Method*, Scripture and Tradition must first be subsumed within the functional specialty of research. They must be submitted to the first, positive historical phase of theology before they can enter into the second, normative phase. As in the previous essay, "The Transition from a Classicist world View to Historical Consciousness", revelation is spoken of in terms of meaning and the historical entry of meaning into human living:

> Divine revelation is God's entry and his taking part in man's making of man. It is God's claim to have a say in the aims and purposes, the direction and development of human lives, human societies, human cultures, human history.[124]

Indeed, instead of speaking in terms of Church authority, Scripture or Tradition, Lonergan speaks of revelation in terms of religious experience and conversion. As I noted above, theology is here variously spoken of as reflection on revelation, on religion and on conversion. As revelation is the entry of new meaning, conversion allows for a new apprehension of meanings and values; and religions arise out of the experience of conversion, which, though personal, is not private. Indeed, it is "communal and historical":

> ... reflection on conversion can supply theology with its foundation and, indeed, with a foundation that is concrete, dynamic, personal, communal, and historical.[125]

This point completes the turn to the subject in Lonergan's understanding of revelation. The foundations of theology are no longer to be found in the teachings of the Church, Scripture or unwavering traditions. They are found in the converted subject, a subject who is "concrete, dynamic, personal, communal, and historical." As McDermott notes, "the problem of historicism has hit home"![126]

I am suggesting, therefore, that just as Lonergan struggled to find a place for historical studies in theological method, so too he struggled to free himself from classicist assumptions about the nature of revelation. In doing so, he developed an implicit understanding of revelation which was thoroughly historical. This was necessitated once Lonergan began to see revelation in terms of the category of meaning. Revelation is regarded as the entry of new meaning into the human situation. Thus, to understand revelation in correlation to Lonergan's theological method, we must pay special attention to the category of meaning as it occurs in *Method*.

2.5 Conclusion

In this chapter I have sought to trace developing themes in Lonergan's thought, from his earliest writings up until the publication of *Method in Theology*. We have seen the emerging interest in existential consciousness, in questions of meaning and historical consciousness, and hints concerning the nature of revelation as the entry of new meaning into human history. All these are correlated with an increasingly sophisticated account of theological method, as Lonergan struggles to locate these new themes into his methodology. In the next

chapter I shall consider the mature fruits of these methodological reflections as found in his major work, *Method in Theology*.

---

1. Crowe, *Lonergan* .
2. Cf. R. Liddy, *Transforming Light* .
3. Crowe, *Lonergan*, 22.
4. Newton's three approximations for planetary motion are 1) bodies move in
straight lines at constant velocity unless a force acts; 2) addition of the law of
gravity between sun and planet yields elliptical motion; 3) the influence of
other planets yields perturbed ellipses.
5. Crowe, *Lonergan*, 25-26. Also "Insight Revisited", *Second Collection*,
271-2. The early work speaks of the ideal line of history, decline and
renaissance, while Lonergan's later word speaks of progress, decline and
redemption. The analogy is not necessarily a happy one. The first
approximation for Newton involves an inverse insight, whereas it is the
second step in Lonergan's approximation which involves the inverse insight.
Secondly, the third approximation for Newton perturbs the ellipses. It does
not attempt to restore things back to the first approximation! The account of
history will be familiar to readers of *Insight* and *Method*. It is remarkable how
early in his intellectual career Lonergan had in place the basic elements of
what is really a theology of history, at least in heuristic form.
6. Lonergan, *Insight*, 748.
7. B. Lonergan, *Grace and Freedom: Operative Grace in the Thought of St.
Thomas Aquinas*, J.P. Burns (ed.) (London: Darton, Longman and Todd,
1970). For an analysis of the context and achievement of *Gratia Operans*, see
D. Tracy, *The Achievement of Bernard Lonergan* (NY: Herder and Herder,
1970) 22-44. Also J. McDermott, "Tensions in Lonergan's Theory of
Conversion" *Gregorianum*, 74/1 (1997), 101-140.
8. B. Lonergan, *Verbum: Word & Idea in Aquinas* (London: Darton,
Longman & Todd, 1968), D. Burrell (ed.).
9. In the introduction to his thesis, *Gratia Operans* (published as *Grace and
Freedom*), Lonergan repeated calls his inquiry, "historical". In *Verbum*, he
notes that, given the failure of others to solve the problems he is facing,
perhaps a "historian" should make an attempt, cf, *Verbum*, 11.
10. Lonergan, "Introduction to *Gratia Operans*", 10.
11. Lonergan, "Introduction to *Gratia Operans*", 11.
12. Lonergan, "Introduction to *Gratia Operans*", 12.
13. Lonergan, "Introduction to *Gratia Operans*", 15.
14. Perhaps this is why the introduction was not published in the book *Grace
and Freedom*. Lonergan was aware of their incomplete nature.
15. In the introduction to *Verbum* Lonergan notes, "if Thomist philosophers
... are reluctant to venture into this field, it remains that a *historian* must do

so" [emphasis added], cf. *Verbum*, xiv. However, later he will note that "to follow Aquinas here, one must practice introspective rational psychology", 11.
16. It is, as Tracy notes, a "recovery of the world of Thomist interiority", in contrast to the earlier work which was, again according to Tracy, a "recovery of the medieval world of theory." Cf. *Achievement*, 22,45.
17. Lonergan, *Verbum*, 11. It must be borne in mind that Lonergan did not come to Aquinas with a clean slate. As the recent studies by Crowe and Liddy make clear, Lonergan had already developed significant notions with regard to interiority through his own reading and thinking. Those masters of interiority, Newman, Plato and Augustine had already left their marks. This process, which had already well and truly begun, was brought to its initial completion with these years of "reaching up to the mind of Aquinas".
18. B. Lonergan, "The Assumption and Theology", *Collection*, 68-83.
19. Lonergan adds a third question concerning Mary's death, which need not concern us here.
20. Lonergan, "Assumption", 68.
21. Lonergan, "Assumption", 69.
22. Lonergan, "Assumption", 74.
23. Lonergan, "Assumption", 75.
24. Lonergan, "Assumption", 76.
25. Lonergan, "Assumption", 80.
26. B. Lonergan, "Theology and Understanding", *Collection*, 121-141.
27. Lonergan, "Assumption", 127.
28. Lonergan, "Theology and Understanding", 129-30.
29. Lonergan, "Theology and Understanding", 132.
30. Lonergan, "Theology and Understanding", 137.
31. Lonergan, "Theology and Understanding", 138.
32. Lonergan, "Theology and Understanding", 139. While this may seem an astonishing statement in our present context, the issue of methodological control in the human sciences and their relationship to theology was a constant concern to Lonergan. See, for example, Doran, *Theology*, Chapter 9, "Reorienting Depth Psychology".
33. B. Lonergan, "Foreword" to D. Tracy, *Achievement*, xi.
34. Lonergan frequently differentiates his view of consciousness from a position which would see consciousness as some form of knowledge. For an illustration of the importance of this differentiation, see his essay, "Christ as Subject: A Reply", *Collection*, 164-197.
35. Cf. Lonergan, *Insight*, 1-12.
36. Cf. Lonergan, *Insight*, 280ff. Lonergan's notion of the virtually unconditioned was influenced by Newman's notion, developed in *Grammar of Assent*, of the illative sense, cf. Liddy, *Transforming Light*, 16ff.
37. Cf. Lonergan, *Insight*, 388.
38. I owe this formulation to Fr. Tom Daly S.J.

39. This is taken up in *Insight,* Chapter 19, on "Special Transcendent Knowledge".

40. Lonergan, *Insight,* 191ff.

41. This spontaneity is characterised by its concern for the present, the immediate, the palpable and its intersubjectivity which radiates from the self as its centre, cf. *Insight,* 218ff.

42. Lonergan, *Insight,* 222ff.

43. Lonergan, *Insight,* 226.

44. Lonergan, *Insight,* 226.

45. Lonergan, *Insight,* 225ff.

46. Lonergan, *Insight,* 672.

47. Lonergan, *Insight,* 319.

48. Cf. Lonergan, *Insight,* 675ff.

49. Lonergan, *Insight,* 662-665. Here Lonergan is reworking in a more systematic and precise manner material from *Grace and Freedom.*

50. Lonergan, *Insight,* 694.

51. Lonergan, *Insight,* 696.

52. Lonergan, *Insight,* 706.

53. Lonergan, *Insight,* 720.

54. Lonergan, *Insight,* 720.

55. Lonergan, *Insight,* 739. Indeed, in *Way to Nicea* (London: Darton, Longman and Todd, 1976), Lonergan comes close to adopting a propositional understanding of revelation, cf. *Way to Nicea,* 8-10.

56. For example, Lonergan questions the need for a metaphysical account of the Incarnation, such as Rahner's notion of quasi-formal causality, or de Taille's notion of actuated act. Lonergan's account is not metaphysical but analogous, using the notion of contingent predication, which describes God's relationship to created being in general, cf. *De Verbo Incarnato* (Rome: Gregorian University, 1960), 254-268.

57. Lonergan, *Insight,* 739.

58. Lonergan, *Insight,* 740.

59. Lonergan, *Insight,* 742.

60. Some of these writings are "pre-*Method*" only inasmuch as they appeared before the publication of *Method.* Many develop themes which are transposed directly into *Method* sometimes verbatim.

61. Cf. Crowe, *Lonergan,* 80

62. B. Lonergan, "*Insight* Revisited", *Second Collection,* 276.

63. Cf. Crowe, *Lonergan,* 80.

64. For this section I am drawing heavily on C. Boly, *The Road to Lonergan's Method in Theology.*

65. Cf. Boly, *Road,* 117-121.

66. Boly, *Road,* 125.

67. Cf. Boly, *Road,* 124-125.

68. Boly, *Road*, 127.
69. Boly, *Road*, 128.
70. Boly, *Road*, 129.
71. Cf. Boly, *Road*, 130.
72. Cf. Boly, *Road*, 132-133.
73. Boly, *Road*, 152.
74. Cf. Boly, *Road*, 151.
75. Boly, *Road*, 153.
76. Cf. Boly, *Road*, 152-154.
77. Boly, *Road*, 128.
78. Boly, *Road*, 175.
79. Cf. Boly, *Road*, 176.
80. Boly, *Road*, 177.
81. Boly, *Road*, 178.
82. Cf. Boly, *Road*, 180.
83. Boly, *Road*, 181.
84. Boly, *Road*, 187.
85. Boly, *Road*, 181.
86. Cf. Boly, *Road*, and the essay by C. Hefling, "On Reading *The Way to Nicea*", in *Religion and Culture* (Albany: SUNY, 1987), 149-166.
87. B. Lonergan, *De Deo Trino I: Pars Dogmatica* (Rome: Gregorian University, 1964), 5.
88. Lonergan, *Pars Dogmatica*, 6.
89. Cf. Lonergan, *Pars Dogmatica*, 11-13. Also Boly, *Road*, 203-205.
90. Cf. Lonergan, *Pars Dogmatica*, 14. Also Boly, *Road*, 206.
91. Hefling, "On Reading", 156-7.
92. Hefling, "On Reading", 156-7.
93. Hefling, "On Reading", 153.
94. B. Lonergan, "Dimensions of Meaning", *Collection*, 252-267.
95. F. Crowe, "Editor's Introduction", *Collection*, xxxiv.
96. Cf. Lonergan, "Dimensions", 252-255.
97. Lonergan, "Dimensions", 258.
98. Cf. Lonergan, "Dimensions", 258-261.
99. Lonergan, "Dimensions", 265.
100. Lonergan, "Dimensions", 266.
101. B. Lonergan, "The Transition from a Classicist World-View to Historical-Mindedness", *Second Collection*, 1-9.
102. Lonergan, "Transition", 6.
103. Cf. Lonergan, "Transition", 6-7.
104. B. Lonergan, "Theology in its New Context", *Second Collection*, 55-67.
105. Lonergan, "New Context", 58-9.
106. Lonergan, "New Context", 62.
107. Lonergan, "New Context", 67.

108. Lonergan, "New Context", 66.
109. B. Lonergan, "The Subject", *Second Collection*, 69-86.
110. Lonergan, "Subject", 79.
111. Lonergan, "Subject", 80.
112. Lonergan, "Subject", 81-2.
113. B. Lonergan, "The Response of the Jesuit as Priest and Apostle in the Modern World", *Second Collection*, 165-187.
114. Lonergan first refers to these authors in the essay "Natural Knowledge of God", cf. *Second Collection*, 132. In *Method*, he footnotes von Hildebrand's work *Christian Ethics* as the source of his discussion on the role of feelings, *Method*, 31.
115. Lonergan, "Response", 168.
116. Lonergan, "Response", 169.
117. Indeed much of this material here on religious experience is repeated verbatim in the later work of *Method*. I will consider it in the next chapter.
118. Lonergan, "Response", 174.
119. Lonergan, "Response", 174-5.
120. For example, the sympathetic critic, J. McDermott notes the fundamental paradigm shift that *Method* represents. He notes that "surely [Lonergan] retained at least until 1964 the permanent necessity of the institutional Church as the authoritative mediator of the truths of faith, but his studies in Aquinas' understanding of understanding forced the subjective elements of his world-view ever more to the fore." cf. J. McDermott, "Tensions in Lonergan's Theory of Conversion", 105.
121. Crowe, *Theology of the Christian Word* (Mahwah: Paulist Press, 1978), 104.
122. McDermott, "Tensions", 117.
123. Lonergan, "Transition", 7.
124. Lonergan, "New Context", 62.
125. Lonergan, "New Context", 67.
126. McDermott, "Tensions", 121.

CHAPTER THREE:
METHOD IN THEOLOGY, ITS STRUCTURE, KEY ELEMENTS AND EXTENSIONS

The book, *Method in Theology*, is Lonergan's crowning achievement in a life-long effort to explicate a critical method for the doing of theology. This achievement can be characterised in many ways. Some have seen it as a shift from a Thomistic intellectualism to an Augustinian existentialism. Many have noted the new emphasis placed on the existential level of consciousness and the central place of conversion. For my part, I wish to emphasise that it represented a radical shift in Lonergan's understanding of the nature of revelation, correlative to his achievement in *Method*.

As David Tracy notes, *Method* represents a "breakthrough towards which all his prior work had been aiming and in the light of which his former work seems relatively unintegrated."[1] No longer was Lonergan struggling to integrate two movements, of analysis and synthesis, or the *ordo inventionis* and the *ordo doctrinae*, with the third area of history. In *Method* he arrives at eight interrelated functional specialties which provide a comprehensive ordering of theological tasks. Correlatively, the strategy of this thesis will be to link these theological tasks to the process of revelation.

3.1 Transcendental Method

Lonergan begins his work with an account of method in general, and transcendental method in particular. Lonergan describes method as a "normative pattern of recurrent and related operations yielding cumulative and progressive results."[2] As such, it is a mixture of both logical and non-logical operations. The logical operations consolidate what has been achieved. The non-logical operations keep all achievement open to further advance.

The basic non-logical operations that Lonergan considers are the intentional operations of the subject. These operations – seeing, hearing, touching, smelling, imagining, inquiring, understanding and so on – are intentional in the psychological sense. That is, by these operations, the subject becomes aware of the object. Such operations are consciously performed by a subject; they are not performed in dreamless sleep or in a coma. As we have seen, Lonergan distinguishes four levels of intentional consciousness: empirical, intellectual, rational and moral. The dynamisms which moves us from the lower empirical level to the higher levels are the transcendental notions of the intelligible, the true, the real and the good.[3] The overall strategy of *Method* is to link these levels of consciousness with different phases in the theological process.

Transcendental method objectifies the structures of consciousness by reflecting on our conscious operations. This is precisely the strategy of Lonergan's earlier work, culminating in *Insight*. Indeed, Lonergan argues in *Insight* that the pattern of these operations, once objectified, is not subject to significant revision. One cannot appeal to new data to eliminate the need for data; nor to new insights to eliminate the need for insight; nor to new reasons to eliminate reason; nor to new decisions to eliminate decision. Anyone who would deny the existence of these conscious and intentional operations "is merely disqualifying himself as a non-responsible, non-reasonable, nonintelligent somnambulist."[4] Transcendental method is, therefore, "a rock on which one can build", though in a footnote Lonergan acknowledges that "an important part of the rock has not yet been uncovered", and refers the reader to Chapter Four of *Method* on religion.[5]

Because of the absolute generality of its object, Lonergan argues, transcendental method is relevant to theology. Its special relevance is "mediated by the special method proper to theology and generated through the reflection of theologians" on past and present success, and failure.[6] Transcendental method is a constituent part of theological method, as it is of all natural and human sciences. Further, the objects of theology do not lie outside the field of transcendental method. Outside that field there is nothing at all. Nonetheless, Lonergan concedes that,

> transcendental method is only a part of theological method. It supplies the basic anthropological component. It does not supply the specifically religious component.[7]

Here again, Lonergan refers the reader to a consideration of religion, that part of the rock yet to be uncovered. Clearly he is responding to criticisms made by Rahner when what was to become Chapter Five of *Method* on functional specialities was published in the journal *Gregorianum*.[8] Rahner claimed that Lonergan had not produced a method for theology, but for the human sciences in general; and that more was needed to meet the requirements of a specifically theological method.

Already, in the above quotation, we can see the tension which arises from the use of transcendental method. For it supplies only the anthropological component of theological method. It does not supply the specifically religious component. That, one must presume, can derive only from revelation, however that may be understood. Yet, how do we know that the anthropological component will do justice to the concrete and particular event of revelation, without distorting it or reducing it to a merely human event? The classic debate on the relationship between grace and nature, or between faith and reason, is now being transposed into a different context.

While Lonergan has already spelt out the basic structure of the anthropological component in terms of his analysis of the different levels of consciousness, he fills out his account by a more detailed consideration of questions of meaning and value. Here he consolidates the advances made during the post-*Insight* period which were identified in the previous chapter. Given Lonergan's earlier references to revelation as the entry of new meaning into human history, the questions of meaning and value are important for the purposes of this thesis.

3.2 The human good and the notion of value

Lonergan begins his discussion of the good with the assertion: "What is good, always is concrete."[9] Thus he begins his account of the good with a very concrete discussion of skills and their acquisition, by drawing on the work of Piaget.[10]

Apart from such specific operational developments, there is a development of feeling within the person. The role of feelings in relation to values differentiates the fourth level of moral consciousness from the previous three cognitional levels.[11] In this regard, Lonergan distinguishes non-intentional feelings (states and trends such as tiredness or hunger) from intentional feelings which respond to satisfactions and/or values. Intentional feelings orient us "massively and dynamically in a world mediated by meaning."[12]

Intentional feelings are related to an objective, normative and transcultural scale of preference: "So we may distinguish vital, social, cultural, personal and religious values in an ascending order." Vital values refer to health, vigour, strength and so on. Social values pertain to the good of order which conditions the supply of vital values for the whole community. Cultural values provide the meanings and values which inform human social living. Personal value is the person as loved and being loved, as originator of values and inspiration to others. Religious values involve a transcendent, unrestricted love which grounds all other values. Further, human moral development entails attention to the "development of feelings" in so far as they assist the subject "towards self-transcendence", and so to respond according to the objective scale of values.[13]

Lonergan goes on to explicate the notion of value, as distinct from the notions of the intelligible – intended in questions for intelligence – and of truth and being – intended in questions for reflection. The notion of value is intended in questions for deliberation, when I ask whether this is truly and not just apparently good, whether that is or is not worthwhile. Just as the drive to understand is satisfied only with understanding, and the drive to truth is satisfied only with suffcent evidence, so the drive to value "rewards success in self-transcendence with a happy conscience and saddens failure with an unhappy conscience."[14]

Feelings, as intentional response to value, elicit judgments of value. These judgments of value differ from judgments of fact, since "one can approve of what does not exist, and one can disapprove of what does." True judgments of value "go beyond merely intentional self-transcendence without reaching the fulness of moral self-transcendence." Judgments of value,

> attain their proper context, their clarity and refinement, only through man's historical development and the individual's personal appropriation of his social, cultural and religious heritage. It is by the transcendental notion of value and its expression in a good and an uneasy conscience that man can develop morally. But a rounded moral judgment is ever the work of a fully developed self-transcending subject or, as Aristotle would put it, of a virtuous man.[15]

Thus, the historical context of moral self-transcendence is discovered in the exercise of human freedom. As one develops both in knowledge and moral feeling, one makes the existential discovery of oneself as a moral being – one's decisions constitute oneself as authentic or inauthentic. There then emerge in consciousness the notions of personal value and personal responsibility.

What Lonergan has achieved here is the disengagement of the transcendental notion of being (as intelligible and reasonable) from the transcendental notion of value or the good. The good is apprehended, not by intelligence, but in the intentional response of feeling.[16] Judgments of value arise not from the intelligent and reasonable cognitive self-transcendence of the subject, but from the moral self-transcendence of the authentic subject.[17] Further, value is created in the responsible, morally self-transcending decisions of the existential subject. This transcendental notion of the good heads for "an encounter with a goodness completely beyond its powers of criticism."[18]

Such a disengagement shifts attention away from a cognitional understand of revelation, evident, for example, in *Insight*, towards a more existential understanding. Questions of authenticity, of existential, historical agency, of moral self-transcendence and love are now acknowledged to be the central questions of human existence.

Because the good is always concrete, because the problems of authenticity always occurs within a social, cultural and religious context, Lonergan includes in his discussion of the human good a treatment of the role of belief. Here Lonergan argues that the appropriation of one's social, cultural and religious heritage, which is the proper context of judgments of value, is largely a matter of belief. As in *Insight*, Lonergan is arguing for the rationality of belief as a principle of personal development and of historical and social progress. Without belief there would be personal, cultural and social stagnation. Just as one moves beyond the world of immediacy into the world mediated by meaning, one moves beyond the necessarily limited world of immanently generated knowledge into a world apprehended through a symbiosis of belief and knowledge.[19]

In the context of revelation, belief can now be seen as a principle of progress. Divine meaning and value work to transform human history for the good, moving it more closely to the ideal line of history, of pure progress.[20] In raising the problem of history, Lonergan sketches an outline of social progress and decline which "will be relevant to an account of the social function of religion"[21] – and, by implication, to the meaning and role of revelation.

Whereas, in *Insight*, progress is a function of intelligence and reasonableness, *Method* presents progress as that which "proceeds from originating value, from subjects being their true selves by observing the transcendental precepts."[22] Progress is the continuous flow of improvements which arise from fidelity to these precepts. Decline begins in the violation of the precepts occasioned by individual, group and general bias, so as to "distort the process of cumulative change and bring to birth a host of social and cultural problems."[23] The compromises and distortions engendered by bias can discredit the very notion of progress itself by leading to objectively absurd situations which do not yield to intelligence: "A civilization in decline digs its own grave with relentless consistency."[24] On this analysis, the basic form of alienation is disregard of the transcendental precepts. Such disregard lies at the foundation of all destructive ideology.

The only solution to such decline lies in a religion capable of promoting self-transcendence "to the point, not merely of justice, but of self-sacrificing love."[25] Such a religion "will have a redemptive role in human society inasmuch as love can undo the mischief of decline and restore the cumulative process of progress."[26] Herein lies the historical purpose of revelation.

3.3 Meaning – carriers, elements, functions, realms and stages

However the meaning of revelation is conceived, it must surely be thought of as meaningful – as opposed to meaningless. Indeed, we have already seen that Lonergan speaks of revelation as the entry of new meaning and value into human history. Thus, any theology of revelation explicated from Lonergan's *Method* must consider his analysis of the "meaning of meaning." Here, there is development in Lonergan's thought, in comparison with his previous writings. Whereas *Insight* spoke of formal and full acts of meaning, *Method* develops a much more nuanced range of categories in its analysis of meaning.

The first of these categories I shall consider is that of "carriers of meaning." These will be of particular importance when we ask the question: how does revelation enter into the human world of meaning? Lonergan distinguishes between five different carriers of meanings: intersubjective meaning, artistic meaning, symbolic meaning, literary meaning and incarnate meaning.

Intersubjective Meaning

Spontaneous intersubjectivity arises from a vital and functional identification with the other. This identification precedes the distinction of subjects into "I" and "Thou", and even the "We" of mutual love. One aspect of this intersubjectivity is the intersubjective communication of meaning. By illustrating this point with a brief phenomenology of the smile, Lonergan stresses that intersubjective meaning "is not about some object. Rather it reveals or even betrays the subject, and the revelation is immediate."[27] We shall consider later whether revelation, in the theological sense, shares in this immediacy of intersubjective meaning.

Artistic Meaning

Following Susanne Langer, Lonergan defines art as "the objectification of a purely experiential pattern." A work of art is a concrete pattern of the internal relations of, say, colors, tones, volumes, movements and so forth. It is a pure pattern in as much as it excludes patterns that instrumentalize experience. The meaning of art is elemental: the meaning and the meant are not distinguished. As art transforms the world, so too the subject who experiences it is transformed. Liberated from the routine structuring of existence, "he becomes just himself: emergent, ecstatic, originating freedom."[28] This liberating, aesthetic aspect of meaning identifies an important dimension of revelation.

Symbolic Meaning[29]

The new context in which Lonergan places feelings, as intentional response to value, leads to a deeper appreciation of the symbolic. Lonergan defines a symbol as "an image of a real or imaginary object that evokes a feeling or is evoked by a feeling." Given the link between feelings and values, our developing moral sensitivity (or its distortion) will involve a "transvaluation and transformation of symbols." Symbols neither obey the laws of logic nor "bow to the principle of excluded middle", preferring to overwhelm the opponent rather than merely prove a point. Prior to logic and dialectic, symbols can express "what logical discourse abhors: the existence of internal tensions, incompatibilities, conflicts, struggles, destructions."[30] Such symbolic meanings clearly suggest the power of revelation for personal transformation and conversion.

Given this context, symbols fulfil a need for internal communication:

> Organic and psychic vitality have to reveal themselves to intentional consciousness and, inversely, consciousness has to secure the collaboration of organism and psyche. Again, our apprehensions of values occur in intentional responses, in feelings; here too it is necessary for feelings to reveal their objects and, inversely, for objects to awaken feelings. It is through symbols that mind and body, mind and heart, heart and body communicate.[31]

Internal communication is the proper mode of functioning and meaning of symbols. Such meaning is elemental, as in a smile or a work of art. This internal field of communication, influenced by the association of images, feelings, memories and tendencies, is the proper explanatory context of the symbolic. Explanation, in turn, provokes a transition from elemental meaning to linguistic meaning.[32]

Linguistic Meaning

In language, Lonergan argues, meaning finds its greatest liberation. The conventional signs of language can be multiplied almost indefinitely. While Lonergan has consistently maintained the prelinguistic nature of the act of understanding,[33] he nonetheless acknowledges the power of language to advancing understanding:

So it is that conscious intentionality develops in and is moulded by its mother tongue. It is not merely that we learn the names of what we see but also that we can attend to and talk about the things that we can name.[34]

Three genera of language are distinguished, as ordinary, technical and literary. The basis of ordinary language is common sense. It is the vehicle by which "the human community conducts its collaboration in the day-to-day pursuit of the human good." Technical language correlates with the division and specialisation of labour to provide the tools of the expert and the specialist. This type of language is indicative of a movement from description to explanation, as when inquiry is pursued for its own sake, as when logic and methods evolve and a tradition of learning is established. Thirdly, there is literary language. It finds expression in the permanent written work, which, aiming at a "fuller statement", attempts to make up for the "lack of mutual presence" in other kinds of language. Consequently it tends to "float somewhere in between logic and symbol." Significantly, for our exploration of Lonergan's notion of revelation, he places high value on the role of literary meaning: "With Giambattista Vico, we hold for the priority of poetry."[35] Indeed, for many, the literary meaning evident in the Scriptures is the primary source of revelation.

Incarnate meaning

Lonergan introduces this brief section by referring to John Henry Newman's motto, *cor ad cor loquitur*. Incarnate meaning is "the meaning of a person, of his way of life, of his words, or of his deeds." It can thus combine intersubjective, artistic, symbolic and linguistic carriers of meaning. Meaning occurs as incarnate in its significance, say, for another person, or more widely, for a group, a nation or a social, cultural or religious tradition.[36]

This list of "carriers of meaning" is a far more nuanced set of distinctions than would commonly be found in theological discussion. Such a variety of possible carriers of meaning has obvious applicability to any account of revelation, particularly the last mentioned category of "incarnate meaning."

However, it is possible to ask whether this list is complete or is meant to be so. It is tempting to see these carriers as linked to Lonergan's usual distinctions of levels of consciousness, of the scale of values, or of functional specialties in theology. A great number of possible correlations could be made; and in the next chapter I shall attempt such an exercise when these various elements are brought together in an explication of the understanding of revelation operative in *Method*.

After his treatment of the carriers of meaning, Lonergan proceeds to consider the elements and functions of meaning. Above all, the manner in which he understands meaning to function will prove of great importance in any exploration of what he means by revelation. In distinguishing the cognitive, efficient (effective),[37] constitutive and communicative functions, Lonergan enriches the context in which the significance of revelation in and for human history can be eventually discussed.

The *cognitive function* of meaning works to take us beyond the child's world of the immediately given and experienced, into the adult's world – the world mediated by meaning. This larger world does not lie within anyone's immediate experience. It is the reality of what is intended in questions. It encompasses a world of objective truth determined not only by experience, but by understanding and judgment.[38] The cognitive function of meaning allows us to consider revelation as the entry of new truth into human history.

The *efficient function* of meaning relates to the world of human activity: "Men work. But their work is not mindless. What we make, we first intend." Through the efficient function of meaning we enter a world of planning, of investigating possibilities, of weighing pros and cons, of entering into contracts, of orders given and received: "The whole of that added, man-made, artificial world is the cumulative, now planned, now chaotic, product of human acts of meaning."[39] The efficient function of meaning suggests revelation's role in promoting progress and reversing decline through the institution of a new praxis.

The *constitutive function* of meaning is found in the intrinsically meaningful component of social and cultural institutions. Such institutions – religions, art-forms, languages, sciences, philosophies, histories – are "inextricably involved in acts of meaning." Moreover, changes in such institutions are often brought about by a change in meaning: "a change of idea or concept, a change of judgment or evaluation, a change of order or request." An apposite example of such change is the reinterpretation of a national constitution.[40] The constitutive function of meaning help us identify the social and cultural impact of revelation in human history.

The *communicative function* of meaning is shown in the actual communication of one person to another, in any or all of the intersubjective, artistic, symbolic, linguistic or incarnate modes. Through the communicative function, meaning can become a rich store of common meaning to attain, if successfully communicated, social and historical significance.[41] By considering the communicative function of meaning we can grasp something of revelation's power to create a new community.

Indeed, for Lonergan, the communicative and constitutive functions of meaning taken together give us notions of community, existence and history. For community is an achievement of common meaning. Such meaning is merely potential in shared experience; it becomes formal in common understandings, and actual in common judgments, to be fully realised through common decisions and choices. Into such communities people are born; and it is only with respect to a community's common meanings that the individual "grows in experience, understanding, judgment and so comes to find out for himself that he has to decide for himself what to make of himself."[42] Thus there arises the notion of existence, which, in its turn, may be authentic or inauthentic:

> There is the minor authenticity or unauthenticity of the subject with respect to the tradition that nourishes him. There is the major authenticity that justifies or condemns the tradition itself.[43]

When the tradition itself is inauthentic one may find that one "can do no more than authentically realize unauthenticity." It is left to history and divine providence to pass judgment on all traditions.[44]

Lonergan's analysis of meaning throws light on the historicity of human existence: "The shape and form of human knowledge, work, social organization, cultural achievement, communication, community, personal development" are shot through with meaning, and these meanings are subject "to cumulative development and cumulative decline."[45] Every human subject lives,

> only in interaction with the traditions of the communities in which he happens to have been born and, in turn, these traditions themselves are but the deposit left him by the lives of his predecessors.[46]

As will be evident in the next chapter, the communicative and constitutive functions of meaning are of special relevance to the understanding both of revelation and of its relationship to tradition and culture.

In his final consideration of meaning, Lonergan introduces the notion of "stages of meaning": "The stages in question are ideal constructs and the key to the constructing is undifferentiation or differentiation of consciousness"[47]:

> In the first stage conscious and intentional operation follow the mode of common sense. In a second stage besides the mode of common sense there is also the mode of theory, where theory is controlled by logic. In a third stage the modes of common sense and theory remain, science asserts its autonomy from philosophy, and there occur philosophies that leave theory to science and take their stand on interiority.[48]

In Western history, as Lonergan sees it, the vital breakthrough into the second stage was initiated by "the Greek discovery of mind." This enabled people to distinguish myth from history, and magic from science. But with the rise of modern science, an ever greater tension between the realms of common sense and theory became apparent. For that tension to be diagnosed and resolved, the modern "turn to the subject", a movement into the realm on interiority, is necessary. What was already initiated by Descartes, furthered by Kant, and accelerated by existentialists and phenomenologists is now systematically exploited by Lonergan himself.[49]

While conceding that these stages are ideal types, Lonergan obviously understands them as having explanatory power in terms of the movements of history. They are "progressive", in that they arise from the exigencies of consciousness itself. Lonergan clearly understands his own work as a contribution to the emergence of the third stage of meaning. In the next chapter, as well as in Chapter 7, I shall consider the ways in which divine revelation contributes to this emergence.

3.4 Religion

In Chapter Four of *Method* Lonergan seeks to provide the "religious component" which a pure transcendental method cannot of itself supply. He felt compelled to add this material in order to overcome the criticism levelled at his project by Karl Rahner. Still, as we shall see, Lonergan prescinds from the concrete content of revelation, even though his thought obviously reflects a particular Christian stance. Again, we can observe an evident tension present in Lonergan's approach to the question of theological method. The religious component is not a pure *a priori*. Hence it is not a "transcendental" in the usual sense, since it arises from the *a posteriori* gift of God's grace.[50] However, Lonergan's approach remains based on an analysis of consciousness. Its focal point is the inner world of religious experience, not the outer world of historical revelation.

Of all the varied responses to *Method* the most comment and criticism has turned on the specifically Christian component of Lonergan's methodological approach. For example, Kelly has criticised the lack of attention to a specifically Christian mode of conversion, while at the same time wondering at the presence of an undoubtedly Christian tradition, instanced in Lonergan's references to Christian Scriptures.[51] Others have criticised Lonergan for his reliance on Heiler, even though, materially speaking, this is minimal given his overall argument. Still, while framing his method within a transcendental analysis of religious experience, he remains significantly nuanced in his comments on the dialectical nature of religious development. It remains, however, that the main criticism of Lonergan deals with his use of Christian religious experience to analyse religious experience in general.[52]

Even though Lonergan would concede that he does in fact draw on Christian religious experience, this is not necessarily a shortcoming. Given all that he says in *Method* about the role of a religious tradition in shaping the religious life of a person, it could hardly be otherwise. Because the "outer word" of a religious tradition has a constitutive role, any attempt to escape this role would simply be another version of that "principle of the empty head" which he so strongly criticises in his treatment of interpretation.[53] The question, then, is not whether Lonergan has drawn on the Christian tradition, but whether, in so drawing upon it, he has produced a coherent *explanatory* account of the phenomena under examination.

3.4.1 Religious experience

While *Insight* presented a variation on the traditional proofs for the existence of God, *Method* concentrates more on the question of

God and the religious experience which underpins the question. He speaks of religious experience in terms of "being in love with God"; it is an experience of "being in love in an unrestricted fashion."[54] Such an experience is the proper fulfilment of our capacity for cognitive and moral self-transcendence. This state is not an achievement; it is a gift:

> That fulfilment is not the product of our knowledge and choice. On the contrary, it dismantles and abolishes the horizon in which our knowing and choosing went on and it sets up a new horizon in which the love of God will transvalue our values and the eye of love will transform our knowing.[55]

Indeed, Lonergan regularly cites Romans 5:5, "God's love flooding our hearts", in speaking of religious experience. In such expressions, it is important to realise that Lonergan, following the Augustinian and Scholastic tradition, uses the phrases, "the love of God", "God's love" in the sense of an objective genitive. Hence, what is referred to is not God's love for us, but our love for God.[56]

In *Method*, Lonergan speak of religious experience as being on the fourth level of intentional consciousness. On this level are located acts of deliberation, judgments of value, decisions and responsible actions:

> But it is this consciousness as brought to a fulfilment, as having undergone a conversion, as possessing a basis that may be broadened and deepened and heightened and enriched but not superseded.[57]

Lonergan understands this gift of God's love to occupy the ground and root of the fourth level of intentional consciousness: "It takes over the peak of the soul, the *apex animae*." He identifies it with what theological tradition, at the second stage of meaning, referred to as the infused entitative habit of sanctifying grace.[58] In later writings Lonergan will speak of this experience as constituting a fifth level of consciousness.[59]

3.4.2 The variety of religious expression

Religious experience, while manifest in spontaneous changes of attitudes, also seeks social and cultural expression. Using Friedrich Heiler's phenomenological researches into world religions, Lonergan itemises seven topics which Heiler identifies as "common areas" among world religions:

> that there is a transcendent reality; that he is immanent in human hearts; that he is supreme beauty, truth, righteousness, goodness; that he is love, mercy, compassion; that the way to him is repentance, self-denial, prayer; that the way is love of one's neighbour, even of one's enemies; that the way is love of God, so that bliss is conceived as knowledge of God, union with him, or dissolution into him.[60]

Note, however, that Lonergan is far from promoting a harmonising account of religion based these common areas. Although the love of God at the heart of religious experience is the fulfilment of our cognitive and moral self-transcendence, self-transcendence is itself ever precarious. Religious development is necessarily dialectical, so that "the seven common areas or features listed above will be matched in the history of religions by their opposites." For example, the neglect of immanence leads to an overemphasis on transcendence so that "God becomes remote, irrelevant, almost forgotten." Religious development is always a struggle "between authenticity and unauthenticity, between the self a transcending and the self as transcended."[61]

3.4.3 The Word

The inner experience of God's love is not the sole constitutive element of religious life. For, associated with this prior "inner word" of religious experience, there is an outer word. It occurs in "any expression of religious meaning or religious value", that is, in art, symbol, language or, most significantly, as remembered in the lives and deeds of persons and groups.[62] This outer word is not incidental but constitutive. Without such expression, religious experience is not objectified, spoken about, or shared. The outer word becomes,

> the word of tradition that has accumulated religious wisdom, the word of fellowship that unites those that share the gift of God's love, the word of the Gospel that announces that God has loved us first and, in the fulness of time, has revealed that love in Christ crucified, dead and risen.[63]

The word is, thus, personal in the religious leader, the prophet, the Christ. It is social, bringing together "into a single fold the scattered sheep."[64] And it becomes historical: it seeks to find its place in the context of other non-religious meanings, by borrowing and adapting language from this world to speak of the realm of transcendence. As it does so, religious expression will move through the different stages of meaning to speak a language appropriate to the various realms of meaning. As it does so the different carriers and functions of the meaning of revelation take on a different significance.

This movement into different realms of meaning becomes problematic as theoretical apprehensions of religious expressions are contrasted with an earlier commonsense apprehension: "So the God of Abraham, Isaac, and Jacob is set against the God of philosophers and theologians." Different carriers and functions of the meaning of revelation may appear in conflict. The greatest controversies arise, however, because of the presence or absence of intellectual conversion. This fundamental tension between commonsense and theoretical apprehensions can only be overcome by a movement into the realm of interiority and the third stage of meaning.[65]

3.4.4 Faith and beliefs

Along with a number of modern authors, Lonergan distinguishes between faith and belief. This distinction underscores a significant shift from the more intellectualist understanding of faith evident in his earlier writings, suggesting a more existential understanding of revelation operative in *Method*.[66]

Method describes faith as "knowledge born of religious love." In reference to Pascal's well-known aphorism, concerning the heart having reasons that reason does not know, Lonergan understands the reasons of the heart as "feelings that are intentional responses to value." Such feelings give rise to a "knowledge reached through a discernment of value and the judgments of value of a person in love."[67] The knowledge of faith, then, stands in contrast to factual knowledge gained through experience, understanding and judgment. To the apprehension of those vital, social, cultural and personal values which are made present through the intentional responses of feeling, is now added the apprehension of transcendent value, as an "experienced fulfilment of our unrestricted thrust to self-transcendence":

the experienced fulfilment of that thrust in its unrestrictedness may be objectified as a clouded revelation of absolute intelligence and intelligibility, absolute truth and reality, absolute goodness and holiness.[68]

Without this affective experience of transcendent value, "the originating value is man and the terminal good is the human good man brings about." However, with this experience,

> originating value is divine light and love, while terminal value is the whole universe. So the human good becomes absorbed in an all-encompassing good.[69]

Faith, by calling us to a higher authenticity of overcoming evil with good, has the historical task of overcoming decline and promoting progress. Instead of being opposed to reason, "religious faith will liberate human reasonableness from its ideological prisons."[70]

Faith also helps us discern the value of believing. By being initiated into a religious tradition, we apprehend the value of "the word of religion, of accepting the judgments of fact and the judgments of value that the religion proposes."[71] These judgments are beliefs. Believing is necessary because religious experience, though personal and intimate, is not solitary, but creative of community. The life of the community generates a variety of expressions: moral imperatives, narratives of the community's origins and development, mystical teachings, theoretical reflections. As a community endures, these expressions become traditional, and religions becomes historical. There is, nonetheless, a far deeper sense in which religion is historical:

> The dynamic state of being in love has the character of a response. It is an answer to a divine initiative. The divine initiative is not just creation. It is not just God's gift of his love. There is the personal entrance of God himself into history, a communication of God to his people, the advent of God's word into the world of religious expression.[72]

Thus, the inner word of God's love is met by "the outer word of the religious tradition" which also comes from God:

> The word of religious expression is not just the objectification of the gift of God's love; in a privileged area it also is specific meaning, the word of God himself.[73]

However, Lonergan argues that a further consideration of these issues is to move beyond purely methodological questions. Such issues are strictly theological, and are to be studied, not by transcendental method, but by historical investigation.   In particular, questions "concerning revelation" fall into this category.[74]

Herein lies the tension in Lonergan's whole project. The *a priori* structures of consciousness and the *a posteriori* gift of God's love, while containing an implicit structure of revelation, cannot specify the full reality of revelation without moving to the concrete, particular details of "historical investigation."

He concludes his discussion of faith and belief with a technical note on the nature of the shift away from a metaphysical faculty analysis of the soul to an intentionality analysis of the subject based on interiority. This shift involves a rejection of two notions: i) that of pure intellect or reason: "A life of pure intellect or pure reason without the control of deliberation, evaluation, responsible choice is something less than the life of a psychopath"; and ii) that of will as arbitrary power: "arbitrariness is just another name for unauthentic-ity."[75]

He extends this analysis to a consideration of the old axiom, *Nihil amatum nisi praecognitum*. While, in the normal course of events, knowledge precedes love, in that "operations on the fourth level of intentional consciousness presuppose and complement corresponding operations on the other three", there are exceptions. For example, there is the case of someone falling in love. Here, "falling in love is a new beginning." But the major exception occurs when God's love floods our hearts to bring about a dynamic state of being in love, as happens in religious conversion. In his later writings, Lonergan will extend the application of these "exceptions" to speak of two vectors within human consciousness: a creative vector which moves up through the four levels of consciousness; and a healing vector which moves down from existential consciousness towards the lower levels.[76] Both of these movements need to be taken into consideration in discussion the process of divine revelation.

3.5 Functional specialties

After his sketch of these "background" considerations, Lonergan introduces a "foreground" analysis of the specifics of theological method.

There are two matters to note in Lonergan's construction of a framework of theological specialties: first, it is arrived at, not by dividing up the field of data, nor by classifying the results of investigations, but by "distinguishing and separating stages of the process from data to results."[77] Hence the eight functional specialties are stages in this process. As such, they cut across many standard divisions between, say, Old and New Testament studies (different fields of data), or between biblical, systematic and moral theologies.

Secondly, these functional specialties are related to the four levels of consciousness, variously described as empirical, intellectual, rational, and moral. Further, in his technical note in the chapter on religion, he introduced the notion of a downward movement in consciousness whereby love precedes knowledge to complement the upward movement whereby knowledge precedes love. These four levels combined with the two movements gives rise to eight functional specialties – research and communications (empirical), interpretation and systematics (intellectual), history and doctrines (rational), and, finally, dialectics and foundations (moral). The first set of each pair – research, interpretation, history and dialectics – constitute the positive, creative phase of theology, while the second set from foundations, doctrines, systematics to communications constitute the normative, healing phase. The hinge on which the two phases swing is then conversion, which has religious, moral and intellectual dimensions.[78] A adequate theology of revelation must take into account both these phases.

I shall make a brief comment on each of the eight functional specialties in turn.

3.5.1 Research

This is the briefest chapter in *Method*, a bare three pages. Lonergan does not want to be too specific here; he suggests that the best way to master research is to work under an expert:

> To them one must go and with them one must work until one is familiar with all the tools they employ and has come to understand precisely why they make their each and every move.[79]

Of most interest to our exploration is the question of the starting point for research. For Lonergan asks:

Is theology to be based on scripture alone, or on scripture and tradition? Is the tradition just the explicit teaching of the apostles, or is it the ongoing teaching of the church? Is it the ongoing teaching of the church up to Nicea, or to A.D. 1054, or up to the reception of Scholastic doctrines, or up to the council of Trent, or up to the days of Pius IX, or forever?[80]

The problem is that these questions cannot be answered by research alone. The answers depend on doctrines, that is, on judgments arising out of foundational commitments. Lonergan's answer to the problem is that it does not matter where one starts, that "the method is designed to take care of the matter."[81]

It is clear, however, that in general Lonergan considers the starting point to be the traditionally identified theological sources of scripture, patristics, church councils and so on.[82] Certainly, given the nature of transcendental method, no data can be *a priori* excluded, since such exclusions are the product of decisions. I shall return to this observation in the more interpretative task of the next chapter, but here I note that an adequate theology of revelation must account for the initial attraction of revelation that captures our attention.

3.5.2 Interpretation

Once more, Lonergan is not about to tell specialists, in this case exegetes, how to do their business. But he is interested in clarifying just what their business is. The need for exegesis occurs when expression arising out of a commonsense realm of meaning is transported from one realm of common sense to another.[83] Lonergan identifies three basic exegetical operations:

(1) understanding the text; (2) judging how correct one's understanding of the text is; and (3) stating what one judges to be the correct understanding of the text.[84]

To understand the text one must have some understanding of the object to which the text refers, of the words employed, of the author and of oneself. This last element is particularly true when the text is a classic, that is, "a writing that is never fully understood." Classic texts ground a tradition which "may be genuine, authentic, a long accumulation of insights, adjustments, re-interpretations, that repeats the original message afresh." On the other hand, a tradition may become unauthentic, thus to water down of the original meaning, and so dodge the issue of conversion.[85] Clearly, revelation, as carried in the linguistic meanings of classic texts, raises fundamental questions about the interpreter, and the authenticity of the tradition to which he or she belongs.

Throughout his reflections on interpretation, Lonergan consistently attacks what he terms the "principle of the empty head." The best interpreter is not the one who has emptied his or her head of all "presuppositions."[86] In contrast, what is demanded is a self-correcting process of learning in which, with an enriched and expanded horizon, an interpreter becomes better placed to understand the text.[87]

3.5.3 History

Notably, Lonergan's treatment of this functional specialty is the largest of the book, taking up two whole chapters of the book. Here I would make two comments on Lonergan's understanding of history.

First, while Lonergan distinguishes between the history that is written about and the history that is written, it is clear that no separation is implied. Given the constitutive role of meaning in history, the history that is written becomes one element within the warp and woof of the history that is written about. For example, the Gospels, though they are writings dealing with historical events, become themselves constitutive of the ongoing life of the Church.

Secondly, there is the issue of the goal of historical study. Clearly Lonergan envisages the final goal to be the total understanding of history *in its particularity*, of what is moving forward within the general schema of progress, decline and redemption. Though such a goal is clearly eschatological and even proper to God alone, it does place the history that is written about under the purview of a providential, universal, salvific horizon.

Lonergan begins his account by distinguishing two meanings of the word "history." "There is history (1) that is written about and there is history (2) that is written. History (2) aims at expressing knowledge of history (1)."[88] Lonergan distinguishes history (1) from nature, by noting the constitutive role of meaning in human history:

> Meaning, then, is a constitutive element in the conscious flow that is the controlling side of human action. It is this constitutive role of

meaning in the controlling side of human action that grounds the peculiarity of the historical field of investigation.[89]

History is thus concerned with meaning, but not in the same way as an exegete. If the exegete is concerned with what a particular person meant in a particular historical context,

> The historian envisages quite a different object. He is not content to understand what people meant. He wants to grasp what was going forward in particular groups at particular places and times. By "going forward" I mean to exclude the mere repetition of a routine. I mean the change that originated the routine and its dissemination. I mean process and development but, no less, decline and collapse.[90]

In grasping what was going forward, the historian will often determine what those experiencing the event do not themselves know, for "in most cases, contemporaries do not know what is going forward."[91]

Lonergan then traces the movement from historical experience, to diary keeping, to autobiography, to biography, to pre-critical history, with its practical functions of maintaining and improving the life of a group, to critical history whose concern is to determining, through probable judgments, what was "going forward." Judgments remain only probable. One cannot exclude the possibility of uncovering new data; and later events may place earlier events in a new perspective. Lonergan recognises the danger here of historical relativism. This problem can be only partially eliminated by the techniques of critical history. What is needed is a further functional specialty, that of dialectics, with its discernment of the influence exerted on historical writings by the limitations of the historian's horizon.[92]

By comparing his own historical approach with that of six different historians, Lonergan partially meets the problem of relativism with the alternative view of perspectivism.[93] The historian is always a person of his or her time and place, so that "the development of historical understanding does not admit systematic objectification":

> The historian finds his way in the complexity of historical reality by the same type and mode of development understanding, as the rest of us employ in day-to-day living. The starting-point is not some set of postulates or some generally accepted theory but all that the historian already knows and believes. The more intelligent and the more

cultivated he is, the broader his experience, the more open he is to all human values, the more competent and rigorous his training, the greater his capacity to discover the past.[94]

As a result historical perspectivism, as distinguished from mere relativism, has not lost the hope of attaining of the truth. It recognises the difficulties of the task and the manner in which the goal of historical scholarship differs from that of other disciplines. There are three factors structuring any given perspectival view: the finiteness of the historian; the fact that the historian is necessarily selective; and that this process of selection and its initial conditions will vary. With regard to the finiteness of the historian we find the comment:

> his information is incomplete; his understanding does not master all the data within his reach; not all his judgments are certain. Were his information complete, his understanding all-comprehensive, his every judgment certain, then there would be room neither for selection nor for perspectivism. Then historical reality would be known in its fixity and its unequivocal structures.[95]

This wording is, of course, evocative of Lonergan's account of divine understanding and providence, since, for God, information is complete, understanding is all-comprehensive and judgment certain. It is quite a different matter for the human historian. Still, we can see in this connection a notion of revelation which encompasses the whole of human history under a divine providential purpose.

While some differences in historical accounts have their origins in different perspectives, others result entirely from differing horizons. An historian's presuppositions will be crucial in determining his judgments about the credibility of witnesses; and these presuppositions, in turn, are "not just his but also the living on in him of developments that human society and culture have slowly accumulated over centuries."[96] To meet the differences of opposed horizons, there is needed another functional specialty, namely, dialectics. It will be concerned with the basic issue of the conversion which elicits "a notable change in horizon."[97]

This raises the issue of whether history is "value free." Certainly, as Lonergan envisages it, the functional specialty aims at "settling matters of fact by appealing to empirical evidence", and value judgments "neither settle matters of fact nor constitute empirical evidence." The historian does not refrain from value judgments, but does so solely "for the purpose of settling matters of fact"[98]: "In fact the historian's value-judgments are precisely the means which make his work a selection of things that are worth knowing."[99]   Still, the making of value judgments is not the specialty of the historian. Rather, such activity pertains to the specialties of dialectics and foundations, to which we now move.

3.5.4 Dialectics

Dialectics, then, deals with the conflicts that arise from the specialty of history, where these conflicts themselves stem "from an explicit or implicit cognitional theory, an ethical stance, a religious outlook." Such conflicts can be overcome only "through an intellectual, moral [or] religious conversion."[100]

To thematise the notion of conversion Lonergan introduces the concept of an horizon. Our differing horizons are determined by the scope of our knowledge, and the range of our interests. Differences in horizon may be complementary, genetic or dialectic. People with complementary horizons live in different, but basically complementary, worlds. Horizons differ genetically when they are related as successive stages of development. But dialectical difference is much more basic. It occurs when,

> what in one is found intelligible, in another is unintelligible. What for one is good, for another is evil. Each may have some awareness of the other and so each in a manner may include the other. But such inclusion is also negation and rejection. For the other's horizon is attributed to wishful thinking, to an acceptance of myth, to ignorance or fallacy, to blindness or illusion, to backwardness or immaturity, to infidelity, to bad will, to a refusal of God's grace.[101]

Consequently, conversion is conceived as a shift across dialectically opposed horizons – a vertical, as distinct from a horizontal, act of freedom. This involves an about-face, a repudiation of the old, and an entry into a new world of meaning and value. At this point, Lonergan makes his usual distinction between the three dimension to conversion, namely, the religious, the moral and the intellectual. Clearly, as far as Lonergan is concerned, a revelation which promotes authentic conversion cannot leave the subject religiously, morally or even intellectually unaffected.

Intellectual conversion concerns the problems of knowledge, truth and reality. It involves overcoming the cognitional myth which envisages knowing as somehow like looking; and objectivity as seeing only what is there to be seen; and reality as being what is out there to be seen. It requires both a rejection of naive realism, empiricism, and idealism, and the adoption of a critical realism.[102] *Insight* aims at achieving this conversion in the reader.

Moral conversion involves a shift in the criteria of decision making, away from satisfactions to true values. It involves existential moments "when we discover for ourselves that our choosing affects ourselves no less than the chosen or rejected." Freedom is then grasped as self-constitution: "it is up to each of us to decide for himself what he is to make of himself."[103]

Religious conversion, in its turn,

> is being grasped by ultimate concern. It is other-worldly falling in love. It is total and permanent self-surrender without conditions, qualifications, reservations. But it is such a surrender, not as an act, but as a dynamic state that is prior to and principle of subsequent acts.[104]

Thus, religious conversion goes beyond moral conversion to provide a new basis for all our valuing and doing good. It places human existence within a cosmic context and purpose, enabling us "to accept suffering involved in undoing the effects of decline." Moreover, religious conversion does not simply add new and efficacious means for attaining moral and intellectual ends; it is an end in itself. Its unrestricted character "corresponds to the unrestricted character of human questioning." Religious conversion brings a distinct dimension of its own, an "other-worldly fulfilment, joy, peace, bliss."[105]

Lonergan relates these different conversions in a Rahnerian notion of sublation.[106] Thus, moral conversion sublates intellectual conversion, and religious conversion sublates moral. Such sublating activity does not imply, however, a temporal sequence of events. He is stressing, rather, a causal relationship. He writes:

> First there is God's gift of his love. Next, the eye of this love reveals values in their splendour, while the strength of this love brings about their realization, and that is moral conversion. Finally, among the values discerned by the eye of love is the value of believing the

truths taught by the religious tradition, and in such tradition and belief are the seeds of intellectual conversion. For the word, spoken
and heard, proceeds from and penetrates to all four levels of intentional consciousness. Its content is not just a content of experience
but a content of experience and understanding and judging and
deciding. The analogy of sight yields the cognitional myth. But
fidelity to the word engages the whole man.[107]

Besides conversion there are also breakdowns. What has been
built up by the individual, the society, or the culture can collapse.
Collapse feeds on itself as each elimination, mutilation or distortion of
past achievements requires more elimination, mutilation and distortion
to maintain the illusion of progress.

Dialectic is concerned, then, with an evaluational turn within the
generalised hermeneutic of the first phase of theology. It deals with
the gross differences in historical accounts which arise not from the
data but from the horizons of the interpreters.

The notion of conversion provides Lonergan with the hermeneutical upper blade, an *a priori*, which can order the multitudinous
results of historical research. While he still speaks of positions and
counter positions, as in *Insight*, he now understands positions to be
"statements compatible with intellectual, moral and religious conversion", while counter positions are considered as incompatible with one
or other conversion.[108]

3.5.5 Foundations

The functional specialty, foundations, marks the transition from
the first, mediating, positive phase of theology to the second, mediated, normative phase. At this stage, we can begin to understand some
of the difficulty in separating out discussion of theological method
from actual theologising. Much of Lonergan's achievement in *Method*
could be subsumed within the functional specialty of foundations. It
arises from Lonergan's own objectification of religious, moral and
intellectual conversion. It embodies Lonergan's own commitments,
arising from his own foundational stance.

This is not meant as a serious criticism of what Lonergan has attempted. It is merely to point out the taut balancing act which he is
forced to achieve in order to discuss theological method while, at the
same time, prescinding as far as possible from direct theological dis-

course. It is little wonder that he has attracted criticism for going too far either in the direction of rationalism or of dogmatic fideism.

In this normative phase, "theological reflection took a much more personal stance", since it arises from the personal commitments of the theologian.[109] The basic foundational reality is, at this juncture, conversion itself; or, perhaps concretely, the personal reality of the theologian as intellectually, morally and religiously converted. Unlike dialectic, foundations calls for a commitment. Such a deliberate act is not arbitrary; it arises from the authenticity of the converted theologian as enacted in a "total surrender to the demands of the human spirit: be attentive, be intelligent, be reasonable, be responsible, be in love."[110]

As Lonergan repeatedly states, while conversion is personal it is not a private event. Concretely, it occurs in relationship to an established religious tradition, for "it is only with century-old traditions that notable developments occur." There remain, however, concrete questions, reserved to another functional speciality, about which tradition one should enter:

> how the group is constituted, who was the founder to whom it bears witness, what are the services it renders to mankind, these are questions not for the fifth functional specialty, foundations, but for the sixth, doctrines.[111]

The presence or absence of conversion is one source of variety in theology. However, there is also that pluralism of expression whose cause is found in the presence or absence of various differentiations of consciousness. The psychological reality of differentiations of consciousness – common sense, theoretic, religious, artistic, scholarly, interiority – enable Lonergan to account for a legitimate pluralism of expression in religious language, but without minimising the exigence for conversion.[112]

Nonetheless, theology, particularly a Christian theology, must go beyond this pluralism to develop theological categories capable of transcending the limitations of various differentiations. Transcendental method meets this need:

> Transcendental method ... is in a sense transcultural. Clearly it is not transcultural inasmuch as it is explicitly formulated. But it is transcultural in the realities to which the formulation refers, for these realities are not the product of any culture, but, on the contrary, the principles that produce cultures, preserve them, develop them.[113]

Apart from transcendental method, there is also the "transcultural" gift of God's love, manifest, more or less authentically, in the diverse religions of humanity.[114] These are two bases from which transcultural categories can be derived, though Lonergan carefully distinguishes between the inner core, which is truly transcultural, and the outer manifestation or expression, which may vary.

Lonergan draws a distinction between general and special categories: "General categories regard objects that come under the purview of other disciplines as well as theology. Special categories regard objects proper to theology."[115] Both *Insight* and the early chapters of *Method* have served to develop the general categories referred to. Special categories, on the other hand, will be developed from historical, phenomenological, psychological and sociological studies of religious experience, and its expression in "the history of salvation that is rooted in being-in-love."[116] More radically still, such special categories are grounded in the historical problem of progress, decline and the events of redemption:

> As human authenticity promotes progress, and human unauthenticity generates decline, so Christian authenticity – which is love of others that does not shrink from self-sacrifice and suffering – is the sovereign means for overcoming evil. Christians bring about the kingdom of God in the world not only by doing good but also by overcoming evil with good.[117]

Lonergan concludes his account of foundations with an eye to the possible criticism of his method as being too subjective. Since the foundational reality is the converted, authentic theologian, Lonergan refuses to make either "*sola Scriptura*", or "Scripture and Tradition", or some "canon within a canon", or even a "hermeneutical privilege of the poor and oppressed", foundational in his precise sense:

> Nor may one expect the discovery of some "objective" criterion or test or control. For that meaning of the "objective" is mere delusion. Genuine objectivity is the fruit of authentic subjectivity. It is to be obtained only by attaining authentic subjectivity.[118]

When Lonergan states that "Genuine objectivity is the fruit of authentic subjectivity", he is in fact expressing a culminating moment in the modern turn to the subject. It implies that all normativity must be sought within the structures of subjectivity, and that all objectivity is expressible only in terms of the authentic subject's commitment to those immanent norms. In those eight words, Lonergan's methodological project is summed up. It reminds us that an adequate theology of revelation must take into account both the objective and subjective poles of revelation, without seeing them as opposed or in conflict.

3.5.6 Doctrines

Clearly the chapter on doctrine must be pertinent to any discussion of the nature of revelation. Though Lonergan speaks of dogmas as revealed mysteries, his account is hardly simplistic – as though revelation were merely propositional or bound up with conceptualist and classicist assumptions. Genuine doctrinal development does occur. Such development may be genetic, when it is occasioned by an ongoing discovery of mind or refinement of feeling, or it may be dialectic, when it occurs in a situation of conflict with contrary error. An understanding of doctrinal development must rely upon the **"intelligibility immanent in historical process"**; it is to be sought, not in some general theory of development, but in concrete historical investigation.[119] While Lonergan rejects *a priori* theorising, this is not to say there is no *a priori*. Indeed he has already spelt out something of the *a priori* upper blade of his generalised evaluative hermeneutic in his discussion of dialectic.

The solution proposed by Lonergan to the problem of the historicity of dogmas differs both from those posed by a number of contemporary authors and from that of Lonergan's own earlier writings. As we have outlined in Chapter 1, many different models of revelation have been developed to challenge a propositional, a-historical, dogmatic understanding of revelation. Rather than simply rejecting the place of dogma, Lonergan seeks to disengage it from conceptualist and classicist assumptions. He is thus able to uphold both the permanence **and** the historicity of dogmas. Indeed, he identifies much of modernity's problems with dogma as due to the lack of intellectual conversion.

Lonergan begins his discussion of the specialty, doctrines, by distinguishing between "primary sources, church doctrines, theological doctrines, methodological doctrines, and the application of a methodological doctrine that results in a functional specialty named doctrines." What is common to all these is that they are taught, though they differ in the authority of the teachers.[120]

Primary sources refer both to the doctrines of the original message and doctrines on these doctrines:

> Thus, there is the divine revelation in which God spoke to us of old through his prophets and most recently in his Son ... There is the church decree in which the decision of assembled Christians coincides with the decision of the Holy Spirit ... There are apostolic traditions ...[121]

Church doctrines arise because new questions emerge which demand new answers which cannot be found simply by repeating the past. Of these, Lonergan notes, "each is a product of its place and time and ... each meets the questions of the day for the people of the day." Theological doctrine, in a Christian context, "denotes a person's reflections on the revelation given in and by Jesus Christ", while methodological doctrine "reflects on theology and theologies [and] ... mentions both the revelation and the church doctrines on which the theologies reflect."[122] But in terms of this particular functional specialty, doctrines are,

> reached by the application of a method that distinguishes functional specialties and uses the functional specialty, foundations, to select doctrines from among the multiple choices presented by the functional specialty, dialectic.[123]

Because doctrines, as taught, are meaningful, they will fulfil "the communicative, effective, constitutive, and cognitive functions proper to meaning." In Lonergan's words, a doctrine may be,

> effective inasmuch as it counsels and dissuades, commands and prohibits. It is cognitive inasmuch as it tells whence we come, whither we go, how we get there. It is constitutive of the individual inasmuch as the doctrine is a set of meanings and values that inform his living, his knowing, his doing. It is constitutive of the community, for community exists inasmuch as there is a commonly accepted set of meanings and values shared by people in contact with one another. Finally it is communicative for it has passed from Christ to the apostles and from the apostles to their successors and from these in each age to the flocks of which they were the pastors.[124]

Along with these functions, doctrines also have a normative role. Being based on conversion, they "are opposed to the aberrations that results from the lack of conversion." In their own way, doctrines actually promote conversion, since the unconverted "have in doctrines the evidence both that there is something lacking in themselves and that they need to pray for illumination and to seek instruction."[125]

Despite this normative function of doctrines, a legitimate pluralism can still be found in doctrinal expression. When doctrines are assimilated into a diversity of cultures, they "bear the stamp of those that assimilate them." Lonergan contrasts this acceptance of pluralism with the classicist position which, viewing its own culture as normative, is suspicious of expression outside its own cultural domain. Nonetheless, he still holds to the permanence of dogmatic doctrines, since they are based not on classicist assumptions, but on "the quite open structure of the human spirit."[126]

The issue which Lonergan then seeks to address, is one that has dominated much of modern theological debate: the development of doctrine. In this context he writes:

> To determine the starting-point, the process, the end-result of any particular development of doctrine calls for an exact historical investigation. To determine the legitimacy of any development calls for evaluational history; one has to ask whether or not the process was under the guidance of intellectual, moral, and religious conversion. But the deeper issue is the more general question that asks how it is that developments are possible. How is it that mortal man can develop what he would not know unless God had revealed it?[127]

For Lonergan the development of doctrine is bound up with stages in the differentiation of consciousness. First, there is the movement out of the world of immediacy, into the world mediated by meaning. There is generated the realm of commonsense meanings, with its varieties in diverse human cultures. The gift of God's love leads to a transcendent differentiation; while the ongoing discovery of mind leads to the emergence of systematic meaning – a theoretic differentiation. The conflict between theoretic and commonsense meaning can be resolved only by a methodic turn to interiority. There thus develops a series of ongoing contexts, each of which will lead to a transposition of the original revelation:[128]

> This series contributes not a little to an understanding of the development of doctrines, for doctrines have meaning within contexts, the ongoing discovery of mind changes the contexts, and so, if the doc-

trines are to retain their meaning within new contexts, they have to be recast.[129]

Though, in earlier writings, he had spoken of a transition from implicit to explicit expression, he now describes the process of doctrinal development as "a transition of Christian consciousness from a lesser to a fuller differentiation."[130] Consequently, the language of "implicit-explicit" language is anachronistic, for it attributes "to scripture and the Fathers an implicit grasp of what the Scholastics discovered." This position he now rejects, along with the archaism antagonistic to "any doctrine that was not to be found in the plain meaning either of scripture or of scripture and patristic tradition." Where, then, does he stand?

> There is, however, a third option: it would contend that there can be many kinds of developments and that to know them, one has to study and analyze concrete historical processes while, to know their legitimacy, one has to turn to evaluational history and assign them their place in the dialectic of the presence and absence of intellectual, moral, and religious conversion.[131]

Lonergan illustrates this series of contexts, related to the ongoing discovery of mind, by giving a brief overview of Western Christian culture from the New Testament era, through the Fathers and early church Councils, to Scholasticism, into the modern era of the scientific revolution, to the turn to the subject, up to contemporary theologians such as Barth and Bultmann.[132] He concludes that there is no one way in which doctrines develop. Rather,

> the intelligibility proper to developing doctrines is the intelligibility immanent in historical process. One knows it, not by *a priori* theorizing, but by *a posteriori* research, interpretation, history, dialectic, and the decisions of foundations.[133]

The ongoing discovery of mind is one way in which doctrine develop. In a sense, it represents what *Insight* would call a genetic process of development. He admits, too, that "often enough development is dialectical. The truth is discovered because a contrary error has been asserted." Finally, apart from an ongoing discovery of mind, Lonergan allows for a "refinement of human feelings", which may help understand the development of Marian doctrines.[134]

It is noteworthy that Lonergan here makes such a close connection between the development of doctrine, which is clearly a key element in understanding the process of revelation, and the "intelligibility immanent in historical process." On such an understanding, revelation enters into the very heart of historical process, transforming human history through the cognitive, effective, constitutive, communicative and normative functions of doctrine. An understanding of revelation drawn from *Method* must conceive it as thoroughly historical.

Using the decree of the first Vatican Council, *Dei Filius*, Lonergan defends the permanence of solemn dogmatic pronouncements of the Church as a permanence of the meaning as it was meant in its original context.[135] Thus, "the meaning it possessed in its own context can never be denied truthfully":

> The meaning of a dogma is not a datum but a truth. It is not a human truth but the revelation of a mystery hidden in God. One is denying divine transcendence if one fancies man has at his disposal the evidence that would enable him to substitute some other meaning for the meaning that has been revealed.[136]

This conclusion about the meaning of dogma as truth leads Lonergan to contrast theology with the physical sciences. The physical sciences seek a fuller understanding of empirical data, with new theories emerging to replace old theories. Theology, on the other hand, seeks a fuller understanding of truth, where "it is still the same truth that is being understood." Dogmas can be better and better understood, but "that ever better understanding is of revealed truth and not of something else."[137] However, this does not mean that dogmas do not suffer from the same problems of historicity as other expressions of meaning. There are still the problems of interpreting something which, emerging within a particular historical context, is,

> revealed in the styles and fashion of one differentiation of consciousness, defined by the church in the style and fashion of another differentiation, and understood by theologians in a third.[138]

What is opposed to the historicity of dogma is not the permanence of dogma, but the assumptions and achievements of classicist culture.

There can still be real pluralism in the unity of faith. For, while the ground of unity is the gift of God's love, the sources of pluralism lie in cultural variety, in the different differentiations of consciousness,

and in the presence or absence of religious, moral and intellectual conversion. Faith does not require the adoption of some particular
culture, as classicism assumes. Nor does it oblige anyone to attain a
more fully differentiated consciousness. Nevertheless, a real menace
to the unity of faith does lie "in the absence of intellectual or moral or
religious conversion."[139]

3.5.7 Systematics

The next functional specialty, systematics, "is concerned with
promoting an understanding of the realities affirmed in the previous
specialty, doctrines."[140] Lonergan returns to well-worked themes of his
earlier writings on method, but now in a changed context. In his
earlier writings, "theology" usually meant "systematic theology."[141]
Now, the specialty, systematics, is only one of eight theological tasks,
placed between doctrines and communications. However, this does
not lessen its importance for an age wary of systematic understanding:

> If one does not attain, on the level of one's age, an understanding of
> the religious realities in which one believes, one will be simply at
> the mercy of the psychologists, the sociologists, the philosophers,
> that will not hesitate to tell believers what it is in which they be-
> lieve.[142]

From this perspective, systematic theology may have a place even
within an understanding of the process of revelation.

The key activity for systematics is understanding. What is at
stake is not the understand of the text, as in interpretation, but the
understanding of the realities to which the text refers. The aim of
systematics is thus not to promote certitude, for certitude arises from
faith. Rather, it is to promote understanding of the judgments proclaimed in doctrines.[143]

Basic to the frame of reference in which systematic theology
operates is an orientation to transcendent mystery, to God. While
adoration is the human response to mystery, it does not exclude words
which,

> in turn, have their meaning within some cultural context. Contexts
> can be ongoing. One ongoing context can be derived from another.
> Two ongoing contexts can interact ... the religions of mankind stand

within a social, cultural, historical context and, by that involvement, generate the problems with which theologians attempt to deal.[144]

Lonergan concedes that these problems can be so great that people no longer know what to believe. For people "want to know what church doctrines could possibly mean. Their question is the question to be met by systematic theology."[145] In such a perspective, even systematic theology has a role to play in the process of revelation. The entry of divine meaning can only be effective in transforming human history if there are those who are dedicated to understanding "what [it] could possibly mean." Systematic theology has a role in protecting the "well-being" of the revelation of the divine meaning.[146]

One of the problems which systematic theology causes is the tension brought about by the transposition of doctrines from one particular differentiation of consciousness, into a theoretic differentiation. For example, Thomistic theology uses terms such as procession, relation and person. What such terms mean within a systematic framework is related to their meaning in their patristic sources "much as in modern physics the terms, mass and temperature, stand to the adjectives, heavy and cold."[147] There is a transposition from a commonsense realm of meaning, where meanings are *quoad nos*, meanings in relation to us, into a theoretic realm of meaning, where meanings are *quoad se*, meanings defined by mutual terms and relations. Lonergan comments:

> The existence of this divergence between religious sources and theological systems is a necessary consequence of the view expressed in the first Vatican council that, while it is the same dogma ... that is being understood, still that understanding grows and advances down the ages.[148]

This shift in context from commonsense to theoretic realms of meaning helps Lonergan explain how systematic theology differs from empirical science. While science understands data, systematic theology understands facts grasped in judgments: the facts of doctrines, expressed in one realm of meaning, become the data for a systematic understanding. Systematic intelligence, as in scientific understanding, aims to be true, even though it "is bound to be imperfect, merely analogous, commonly no more than probable."[149]

In his final consideration on doctrine, Lonergan reflects on the problems of continuity, development and revision of systematic theology.   Continuity arises from a number of factors.   These relate to the normative structure of conscious and intentional acts (implicit transcendental method), God's gift of his love (religious experience), the permanence of revealed dogma, and lastly the occurrence of those genuine achievements in the past (particularly, for Lonergan, those of Thomas Aquinas), the neglect of which would leave the present "a substantially poorer affair." Development also occurs as human consciousness achieves further, more refined differentiations.[150]   Last of all, there are the revisions which arise from significant shifts in culture, as is occurring in our own day.   Lonergan illustrates this with an example:

> Thus, the shift from a predominantly logical to a basically methodological view-point may involve a revision of the view that doctrinal developments were "implicitly" revealed.[151]

Because to establish such a point would lead to a specifically theological question, Lonergan concedes that it lies "outside the scope of the present work on method."[152]

3.5.8 Communications

The last of the functional specialties is communications.   Its task is to communicate to a particular situation the results of systematics. Once more, Lonergan refers to the communicative function of meaning within a community constituted by common meanings.   Common meanings arise in an ongoing process of communication, a shared activity "of people coming to share the same cognitive, constitutive, and effective meanings."[153]

In this context, the Christian church is described as "the community that arises from the outer communication of Christ's message and from the inner gift of God's love."   Communications is concerned, therefore, with the "effective communication of Christ's message", a message which has cognitive, constitutive and effective dimensions. Lonergan allows that this task should not demand the acceptance the message "as it has been developed within one's own culture"; for that would require that the recipients "renounce their own culture and accept one's own."[154]

Rather than speaking of the church as a perfect society, as in more traditional ecclesiologies, Lonergan understands it as a structured, ongoing, redemptive process of self-constitution – constituting and perfecting itself through communication of the Christian message.[155]

Clearly these comments indicate a vital role of the Christian Church in the process of revelation. The Church arises from the communication of divine meaning, through both outer and inner words. It must concern itself with the effective communication of the divine meanings of "Christ's message." An adequate theology of revelation cannot ignore the role of the Christian community in the overall process of revelation.

In admitting the inadequacy of his comments on practical theology, our author refers the reader to the "five-volume *Handbuch der Pastoraltheologie*, edited by F.X. Arnold, F. Klostermann, K. Rahner, V. Schurr, and L. Weber."[156] One could ask here, how, in the communication of the Gospel message, does one distinguish between the message, and the message "as it has been developed within one's own culture"?[157] In many ways this is **the** classical missiological question. However, the methodological answer to such a question is not to be found in the specialty, communications, but through the interplay of foundations, doctrines and systematics which use categories which aim to be transcultural.

3.5.9 Concluding remarks on *Method*

Clearly the above summary of the structure and content of *Method in Theology* must, of necessity, leave out much of the rich texture and fine nuance of this profound work. Selections have had to be made; and the criteria of selection are defined by the focus of this thesis on revelation. Given the preliminary findings of the previous chapter, that Lonergan conceives of revelation in terms of the entry of divine meaning into human history, the issues of meaning, particularly the concepts of carriers and functions of meaning, are of greatest importance. Also of interest is Lonergan's account of religious experience, which is, if you like, the key entry point of divine meaning into human experience. Finally, the functional specialities will provide us with the basic structure around which to explicate the theology of revelation implicit in *Method*. As theology works methodically through the process of moving "from data to results" – mediating the past to the present, for the sake of the future – so too, the process of revelation involves both a receiving and a handing on of what is revealed. These preliminary observations will be expanded in the next chapter.

3.6 Extension in the Post-*Method* era

While *Method in Theology* marks the high-point of Lonergan's reflections in theological method, it also marks the beginning of the end of his preoccupation with particular theological issues. Lonergan himself admitted that much of his earlier work in Christology and Trinity would need to be totally recast in light of his reflections in *Method*. This is one of the reasons why he was reluctant to have his Latin treatises translated and published.[158] The post-*Method* writings do, however, shed light on how Lonergan conceived of his method, and give indications as to how it could be applied to concrete examples.

3.6.1 "The Origins of Christian Realism" [1972][159]

This essay was written in response to certain proposals of Hulsbosch, Schillebeeckx and Schoonenberg for a revision of Christological doctrine. Lonergan meets these proposals with a discussion of Christianity's engagement with the problems of realism since the time of the early Trinitarian and Christological debates. He outlines how Christianity is inextricably involved in the problems of realism. In fact, Christian meanings demand a critical, or at least, dogmatic realism to make sense of its basic doctrines.[160] And so, after reviewing the distinction between the world of immediacy and the world mediated by meaning, he considers the early Trinitarian debates. The way in which to understand "what was moving forward" is, he argues, to observe that Tertullian was a naive realist, that Origen was a neo-Platonic idealist, while Athanasius, and the definition of Nicea, demand at least a dogmatic realism. This realism is based in accepting the assertion that reality corresponds to true meaning, mediated by propositions.[161]

Lonergan then goes on to discuss specifically Christological issues and the Chalcedonian understanding of "one person" in Christ. Rather than viewing the terms *person, prosopon* and *hypostasis* as technical terms taken from Greek philosophy, Lonergan conceives them as heuristic, as naming an unknown.[162] He argues that Chalcedon gave them only an implicit definition; so that *person* is that of which there is one in Christ.[163]

Lonergan then seeks to explain the distinction between person and nature in the Chalcedonian definition by considering three meanings of the term *one*. There is one, in the numerical sense, corresponding to experiential activity. There is one, grasped in terms of the unity of a thing, corresponding to intellectual activity. And then there is one, as in one and the same, as distinct from another, corresponding to judging. Here Lonergan is clearly invoking the three levels of intentional consciousness in a way which transposes into cognitional terms the classical distinction between essence and existence. Person is then defined in terms of the one and the same identity which is affirmed in judgment.[164]

His concluding comments deal with Christianity's involvement with both the world of immediacy and the world mediated by meaning:

> the world of immediacy because of religious experience, because of God's love flooding our hearts through the Holy Spirit given to us (Rom. 5:5); the world mediated by meaning because divine revelation is God's own entry into man's world mediated by meaning.[165]

In its own way, this essay is illustrative of comments made in *Method* concerning the Christian tradition as containing the "seeds of intellectual conversion."[166] This raises crucial questions about the relationship between revelation and Lonergan's entire transcendental project which we will address in the chapters which follow. I shall consider this essay in more detail in Chapter 7 of this thesis.

3.6.2 *A Third Collection*[167]

It would be worthwhile to trace the development of Lonergan's thought in the post-*Method* era as it is represented by the essays in *A Third Collection* and the recently published essay, "Philosophy and the Religious Phenomenon", even though the limited scope of this present thesis cannot permit such an investigation. At the moment, our primary focus is on the established positions found in the work, *Method in Theology*. Though the later works clearly operate within these positions, clarifying and extending them, the basic invariant patterns are to be found in *Method*. While in the coming chapters of this thesis I shall have occasion to refer to these later writings in order to illustrate and clarify issues under consideration, I merely identify certain themes which are developed in these writings and which I feel to be significant for the focus of this thesis. I am assisted in this task by Robert Doran in his major study, *Theology and the Dialectics of History*.[168]

Existential and Historical Agency

The essays of *A Third Collection* continue the direction evident in *Method* of increasingly focussing on questions of existential and historical agency. This is particularly evident in the essays, "Dialectic of Authority", "Prolegomena to the Study of the Emerging Religious Consciousness of our Time", "Healing and Creating in History", "Natural Right and Historical Mindedness" and, "A Post-Hegelian Philosophy of Religion"[169]. Doran focuses his attention on a passage in the essay, "Natural Right and Historical Mindedness", an essay he describes as an attempt to "mediate a concern with human nature found in classical political philosophy ... with the historical consciousness of modern and specifically post-Hegelian thought."[170] The passage deals with the emergence of questions for deliberation, with their "practical, interpersonal and existential dimensions." Such questions emerge because "the successful negotiation of questions for intelligence and questions for reflection are not enough", since they are "strangely dissociated from the feelings that constitute the mass and momentum of our lives."[171] Thus, there emerges the question, "Is it worthwhile?":

> It is a searching question. The mere fact that we ask it points to a distinction between feelings that are self-regarding and feelings that are disinterested. Self-regarding feelings are pleasures and pains, desires and fears. But disinterested feelings recognize excellence: the vital value of health and strength; the communal value of a successfully functioning social order; the cultural value proclaimed as a life to be sustained not by bread alone but also by the word; the personal appropriation of these values by individuals; their historical extension in progress; deviation from them in decline; and their recovery in self-sacrificing love. ... Feelings reveal values to us. They dispose us to commitment. But they do not bring commitment about. For commitment is a personal act, a free and responsible act, a very open-eyed act in which we would settle what we are to become.[172]

Doran sees this passage as "a summation of the principal dimensions of the position on the subject advanced in what I am calling the second phase of Lonergan's thought on the human subject." In particular, he draws attention to the features of "feelings, moral self-transcendence, a scale of values, judgments of value, and decision."[173] I would add the link Lonergan makes between all these and the historical categories of progress, decline and redemption, in order to emphasise the historical role of revelation.

The Centrality of Love

The second theme which Doran identifies in Lonergan's post-*Method* writings is "the increasing centrality of love. The discussion of love constitutes one of the principal distinguishing and unifying themes in the book *A Third Collection*."[174] Whereas Doran focuses on passages from other essays, I am attracted to a passage from the essay, "Christology Today: Methodological Reflections." Here Lonergan draws attention to the ordinary path of development of advancing through the levels of consciousness, only to conclude that this ordinary process does in fact admit exceptions. There is another factor to be considered:

> Man's insertion in community and history includes an invitation for him to accept the transformation of falling in love: the transformation of domestic love between husband and wife; the transformation of human love for one's neighbor; the transformation of divine love that comes when God's love floods our inmost heart through the Holy Spirit he has given us (Rom. 5:5).
> Such transforming love has its occasions, its conditions, its causes. But once it comes and as long as it lasts, it takes over. One on longer is one's own ... There has begun a life in which the heart has reasons which reason does not know. There is opened up a new world in which the old adage, *nihil amatum nisi prius cognitum*, yields to a new truth, *nihil vere cognitum nisi prius amatum*.[175]

One should also add that the key text of Romans 5:5 is quoted or referred to at least nine times in the essays of *A Third Collection*. In the context of this thesis, the centrality of love emphasises the importance of the existential dimensions of revelation.

Healing and Creating in History

The recognition of the centrality of love, initiating us into a new life of self-transcendence, leads to the discernment of a new movement within consciousness. This is made explicit in the essay "Healing and Creating in History", but it is also contained in a number of other essays in *The Third Collection*. In the essay under consideration, Lonergan refers to the upward dynamism "from experience to growing understanding, from growing understanding to balanced judgment, from balance judgment to fruitful courses of action, and from fruitful courses of action to new situations." This is a creative vector within consciousness. He then identifies a reverse vector that moves "from above downwards." This healing vector he describes in the following terms:

> ... there is also development from above downwards. There is the transformation of falling in love: the domestic love of the family, the human love of one's tribe, one's city, one's country, mankind; the divine love that orientates man in his cosmos and expresses itself in worship. Where hatred only sees evil, love reveals values. At once it commands commitment and joyfully carries it out, no matter what the sacrifice involved. Where hatred reinforces bias, love dissolves it, whether it be the bias of unconscious motivation, the bias of individual or group egoism, or the bias of omnicompetent, shortsighted common sense. Where hatred plods around in ever narrower vicious circles, love breaks the bonds of psychological and social determinisms with the conviction of faith and the power of hope.[176]

Lonergan goes on to indicate the interdependence and necessity of both vectors operating within consciousness: "For just as the creative process, when unaccompanied by healing, is distorted and corrupted by bias, so too the healing process, when unaccompanied by creating, is a soul without a body."[177]

It is not as if these three features are not present in *Method*, at least implicitly. What Doran is pointing out is the sharpening focus and fuller explication of these themes. I shall have occasion to refer to these features as this thesis develops and gathers all these points together under the heading of revelation and *Method*.

3.7 Conclusion

In this chapter I have given an exposition of Lonergan's *Method in Theology* in light of the concerns of this thesis, dealing as it does with the theme of revelation. Most important for our present concerns is *Method*'s nuanced account of meaning. Given that Lonergan evidently understands revelation as the entry of "new meaning" into human history, his discussion of meaning will be of great assistance in exploring what he means by revelation. We take up this matter in the next chapter.

---

1. Tracy, *Achievement*, 266. For a thorough analysis of the development in Lonergan's thought on theological method, see C. Boly, *Road* .
2. Lonergan, *Method*, 4.
3. *Notion* is a technical term in Lonergan's writings. It refers to an immanent, dynamic orientation within consciousness, cf. *Insight*, 354ff. For example, Lonergan distinguishes between the idea of being which would express an understanding of everything, with a notion of being which is the pure unrestricted desire to know everything about everything. In *Insight*, Lonergan inadequately distinguishes between the notion of being and the notion of value.
4. Lonergan, *Method*, 17.
5. Lonergan, *Method*, 19.
6. Lonergan, *Method*, 23.
7. Lonergan, *Method*, 25.
8. B. Lonergan, "Functional specialties in theology", *Gregorianum*, Vol.50, fasc.3-4, (1969), 485-505 and K. Rahner, "Kritische Bemerkungen zu B.J.F. Lonergan's Aufsatz: 'Functional Specialties in Theology'", *Gregorianum*, 51/3 (1970), 537-540.
9. Lonergan, *Method*, 27.
10. Lonergan, *Method*, 27-30.
11. While, in *Insight*, feelings are by-passed, in *Method* they begin to take on a positive significance. Cf. "An interview with Fr. Bernard Lonergan", *Second Collection*, 221-3.
12. Lonergan, *Method*, 31.
13. Lonergan, *Method*, 30-32.
14. Lonergan, *Method*, 35.
15. Lonergan, *Method*, 40-1. Lonergan is drawing on a morality of virtue, as found in Aristotle's *Nicomachean Ethics*.
16. Lonergan states: "the apprehension of values and disvalues is not the task of understanding but of intentional response", *Method*, 245.
17. Lonergan, *Method*, 37.
18. Lonergan, *Method*, 36.

19. Lonergan, *Method*, 41-47.

20. Cf. Crowe, *Lonergan*, 25-26.   Also "Insight Revisited", *Second Collection*, 271-2.

21. Lonergan, *Method*, 52.

22. Lonergan, *Method*, 53.

23. Lonergan, *Method*, 54.

24. Lonergan, *Method*, 55.

25. Lonergan, *Method*, 55.

26. Lonergan, *Method*, 55.

27. Lonergan, *Method*, 59-61.

28. Lonergan, *Method*, 61-64.

29. For a critical evaluation of Lonergan's understanding of the role of symbols, see E. Braxton, "Bernard Lonergan's Hermeneutic of the Symbol", *Irish Theological Quarterly*, XLIII/3 (1976), 186-197. Braxton argues that Lonergan's understanding of symbol is underdeveloped, a point even as ardent a Lonergan scholar as Doran would concede. However Braxton does not allow Lonergan his own systematic control of language (i.e. Lonergan's own use of the terms myth and mystery), nor does he attend sufficiently to the relationship between symbol and affectivity Lonergan suggests. Because Doran attends to this he can constructively develop Lonergan's position, whereas Braxton rejects it.

30. Lonergan, *Method*, 64-69.

31. Lonergan, *Method*, 66-67.

32. Lonergan's account of symbols is much more precise and limited than that of, say, Paul Ricoeur. It is influenced by various psychotherapeutic theorists, as his list of references and footnotes suggests. Significantly there is a shift from the more rationalist psychotherapies of Stekel, referred to in *Insight*, toward the more affectively and symbolically oriented approaches Freud, Jung, Horney and Rogers. Cf. *Insight*, 202ff. Stekel's approach is to lead the patient from a blind spot towards a "lightening flash of illumination", which Lonergan identifies with insight. Affective approaches focus much more on removing, through symbolic negotiation, the affective blocks and biases which prevent insight.

33. For an analysis of the emergence of the distinction between insight and concept, and the significance of the distinction in the relativisation of concepts, see J. McDermott, "Tensions in Lonergan's Theory of Conversion", *Gregorianum*, 74/1 (1997), 114-117. McDermott draws largely on the *Verbum* articles.

34. Lonergan, *Method*, 71.

35. Lonergan, *Method*, 70-73.

36. Lonergan, *Method*, 73.

37. Note that Lonergan uses the terminology *efficient* and *effective* interchangeably. On 76-78 of *Method* he speaks of cognitive, *efficient*,

constitutive and communicative functions of meaning. On 356 of *Method*, in refering to this same material, he speaks of cognitive, constitutive, communicative and *effective* functions.

38. Lonergan, *Method*, 76-77.
39. Lonergan, *Method*, 77-78.
40. Lonergan, *Method*, 78.
41. Lonergan, *Method*, 78-9.
42. Lonergan, *Method*, 79.
43. Lonergan, *Method*, 80.
44. Lonergan, *Method*, 80.
45. Lonergan, *Method*, 81.
46. Lonergan, *Method*, 81.
47. Lonergan, *Method*, 85.
48. Lonergan, *Method*, 85.
49. Lonergan, *Method*, 90-96.
50. M. Vertin refers to this gift as an *agapic datum*, to distinguish it from the transcendental notions. This has significance for Lonergan's terminology of "levels of consciousness, cf. M. Vertin, "Lonergan on Consciousness: Is There a Fifth Level?", *Method : Journal of Lonergan Studies*, 12/1 (1994), 1-36, esp. 21ff.
51. Kelly, "Is *Method* Adequate?"
52. For one response to such criticism, see B. Carmody, "A Note of the Transcultural Nature of Lonergan's Religious Experience", *Irish Theological Quarterly*, 49/1 (1982), 59-64.
53. Lonergan, *Method*, 156-158. See in particular n.2 and its reference to Bultmann.
54. Lonergan, *Method*, 105.
55. Lonergan, *Method*, 106.
56. Modern exegetical opinion now sees the text as a subjective genitive, that is, as referring to God's love for us. Doran has questioned Lonergan's use of the objective genitive reading in a recent article, "Consciousness and Grace", *Method: Journal of Lonergan Studies*, 11/1 (1993), 51-75. While Lonergan's position is weak exegetically, I would still hold that, systematically, his use of the objective genitive is defensible.
57. Lonergan, *Method*, 107
58. Lonergan, *Method*, 107.
59. See the debate between R. Doran, "Consciousness and Grace", and M. Vertin, "Lonergan on Consciousness", on the significance of Lonergan's references to a fifth level of consciousness.
60. Lonergan, *Method*, 109.
61. Lonergan, *Method*, 110-1.
62. Lonergan, *Method*, 112.

63. Lonergan, *Method*, 113. This interplay of "inner word" and "outer word" gives Lonergan's account of religious experience a Trinitarian structure, though his terminology of inner "word" is perhaps a bit unfortunate. It raises the question as to whether the Spirit is a second word. He gives a more explicitly Trinitarian analysis in his later essay, "Mission and the Spirit", where he states that: "Without the visible mission of the Word, the gift of the Spirit is a being-in-love without the proper object; it remains simply an orientation to mystery that awaits its interpretation. Without the [in]visible mission of the Spirit, the Word enters into his own, but his own receive him not." "Mission and the Spirit", *Third Collection*, 32.

64. Lonergan, *Method*, 113.

65. Lonergan, *Method*, 114-5.

66. See, for example, his criticism of Leslie Dewart's book, *The Future of Belief*, in the essay, "The Dehellenization of Dogma", *Second Collection*, 11-32. He notes that Dewart's notion of faith "seems to coincide with religious experience" (17). Ironically, this is not far from Lonergan's own account of faith in *Method*.

67. Lonergan, *Method*, 115.

68. Lonergan, *Method*, 116.

69. Lonergan, *Method*, 116.

70. Lonergan, *Method*, 117.

71. Lonergan, *Method*, 118.

72. Lonergan, *Method*, 119.

73. Lonergan, *Method*, 119.

74. Lonergan, *Method*, 119.

75. Lonergan, *Method*, 122.

76. Lonergan, *Method*, 122. Cf., "Healing and Creating in History", *Third Collection*, 100-109.

77. Lonergan, *Method*, 126.

78. Lonergan, *Method*, 133-136.

79. Lonergan, *Method*, 149.

80. Lonergan, *Method*, 150.

81. Lonergan, *Method*, 150.

82. However, Robert Doran has argued, on the basis of Lonergan's discussion of the final specialty of communications, that the present situation of the cultural matrix is also a source for theology, cf. Doran, *Theology*, 12-16. Specifically, Doran is seeking to overcome the conceptualism he sees as being inherent in the "method of correlation" employed by theologians such as David Tracy. If the situation is already a theological source it cannot simply be correlated, as "non-religious", with religious symbols drawn from the tradition.

83. In general, systematic expression does not need exegesis. As Lonergan notes, there is no body of exegetical literature on Euclid's *Elements*, cf. *Method*, 154.

84. Lonergan, *Method*, 155.

85. Lonergan, *Method*, 161-2.

86. Lonergan, *Method*, 156-8.

87. On the self-correcting process of learning, see *Insight*, 174-75.

88. Lonergan, *Method*, 175.

89. Lonergan, *Method*, 178.

90. Lonergan, *Method*, 178-9.

91. Lonergan, *Method*, 179. Lonergan could illustrate the point by reference to his work on the Council of Nicea, cf. *The Way to Nicea*. One thing which was going forward at the time of Nicea was the very notion of doctrine, though most of those involved could not have formulated this forward movement.

92. Lonergan, *Method*, 181-196.

93. Lonergan, *Method*, 198-214.

94. Lonergan, *Method*, 216.

95. Lonergan, *Method*, 218.

96. Lonergan, *Method*, 223.

97. Lonergan, *Method*, 224.

98. Lonergan, *Method*, 232-233.

99. Lonergan, *Method*, 233.

100. Lonergan, *Method*, 235.

101. Lonergan, *Method*, 236-7.

102. Lonergan, *Method*, 238-240.

103. Lonergan, *Method*, 240.

104. Lonergan, *Method*, 240.

105. Lonergan, *Method*, 242.

106. Lonergan, *Method*, 241. Lonergan uses the term as follows: "what sublates goes beyond what is sublated, introduces something new and distinct, puts everything on a new basis, yet so far from interfering with the sublated or destroying it, on the contrary needs it, includes it, preserves all its proper features and properties, and carries them forward to a fuller realization within a richer context". Though Lonergan refers to Rahner's *Hearers of the Word* (London: Sheed and Ward, 1969) for his notion of sublation, it seems to be as much his own as Rahner's. See Crowe's editorial notes to the recently published article by B. Lonergan, "Philosophy and Religious Phenomenon", *Method: Journal of Lonergan Studies*, 12/2 (1994), 145, note.e.

107. Lonergan, *Method*, 243.

108. Lonergan, *Method*, 249.

109. Lonergan, *Method*, 267.

110. Lonergan, *Method*, 268.

111. Lonergan, *Method*, 269.
112. Lonergan, *Method*, 271-81.
113. Lonergan, *Method*, 282.
114. Lonergan, *Method*, 282-3.
115. Lonergan, *Method*, 282.
116. Lonergan, *Method*, 290-1.
117. Lonergan, *Method*, 291.
118. Lonergan, *Method*, 292.
119. Lonergan, *Method*, 319.
120. Lonergan, *Method*, 295.
121. Lonergan, *Method*, 295.
122. Lonergan, *Method*, 296-7.
123. Lonergan, *Method*, 298.
124. Lonergan, *Method*, 298.
125. Lonergan, *Method*, 299.
126. Lonergan, *Method*, 302.
127. Lonergan, *Method*, 302.
128. Lonergan, *Method*, 302-5.
129. Lonergan, *Method*, 305.
130. Lonergan, *Method*, 309.
131. Lonergan, *Method*, 312.
132. Lonergan, *Method*, 312-8.
133. Lonergan, *Method*, 319.
134. Lonergan, *Method*, 319-20.
135. As Lonergan notes in the introduction to *Method* (p.xii), this is one of the few instances where he makes explicit reference to Catholic Church teaching.
136. Lonergan, *Method*, 323.
137. Lonergan, *Method*, 325.
138. Lonergan, *Method*, 325.
139. Lonergan, *Method*, 326-330.
140. Lonergan, *Method*, 335.
141. For example, Boly comments: "when Lonergan spoke of theology, he meant speculative theology in the strict sense, the operation of faith seeking understanding", *Road*, 157.
142. Lonergan, *Method*, 351.
143. Lonergan, *Method*, 336.
144. Lonergan, *Method*, 344.
145. Lonergan, *Method*, 345.
146. Cf. Doran, *Theology*, 629.
147. Lonergan, *Method*, 346.
148. Lonergan, *Method*, 346-7.
149. Lonergan, *Method*, 348.

150. Lonergan, *Method*, 351-352.
151. Lonergan, *Method*, 353.
152. Lonergan, *Method*, 353.
153. Lonergan, *Method*, 357.
154. Lonergan, *Method*, 362-3.
155. Lonergan, *Method*, 363-4.
156. Lonergan, *Method*, 355-6.
157. Lonergan, *Method*, 362.
158. Note, however, that he did allow the historical part of *De Deo Trino* to be published as *The Way to Nicea* since he may have felt that it was illustrative of what he meant by the functional specialty, dialectics. Cf. C. O'Donovan, "Translator's Introduction", *Way to Nicea*, xxvi-xxviii.
159. B. Lonergan, "The Origins of Christian Realism", *Second Collection*, 239-261.
160. Lonergan, "Origins", 239-40.
161. Lonergan, "Origins", 244-50.
162. In this regard, Lonergan regularly refers to Augustine's *De Trinitatae* where Augustine basically defines person as what there are three of in the Trinity.
163. Lonergan, "Origins", 253-57.
164. Lonergan, "Origins", 258.
165. Lonergan, "Origins", 260.
166. Lonergan, *Method*, 243.
167. B. Lonergan, *A Third Collection: Papers by Bernard J.F. Lonergan s.j.*, F. Crowe (ed.) (Mahwah: Paulist Press, 1985).
168. Doran, *Theology*, 19-37.
169. Lonergan, *A Third Collection*, "Dialectic of Authority" 5-12, "Prolegomena to the Study of the Emerging Religious Consciousness of our Time" 55-73, "Healing and Creating in History" 100-109, "Natural Right and Historical Mindedness" 169-183 and, "A Post-Hegelian Philosophy of Religion", 202-223.
170. Doran, *Theology*, 26.
171. Lonergan, "Natural Right", 172-3.
172. Lonergan, "Natural Right", 173.
173. Doran, *Theology*, 27.
174. Doran, *Theology*, 31.
175. B. Lonergan, "Christology Today: Methodological Reflections", *A Third Collection*, 77.
176. B. Lonergan, "Healing and Creating", *A Third Collection*, 106.
177. Lonergan, "Healing and Creating", 107.

CHAPTER FOUR:
METHOD AND REVELATION

In the last two chapters I have given an exposition of Lonergan's developing thought from his earliest writings to his mature position in *Method in Theology* and beyond, with an eye to the themes of method and revelation. In this chapter I shall move to a more constructive mode. At the end of chapter two, I presented evidence that the major developments in Lonergan's understanding of theological method also involved a shift in the underlying understanding of the nature of revelation. In this chapter, I shall attempt to explicate an understanding of revelation which I find to be implicit in *Method*. In the next chapter I shall compare and contrast this understanding with the work of three key authors in the theology of revelation. There, I hope to be able to vindicate my claim that *Method* implicitly contains a much more nuanced account of revelation than is present in contemporary theology.

4.1 Revelation and divine transcendence

The absolute starting point for any analysis of divine revelation is obviously God. As I concluded at the end of chapter two, Lonergan conceives revelation as the entry of new, transcendent meaning and value into human history. Revelation is a divine act of communicating meaning to humanity; so we must begin with some observations about the general nature of the relationship between transcendent being and creation.

On this matter, Lonergan has been a constant and unwavering upholder of divine transcendence. God is completely other than creation, other than the spatio-temporal material universe which we inhabit. Lonergan affirms this as the teaching of Thomas Aquinas in his doctoral thesis, *Gratia Operans*, and adopts it as his own in *Insight*, Chapter 19, "General Transcendent Knowledge." There, Lonergan conceives God as an unrestricted act of understanding that primarily understands itself, and, hence, understands every other intelligible reality. Among the many assertions that Lonergan affirms about such being in his long and subtle discussion is that "the unrestricted act understands, affirms and wills contingent beings to be, without any increment or change in its [own] reality."[1] A number of important corollaries follow, which he discusses under the heading of contingent predication. I shall focus attention on two of these corollaries:

> The third corollary is divine efficacy. It is impossible for it to be true that God understands, affirms, effects anything to exist or occur without it being true that the thing exists or the event occurs exactly as God understands, affirms, or wills it. For one and the same metaphysical condition is needed for the truth of both propositions, namely, the relevant contingent existence or occurrence.
>
> The fourth corollary is inverse to the third, namely, that divine efficacy does not impose necessity upon its consequents. In the light of divine efficacy it is quite true that if God understands or affirms or wills or effects this or that to exist or occur, then it is impossible for the this or that not to exist or not to occur. Still, the existence or occurrence is a metaphysical condition of the truth of the antecedent, and so, if there is the existence or occurrence, then there is the existence or occurrence.[2]

These corollaries establish a framework for affirming a universally efficacious divine providence consistent with human freedom. Providence continues even after the "occurrence" of evil, since "there are no divine afterthoughts."[3] Divine providence remains all-encompassing and totally efficacious. Thus, Chapter 20 of *Insight*, "Special Transcendent Knowledge", takes up the problem of evil and the divine solution to the problem of evil, without any backing away from his previous position on providence. This distinction, between general and special transcendent knowledge, is clearly parallel to the classical distinction between natural and supernatural revelation.

The notion of providence clearly involves a rejection of the many theological positions currently proposed which seek to compromise divine transcendence in some way or other, most notably as found in process theology, but also present in thinkers such as Moltmann, Pannenberg, and some would suggest, Rahner. I shall contrast Lonergan with Rahner at a later stage of this thesis on this point. However, for the moment, I will note that a universally efficacious providence, based on divine transcendence, is a secure basis for grounding a notion of divine revelation. God stands in a creative relationship to the totality of occurrences and things, including both the events of the outer world and the inner movements of the heart and mind, in a way which remains consistent with human freedom and responsibility.

Lonergan's position on divine transcendence is a consequence of intellectual conversion. This conversion grounds the relationships between knowing, being and reality, which are pivotal to his argument in *Insight* for the existence of God, and for understanding the relationship between God and creation. While this may seem like a purely philosophical starting point, for Lonergan, the religious and dogmatic tradition contains the seeds of intellectual conversion.[4] Thus, Christian revelation is already implicated in the philosophical tradition within which Lonergan operates.

That Lonergan himself would begin a discussion of divine revelation with a discussion of providence may be inferred from a footnote at the start of *The Way to Nicea*. We find him discussing dogmatic development, and presuming in his students some familiarity with the issues at stake. In the footnote he states:

> We presume familiarity with the theological treatises on God's special providence, divine revelation, the inspiration of sacred Scripture and the *magisterium* of the Church.[5]

I would propose that here we see Lonergan's own suggestion as to the proper ordering of these treatises. The key controlling notion, which would order the whole, is "special divine providence." It would stand to general providence as special transcendent knowledge (*Insight*, Chapter 20), stands to general transcendent knowledge (*Insight*, Chapter 19). From this one controlling notion, Lonergan can move to explicate notions of revelation, inspiration and magisterium.

While Lonergan later moved beyond the approach adopted in these later chapters of *Insight*, inasmuch as he sought to ground his approach more in religious experience, and to move from questions of proof to the issue of conversion,[6] there is no indication that he moved away from his uncompromising position on divine transcendence, nor from the consequent position on providence.

4.2 Revelation and meaning

As I have already indicated, the concept of revelation found in Lonergan's later writings is primarily concerned with the issue of meaning. Revelation is God's entry into the world mediated by meaning:

> ... however trifling the uses to which words may be put, still they are the vehicles of meaning, and meaning is the stuff of man's making of man. So it is that *divine revelation is God's entry and his taking part in man's making of man.* It is God's claim to have a say in the aims and purposes, the direction and development of human lives, human societies, human cultures, human history ... For revelation is God's entry into man's making of man, and so theology not only has to reflect on revelation, but also it has somehow to mediate *God's meaning into the whole of human affairs.*[7] [emphasis added]

Lonergan identifies this entry by God into the world of meaning with "revealed religion", as distinct from "natural religion"[8]. This parallels the distinction between general and special transcendent knowledge, or natural and supernatural revelation.

4.2.1 Revelation, carriers of meaning and the functional specialties

If revelation is about the entry into human history of a new divine meaning, then such meaning must be "carried"; that is, it must present itself within the world of meaning as one of the many meanings which humans encounter. While, in the above citation, Lonergan pays particular attention to linguistic carriers of meaning (words), in other material he refers to the entry of the divine Word into human history as involving both linguistic and incarnate meaning.[9] More generally, we need make no *a priori* restrictions, but should consider revelation in terms of all the carriers of meaning which Lonergan itemises in *Method.*

As the reader will recall, *Method* treats a number of carriers of meaning. Intersubjective meaning has it basis in a vital and functional identification with the other, which precedes the distinction between "I" and "You", and is carried over into the "We" of mutual love. Artistic meaning is found in the concrete pattern of internal relations of colours, tones, notes and volumes and so on, which constitute the work of art. This pattern excludes instrumentalized experience, in order to liberate the subject to be himself or herself. Symbolic meaning involves the internal communication between heart and mind, mind and body, body and heart, whereby images release feeling, feeling evokes image and apprehends value. Linguistic meaning is meaning as spoken or written, in commonsense, theoretic or literary modes. Incarnate meaning is the meaning of a person, of his or her life, deeds, and actions.

In the previous chapter I suggested that these different carriers of meaning could be correlated with different levels of consciousness. Thus, intersubjective, artistic and symbolic meaning correlate with experiential consciousness. Linguistic meaning correlates with intellectual consciousness. Incarnate meaning correlates with existential consciousness.

Moreover, it could also be suggested that historical carriers of meaning correlate with rational consciousness. Here, historical meaning is found in "what is moving forward", to use Lonergan's phrase. The identification of historical meaning is important for understanding the ways in which history itself can be revelatory. Historical events can "carry" divine meaning into human living. Lonergan seems to subsume the possibility of historical meaning within his category of incarnate meaning. Here I would prefer to keep the two distinct, though related – as rational consciousness is distinct from, though related to, existential consciousness.

I would further suggest that these carriers of meaning should be correlated with the eight functional specialties. Thus, intersubjective, artistic and symbolic meaning correlate with research and communications. Linguistic meaning correlates with interpretation and systematics. Historical meaning correlates with history and doctrine. Incarnate meaning correlates with dialectics and foundations. **This kind of correlation provides the basic structural isomorphism between revelation, as carried into human history, and Lonergan's theological method.** The two-fold nature of the correlation, as, for example, when historical meaning correlates with both history and with doctrines, follows from the two-fold dynamic of the creating and healing vectors within human consciousness. I shall explore this more fully below.

Clearly, one and the same reality may be a multiple carrier of meanings: "Incarnate meaning combines all or at least many of the other carriers of meaning."[10] Thus, the life of Jesus has intersubjective, artistic (in this case, dramatic), symbolic (for example, the parables), linguistic, historical (crucifixion, resurrection) and incarnate meanings. One may argue that revelation, as "carried", is concerned with all eight of the theological tasks, from research all the way through to communications. All are parts of the process whereby divine meaning enters, or is carried, into the world mediated by meaning.

4.2.2 Functions of meaning

Any discussion of revelation as meaning must also consider the various functions of meaning. If revelation is the entry of a new, divine meaning into human history, it must fulfil various functions in that history; and those functions can be analysed in terms of the various functions of meaning. Lonergan speaks of the cognitive, effective, constitutive and communicative functions of meaning. He relates these particularly to the role of doctrines in religion: doctrines fulfil "the communicative, effective, constitutive, and cognitive functions proper to meaning." Lonergan gives a fuller statement of how doctrine functions:

> It is effective inasmuch as it counsels and dissuades, commands and prohibits. It is cognitive inasmuch as it tells whence we come, whither we go, how we get there. It is constitutive of the individual inasmuch as the doctrine is a set of meanings and values that inform his living, his knowing, his doing. It is constitutive of the community, for community exists inasmuch as there is a commonly accepted set of meanings and values shared by people in contact with one another. Finally it is communicative for it has passed from Christ to the apostles and from the apostles to their successors and from these in each age to the flocks of which they were the pastors.[11]

The different functions of meaning, then, spell out the various functions of divine revelation.

Firstly, it has an effective, moral function. Revelation will establish various moral norms and guides for human conduct. It will order human values and place them in relationship to the experience of religious value, which involves a transvaluation of all our human values. Without an affective experience of transcendent value, "the originating value is man and the terminal good is the human good man brings about." However, with this affective religious experience,

> originating value is divine light and love, while terminal value is the whole universe. So the human good becomes absorbed in an all-encompassing good.[12]

Recognition of a moral role in revelation does not solve the problem of the relationship between revelation and a natural moral law attainable by reason alone. Lonergan clearly does not want to reduce revelation to its moral and intellectual functions:

> It is not to be thought, however, that religious conversion means no more than a new and more efficacious ground for the pursuit of intellectual and moral ends.[13]

Grace is not reduced to nature. Religious experience is an end in itself, needing no further justification: "There is no need to justify critically the charity described by St Paul" (I Corinthians 13).[14] However, revelation is not without moral implications, since religious conversion sublates moral conversion.

To say more would require a thorough investigation of the relationship between grace and nature as found in Lonergan's writings, an investigation which goes beyond the scope of this thesis. Nonetheless, what the above discussion does establish is that revealed meanings can have an effective function in human living. Moreover, given the priority Lonergan gives in *Method* to the existential over the cognitive, we can see the essential importance played by the effective function of revealed meanings.

Secondly, revelation has a cognitive, intellectual function. It informs us about reality, being, truth, about what is. Unlike many of his contemporaries, Lonergan maintains that revelation has this cognitive role. It does, in fact, tells us something about God, about humanity in relationship to God, about our origins and our ends. Still, revelation can never be reduced to this cognitive function, nor can such a function be ignored or denied. The cognitive function of revelation is not simply a matter of imparting facts; it is also a matter of creating the framework within which revelation can be coherently understood. The cognitive function of revelation demands and promotes intellectual conversion:

> among the values discerned by the eye of love is the value of believing the truths taught by the religious tradition, *and in such tradition and belief are the seeds of intellectual conversion.*[15] [emphasis added]

Indeed, Lonergan identifies the role of the tradition in promoting intellectual conversion as the normative function of doctrines.[16] Revelation has a normative function inasmuch as it creates the very framework needed for its own explication. It promotes an intellectual conversion congruent with that explication.

Next, we may consider the constitutive and communicative functions of meaning and the notions of community, existence (as authentic or unauthentic), and history. Significantly, it is in his discussion of these notions that Lonergan first introduces the crucial role of tradition.[17] Clearly, taking into account the constitutive and communicative functions of meaning, revelation creates a community with its own tradition of belief and practice. Such a community is held together by the common meanings and values drawn from the basic revelation which founds the community in the first place.[18] More than this, it is a community which generates a tradition of moral and intellectual reasoning. The effective and cognitive functions of revelation occur within that tradition, to drive it to greater coherence and completeness. I return to this issue later in this chapter and in a chapter seven, where I examine the relationship between revelation and transcendental method.

While Lonergan talks about cognitive, effective, constitutive and communicative functions of meaning in relation to doctrines, these functions are not restricted to doctrines alone, even though doctrine may be the most conspicuous example of these. Indeed, the efficient, moral component of revelation is far more potently fulfilled by the concrete examples of Jesus' life, and the lives of the saints, than by any moral doctrine or treatise. Once more, this turns our attention to the question of how meaning is carried, since doctrines are only one of many carriers of divine meaning into the human situation. For the moment, let me complete our discussion on the various carriers of meaning and their relation to revelation.

4.3 Revelation and incarnate meaning

While the absolute *prior quoad se* of revelation is God, in terms of the entry of God's meaning into the human world mediated by meaning, ontological priority must be given to incarnate meaning. Human beings, through their experience of God's love poured into their hearts and inspiring conversion, are transformed into carriers of divine meaning. Human beings are the relative *prior quoad se* of divine revelation, and are, in turn, the proximate sources of historical, linguistic, symbolic, artistic and intersubjective carriers of meaning, through their words and deeds, and the triumphs and failures of their lives. In this sense, revelation is thoroughly **personal**, since it is expressed in and through the lives of persons.

4.3.1 Incarnate meaning and authentic subjectivity

But incarnate meaning cannot be taken for granted. As Lonergan notes, "as meaning can be incarnate, so too can be the meaningless, the vacant, the empty, the vapid, the insipid, the dull."[19] The key issue in incarnate meaning is that of personal authenticity. Authenticity alone generates progress, while unauthenticity generates decline, and so discloses the need for redemption.[20] As the purpose of revelation is the redemptive action of God in reversing decline and promoting progress, revelation is incarnate in the lives of men and women who make authenticity their own apostolate.[21] Of course, as Lonergan repeatedly affirms, not only individuals but also traditions must face the problems of authenticity and unauthenticity.

The authenticity of human beings is the sole guarantor of the truthfulness of incarnate meaning, and of the various other meanings expressed through the diverse carriers of meaning which human beings employ. "Genuine objectivity is the fruit of authentic subjectivity. It is to be attained only by attaining authentic subjectivity."[22] Incarnate meaning is true meaning inasmuch as a human being lives authentically. The historical, linguistic, symbolic, artistic and intersubjective meanings a person creates are true inasmuch as he or she lives authentically, in accord with the transcendental precepts, Be attentive, Be intelligent, Be reasonable, Be responsible, Be in love.

Ultimately, however, authenticity is not so much an achievement, as a gift:

> I have argued that man exists authentically in the measure that he succeeds in self-transcendence, and I have found that self-transcendence has both its fulfilment and its enduring ground in holiness, in God's gift of his love to us.[23]

We should see this final phrase as an abbreviated reference to one of Lonergan's favourite texts, Romans 5:5, expressive of the gift of God's love as "the Holy Spirit given to us." In his later post-*Method* essay, "Mission and the Spirit", Lonergan speaks of the invisible mission of the Holy Spirit in terms of *fides ex infusione*, the inner gift which "descends from the gift of God's love through religious conversion to moral, and through religious and moral to intellectual conversion."[24] Thus, the "achievement" of human authenticity is grounded in the prior gift of the Holy Spirit. In this way, a Trinitarian dimension of revelation is implied, and so provokes a Trinitarian account of the process of revelation, through the incarnate meaning of authentic subjectivity.

4.3.2 Authentic subjectivity and personal value

Authenticity raises the issue of personal value. Human beings are originating values inasmuch as they choose. Yet the object of those choices, which are terminal values, may itself be authenticity or self-transcendence. Through their decisions they make themselves who they are to be; that is, human freedom is a process of self-constitution:

> Since man can know and choose authenticity and self-transcendence, originating and terminal values can coincide. When each member of the community both wills authenticity in himself and, inasmuch as he can, promotes it in others, then the originating values that choose and the terminal values that are chosen overlap and interlace.[25]

Thus, incarnate meaning relates to authenticity, to objectivity and so to personal value. The greater the authenticity, the greater the objectivity; and the greater the ontic value of the person, both in themselves and as a source of value for others. The authentic human being is the measure of all things, the true teacher, the true prophet, the true judge.[26]

4.3.3 Personal value and transcendent value

I have linked the issues of revelation, incarnate meaning, authenticity and personal value. In this connection, personal value is one level of a hierarchy or scale of values which Lonergan introduces in his discussion of the human good. This scale consists of vital, social, cultural, personal and religious value. Lonergan argues that without the experience of religious value, without religious experience and the faith that it engenders,

> the originating value is man and the terminal value is the human good man brings about. But in the light of faith, originating value is divine light and love, while terminal value is the whole universe.[27]

Yet how does religious value enter into the human world mediated by meaning? In Lonergan's account, this generally occurs through the religious experience of human beings throughout history. However, there is another possibility, which, anticipated by transcendental method as a possibility, lies beyond it in terms of any historical identification. It is possible that, in some particular human being, religious value coincides with personal value. The personal value of such a person would be transcendent, divine. This would instance the most intimate entry of God's meaning into human history, as a divine self-communication of the most definitive kind. Such a human being would have a value which was not just quantitatively different, but qualitatively different from other human beings.[28] Without ceasing to be a human being, that person would have transcendent value; he or she would be, in some sense, a divine person.[29]

As noted above, such a person, as absolutely authentic subject, would be a true teacher, prophet and judge.[30] The teachings would include statements of self knowledge, self affirmation, self identity. Such a subject is not simply the carrier of revealed meanings and values, but is also the content of revelation: both revealer and revealed. Such a subject could demand faith, not simply in what he or she said, but in him or herself.[31]

Lonergan saw no need to give a metaphysical account of such an incarnation of a divine person:

The theologian is under no necessity of reducing to the metaphysical elements, which suffice for an account of this world, such super-natural realities as the Incarnation, the Indwelling of the Holy Spirit, and the Beatific Vision.[32]

He thus sees no need for the programme of theologians such as Karl Rahner, who attempt to speak of these realities in terms of quasi-formal causality.[33]   Instead he invokes the notion, which we have already spoken of as grounding the whole account of revelation, of contingent predication (see p.136).[34]   The incarnation of a divine person, as envisaged by Lonergan's transcendental method, is a special instance of the general problem of the relationship between transcendent being and created being.

Because personal value is linked with authenticity, such a human being would have an absolute authenticity, appropriate to the developmental level of whatever stage of human psychological, cognitional and moral development he or she was at.   Such a person could truly be said to be the way, the truth and the life.

Lonergan's transcendental method can envisage such a human being as a real possibility.   It can conceive of such a human being as the definitive entry of God into the human world mediated by meaning and motivated by value.   Further, it can suggest that such a human being would play a definitive role in the drama of human history.   Still, transcendental method, solely, cannot identify any existing human being as fulfilling such conditions.

However, inasmuch as transcendental method can conceive of such possibilities, it can develop a heuristic, or "searching", Christology, in the sense of Karl Rahner.[35]   In much the same way that Rahner develops the notion of the absolute saviour, so Lonergan's transcendental method can be used to envisage the absolutely authentic subject in whom personal and divine value coincide.   In its way, this searching Christology enjoins us to seek out such a human being, to "follow him", "listen to him", as a model and source of authenticity, as one who takes on the task of reversing human decline through self-sacrificing love.

4.3.4 Falling in love with the incarnate one, the interpersonal element

When the conditions indicated above are fulfilled, then falling in love with God and falling in love with the incarnation of divine value are one and the same thing. As Lonergan notes, Christianity adds an interpersonal element to religious experience. The mystery, which is at the heart of being, is now to be identified with this particular historical human being, whom I can relate to and fall in love with. Religious experience, no longer an anonymous falling in love without restriction, is falling in love without restriction with this human being. Faith is not just knowledge born of religious love. It becomes commitment to the life and teaching of this one historical person. The quest for authenticity is, then, not just a solitary journey. It is revealed to be discipleship, following the one who has gone before us all. Indeed, it may even involve a commitment to a tradition of religious belief initiated by such a person.

This would seem to be the experience of generations of Christians who have fallen in love with Jesus Christ, who have committed themselves to his life and teaching, and who have given up all to follow him in discipleship, humbly following their master even unto death. While transcendental method can envisage such a possibility, it is only the eye of love which discerns the realisation of such a possibility in the poor carpenter from Nazareth who died, cursed on a cross, to be raised to new life by the Father.

These comments might be sufficient to suggest that Lonergan's transcendental method anticipates a classically orthodox Christology. The jump from this searching Christology to an explicit Christology is clearly beyond a purely transcendental method. It can be made, not by attending to the data of consciousness, but only by attending to the data of history. However, a searching Christology is still not the complete response to those critics of Lonergan who are dissatisfied with the lack of a Christological basis in his methodology. A more complete solution will depend on later discussion on the relationship between Christian revelation and transcendental method.

I conclude this section by noting the relationship between incarnate meaning and the functional specialties, dialectic and foundations. These two specialties are particularly concerned with the turn to the subject in the hermeneutical process. Dialectic determines the patterns which represent the presence or absence of various conversions. Foundations grounds the normative phase of theology in the authenticity of the converted theologian. These two specialties raise the question of incarnate meaning present in sources to be believed or not, to be followed or not, and of the incarnate meaning of the theologian him/herself. In these specialties the theologian is inextricably bound up with the concrete and personal issues implicit in a searching Christology. In this context, we can see how Lonergan's theological method does orient the theologian to a Christological conversion as well as to the personal appropriation of authenticity.

4.4 Revelation and experiential carriers of meaning

In the preceding analysis, I have argued for the personal nature of revelation, grounded in incarnate meaning. This is the relative *prior quoad se* of revelation, the basic entry point of divine meaning into the human world of meaning and value. But what is *prior quoad se* is not *prior quoad nos*. As Lonergan repeatedly states, the ontological order and the intentional order are reversed.[36] What is ontologically first, is last in the order of knowledge. Now, what is first in the order of knowledge is the content of experiential consciousness. So we may turn our attention to the carriers of meaning which correlate to experiential consciousness; that is, intersubjective, artistic and symbolic carriers of meaning. Here I shall focus on the latter two in relation to revelation.

4.4.1 Revelation and dramatic artistry

There is another reason for turning our attention to these particular carriers of meaning. Not only are they the *prior quoad nos*, but also, as Robert Doran has shown in a number of his works,[37] there is an intimate connection between the dramatic artistry of experiential consciousness and the struggle for authenticity of the existential subject.[38] The following quotation from *Method* illustrates this important point:

> First, there is God's gift of his love. Next, the eye of this love reveals values in their splendour, while the strength of this love brings about their realization, and that is moral conversion. Finally, among the values discerned by the eye of love is the value of believing the truths taught by the religious tradition, and in such

tradition and belief are the seeds of intellectual conversion. For the word, spoken and heard, proceeds from and penetrates to all four levels of intentional consciousness. Its content is not just a content of experience but a content of experience and understanding and judging and deciding. The analogy of sight yields the cognitional myth. But fidelity to the word engages the whole man.[39]

Doran draws attention to the tension between Lonergan's rejection of the "analogy of sight" and his acceptance of "the *eye* of love." Apparently some visual analogy is being kept. Doran seeks to resolve this tension by appealing to an aesthetic quality of the experience of God's love.[40]

An explicit role is given above to the aesthetic criterion of *splendour* in the awakening of the subject to both its moral object (value and moral conversion) and its intellectual object (truth, particularly doctrine and intellectual conversion). The aesthetic criterion proceeds from the prior gift of God's love poured into our hearts, but precedes our attunements to the moral and intellectual objects of conscious intentionality. We are awakened to these by the *splendour* of God's truth and goodness. Beauty, in particular, dramatic artistry, thus has a role to play in the process of revelation. The beauty of revelation may be the first aspect which captures and holds our attention, prior to any moral or intellectual apprehension on our part.

This is not to argue for an aesthetical theology, but rather, as von Balthasar would claim, to allow for a theological aesthetics. Prior to all is the gift of God's love. It is this gift which establishes the necessary aesthetic criterion; just as the same gift grounds the later moral and intellectual conversions. The priority remains with the revealing God, who establishes the aesthetic, moral and intellectual criteria needed within the receiving subject to appropriate the fullness of revelation.

4.4.2 Revelation and symbol

While artistic meaning is one aspect of the experiential carriers of meaning, special mention should also be made, given the prominence of the term in current theology, to symbolic carriers of meaning. Lonergan defines a symbol as "an image of a real or imaginary object that evokes a feeling or is evoked by a feeling."[41] This definition is much more precise and technical than is common in theological literature.

But it allows Lonergan to establish an exact link between symbol, affect and value which mediates the connection between existential and experiential consciousness. Lonergan expresses this link by attending to the communicative function of symbols:

> This need is for internal communication. Organic and psychic vitality have to reveal themselves to intentional consciousness and, inversely, consciousness has to secure the collaboration of organism and psyche. Again, our apprehensions of values occur in intentional responses, in feelings; here too it is necessary for feelings to reveal their objects and, inversely, for objects to awaken feelings. It is through symbols that mind and body, mind and heart, heart and body communicate.[42]

Internal communication allows for a symbolic expression of our affective development:

> Affective development, or aberration, involves a transvaluation and transformation of symbols. What before was moving no longer moves; what before did not move now is moving. So the symbols themselves change to express the new affective capacities and dispositions.[43]

Lonergan seems to suggest that attention to our personal symbol systems, and to the internal communication they represent, allows us to identify our personal affective development. Affective development is a core issue for existential authenticity:

> Now the apprehension of values and disvalues is the task not of understanding but of intentional response. Such response is all the fuller, all the more discriminating, the better a man one is, the more refined one's sensibility, the more delicate one's feelings.[44]

Now, the most significant development in one's affectivity, the most powerful existential event promoting authenticity, is conversion. In short, conversion is symbolically mediated.

Commenting on Lonergan's analysis of symbol, Doran observes that they have a transforming and disclosive power.[45] This disclosive and transforming power of symbols makes them significant for any theology of revelation. Symbols not only capture the attention of the subject. By mediating the transformation of the subject, they allow for the negotiation of affective blocks and biases which distort the subject's current horizon. In revelation, the symbol becomes sacrament as it mediates the transforming love of God, poured into our heart. The result is the transvaluation of all our values and the opening of the eyes of love which transforms our knowing.[46]

These observations indicate something of the role of symbols in revelation. What Lonergan identifies is a connection between symbols and the personal, existential event of conversion. Converted subjects become incarnate carriers of divine meaning as it makes its entry into our human world of meanings and values.

The above discussion has dealt with the issue of experiential carriers of meaning, on dramatic and symbolic carriers of meaning in particular. I should repeat that this differentiation of carriers does not necessarily imply distinct objects, for the same object may be a carrier of different types of meaning. For instance, a dramatic life-story may contain many symbolic aspects.

Indeed, the primacy, as *prior quoad nos*, of these experiential carriers of meaning is evident in Christian experience. Most, if not all, Christians are first captured through the telling of the Christian story, the dramatic narrative of the life, death and resurrection of Jesus, often in an aesthetically rich setting of the Christian liturgy. The Christian narrative is itself embedded in the fuller biblical narrative of the people of Israel; to be expanded out into a universal narrative of humankind through the soteriological reflections of the Patristic era. Few Christians would not have been caught by the symbolic stories told (parables) and actions performed (miracles, table fellowship with sinners) by Jesus. These stories and actions, arousing wonder and puzzlement, are directed towards the conversion of those who apprehend them. The dramatic artistry of the life of Jesus Christ and the symbolic power of his words and actions mediate the grace of conversion. So that Jesus is the sacrament of the Father's love for humanity.

By focusing on experiential carriers of meaning, we can connect our explorations with a number of current theological themes. Examples here are von Balthasar's theological aesthetics,[47] Metz's narrative theology,[48] and Dulles' theology of revelation as symbolic mediation.[49] But by drawing attention to other carriers of meaning and functions of meaning, Lonergan's method allows for a much fuller account than these and other approaches.

I conclude this analysis of the role of experiential carriers of meaning and their role in revelation by linking them with the functional specialties of research and communication. Clearly, communication makes ample use of intersubjective, artistic and symbolic carriers of meaning as it seeks to articulate the meaning of the Christian story for each generation and each culture.

With regard to the specialty of research, we can utilise our reflections on experiential carriers of meaning to address an issue raised in Lonergan's brief chapter on that topic in *Method*. What is the starting point of theology?

> Is theology to be based on scripture alone, or on scripture and tradition? Is the tradition just the explicit teaching of the apostles, or is it the ongoing teaching of the church? Is it the ongoing teaching of the church up to Nicea, or to A.D. 1054, or up to the reception of Scholastic doctrines, or up to the council of Trent, or up to the days of Pius IX, or forever?[50]

As Lonergan notes, it does not matter which starting point one chooses. The method itself is designed to sort out the central theological issues through the normativity of its own procedures. Nonetheless, the above discussion of experiential carriers of meaning does, to some extent, provide an answer. One starts where one's attention has been captured artistically and symbolically; where one feels oneself being moved towards a fuller or radically different horizon. Such an option may have a variety of contexts but its basic causes are the prior inner gift of God's love and the outer ordering of events under God's efficacious providence.

4.5 Revelation and historical meaning

While one may give a relative ontological priority to incarnate carriers of meaning and an intentional priority to experiential carriers of meaning, it would be wrong to attempt to restrict the discussion of revelation to these two carriers alone. Incarnate meaning resides in a social, cultural and historical context: "It may be his meaning for just another person, or for a small group or for a whole national, or social, or cultural, or religious tradition."[51] The dramatic impact of a person's life stands in relation to the broad sweep of human history within which he or she acts. Persons both shape history and are overtaken by it. They can contribute to progress, decline and redemption within the unfolding history of a particular people, or within the whole framework of human history. The flow of historical events itself begins to take on meaning. What is moving forward constitutes the larger historical drama of progress, decline and redemption.

The previous chapter outlined Lonergan's account of the goal of the functional specialty, history, in terms of the total understanding of history *in its particularity*, of what is moving forward within the general schema of progress, decline and redemption. It drew attention to the similarity of this to Lonergan's discussion of God's knowledge of the world. The discussion of divine transcendence in *Insight* makes clear that God's knowledge is identical to God's creation and providence.[52] The whole of human history is under divine providence; and it is through history that God acts and speaks. We can see similarities here with the position of Wolfhart Pannenberg, a leading contemporary theologian who has developed a theology of revelation as universal history.[53]

However, there are significant differences between what Pannenberg suggests and what can be developed from Lonergan's transcendental methodology. Pannenberg has not made the transition to what Lonergan calls critical realism. Hence his account is restricted by his empiricist assumptions. The next chapter will provide a more detailed comparison between these two theologians.

4.5.1 History, Doctrine and a Tradition of Rationality

In *Method*, Lonergan emphasises the close connection between the specialties of dialectics and foundations. I would now like to explore the connection between history and doctrine. As has already been observed, Lonergan's whole effort in theological method has been directed towards the integration of history into theology. And nowhere is the struggle to achieve this integration more keenly felt than in the issue of the historical development of doctrine. Lonergan's reflections place this development in the broad contexts of the ongoing discovery of mind, in the refinement of affectivity and in the dialectic context of overcoming error. Indeed, he suggests that "the intelligibility proper to developing doctrines is the intelligibility immanent in historical process."[54]

I would like to suggest that doctrines pertain to historical process in two distinct manners.

In the first place doctrines "express judgments of fact and judgments of value"[55], and these judgments relate to historical realities. If doctrines are judgments of fact and value, to what do these judgments relate? They are "the content of the church's witness to Christ."[56] That is, they are judgments which pertain to the life, death, resurrection, mission, purpose, the meaning and value of Jesus Christ. They are judgments of fact and value about "what was going forward", about the redemptive entry of God into human history in the person of Jesus. Indeed, this is precisely the concern of the early Church councils, of Nicea, Constantinople, Ephesus and Chalcedon. This is one way, then, in which doctrines pertain to historical process.

Secondly, doctrines **as proclaimed** are themselves historical events. As such, they are part of the unfolding process of revelation. They help create a tradition of rationality whose purpose is to offset decline by the promotion of intellectual conversion; more adequately, by the promotion of transcendental method.

This second point perhaps needs a fuller explication. I have already discussed the constitutive and communicative functions of revelation which "yield the three key notions of community, existence, and history."[57] Doctrines, as historical events in the life of the Christian community, fulfil these constitutive and communicative functions of revelation by establishing a community of common meanings and values. The truth of such meanings and values is expressed in the judgments that are doctrines. Community is, then, the bearer of a tradition, of a set of meanings and values, which establish its identity as a community of faith. Lonergan writes:

> Communities endure. As new members replace old, expression be-
> comes traditional. The religion becomes historical in the general
> sense that it exists over time and that it provides basic components
> in the ongoing process of personal development, social organization,
> cultural meaning and value.[58]

Lonergan raises difficult questions about the authenticity or un-authenticity of such traditions. They may be faithful or not to the originating experience of God's entry into history. When the tradition itself is unauthentic, then, "in the measure a subject takes the tradition, as it exists, for his standard, in that measure he can do no more than authentically realize unauthenticity."[59] Authenticity can in that case be attained only by reforming the tradition to which one belongs.

Here, Lonergan's transcendental method must necessarily face the issue of the magisterium, the Church's teaching office, if it is to be part of an authentic Catholic theology. All communities clearly need ways of resolving the conflicts that arise in the central meanings and values constitutive of their common life. A community which has no such resolution process will inevitably cease having common meanings and values. It will cease to be a real community. Though the objectivity of the judgments in such a process are the outcome of the authenticity of those who make them, such authenticity is ever a precarious achievement:

> So human authenticity is never some pure and serene and secure possession. It is ever a withdrawal from unauthenticity, and every successful withdrawal from unauthenticity only brings to light the need for still further withdrawals.[60]

How, then, is the authenticity of those whose task it is to judge on the central meanings and values of the community, those who preserve the tradition, guaranteed? The only solution, I would suggest, is an appeal to the same efficacious providence, which arches over the whole of human history, that I have invoked as grounding the present account of revelation. The guarantee is, then, found, not in particular individuals, but in the provident fidelity of God.

Still, this is not the complete account of the meaning of doctrines as historical events. Doctrines not only have a constitutive and a communicative function, and so establish a tradition. They also have a cognitive function: "It is cognitive inasmuch as it tells whence we come, whither we go, how we get there."[61] This cognitive function grounds what Lonergan calls the normative function of doctrines:

> Men may or may not be converted intellectually, morally, religiously. If they are not, and the lack of conversion is conscious and thorough-going, it heads for loss of faith ... But against such deviations there is the normative function of doctrines ... and so, doctrines based on conversion, are opposed to the aberrations that result from the lack of conversion.[62]

Doctrines, then, contain "the seeds of intellectual conversion."[63] Indeed, Doran has gone so far as to suggest that "perhaps only a Christian theologian could have articulated critical realism."[64]

In other words, one of the effects of revelation is to initiate, sustain and prolong what Alasdair MacIntyre calls a "tradition of rationality."[65] The notion of a "tradition of rationality" was introduced

by MacIntyre in order to overcome what he saw as the abstract a-
historical understanding of rationality which sprang from the
Enlightenment. The Enlightenment proclaimed reason as opposed to
tradition, yet, on MacIntyre's analysis, it did nothing but establish its
own tradition of rationality – the liberalism of the modern era. He
conceives of a tradition of rationality as a socially established and
culturally accepted way of reasoning or arguing. As such it is never an
individual accomplishment but is always culturally and socially
located. Reasoning requires the support of a cultural and social
embodiment if it is to have enduring force, and is not to be a mere blip
in the intellectual history of humankind. Thus, MacIntyre concludes
his argument:

> The conclusion to which the argument so far has led is not only that
> it is out of the debates, conflicts, and enquiry of socially embodied,
> historically contingent traditions that contentions regarding practical
> rationality and justice are advanced, modified, abandoned, or
> replaced, but that there is no other way to engage in the formulation,
> elaboration, rational justification, and criticism of accounts of prac-
> tical rationality and justice except from within some particular
> tradition in conversation, cooperation, and conflict with those who
> inhabit the same tradition. There is no standing ground, no place of
> enquiry, no way to engage in the practice of advancing, accepting,
> and rejecting reasoned argument apart from that which is provided
> by some particular tradition or other.[66]

While such a position is not dissimilar to that proposed by Lindbeck in his cultural linguistic account of religion, it is far more
sophisticated. For MacIntyre allows for interaction, dialogue and even
merger between competing traditions of rationality as they struggle to
address issues of justice and practical rationality. Nor is MacIntyre
bound by the static conceptualist assumptions of Lindbeck, understanding intellect in more dynamic terms of questions, problems and
answers.[67]

On such an understanding, revelation demands the emergence of a
tradition of rationality culminating in critical realism, and more precisely, of transcendental method, for its comprehension. Indeed, I
would argue that, historically, revelation has provoked the emergence
of critical realism and transcendental method. Further, this emergence, I suggest, is part of the redemptive action of God in human

history, as the move to interiority is necessary to reverse the longer cycle of decline which threatens to bring about the end of history. The relationship between revelation and transcendental method will be the specific topic of chapter seven of this thesis. For the moment, three indicators of such a relationship can be found in Lonergan's own work. Firstly, there was the early impact of the lectures on Christology by Bernard Leeming, in which Lonergan first grasped the necessity of the distinction between essence and existence, as it was required by the Chalcedonian distinction between nature and person.[68] Secondly, there is Lonergan's own work on the emergence of a "dogmatic realism" in the decree of Nicea, as outlined in *Way to Nicea* and in the essay, "The Origins of Christian Realism." Thirdly, there is Lonergan's long term interest in the trinitarian psychological analogy, which demands a most meticulous "turn to the subject." In a later chapter, I shall add to these indicators reflections on the term "person", used in Trinitarian and Christological doctrines. Such reflections go beyond what Lonergan has written, even if, as I believe, they are consistent with his transcendental method.

Provisionally, then, we may suggest that revelation initiates, sustains and prolongs a tradition of rationality. How this tradition of rationality operates so as to offset, or even reverse, the longer cycle of decline remains a question to be addressed. Lonergan has repeatedly written, in almost apocalyptic terms, of the consequences of the longer cycle of decline in human history. If "a civilization in decline digs its own grave with a relentless consistency"[69], the process can be described thus:

> In this fashion, the objective social surd will be matched by a disunity of minds all warped but each in its own private way. The most difficult of enterprises will have to be undertaken under the most adverse circumstances and ... one cannot but expect the great crises that end in complete disintegration and decay.[70]

Insight locates the source of the longer cycle of decline in general bias, that inability of common sense to address the social surd with effective long term action. Meanwhile, philosophy, which could be part of the solution, shows itself to be "under the reign of sin", reflecting, not the disinterested desire to know, but the polymorphism of human consciousness.[71] Lonergan elaborates a notion of cosmopolis as the solution to the longer cycle of decline. It makes operative fruitful ideas, prevents the formation of the falsification of history, promotes critical intelligence and long term theoretical learning, and so on. Still, the only really effective counter to the supposed omni-competence of common sense in the realm of practical activity is the emergence of the third stage of meaning, which Lonergan speaks of in *Method*. This stage of meaning is grounded in interiority; and is the fruit of transcendental method. Inasmuch as revelation initiates, sus-tains and prolongs a tradition of rationality, culminating in a transcendental method, it promotes the reversal of the longer cycle of decline which presently grips human history.

4.6 Revelation and linguistic meaning

Thus far I have considered incarnate, experiential and historical carriers of meanings. It is now time to turn attention to linguistic carriers of meaning. In these, meaning attains its greatest liberation, since the conventional signs of language can be multiplied almost in-definitely. For some, linguistic carriers of meaning have become the only "true" carrier of meaning. The consequence is that revelation has been understood simply in propositional terms, as, for example, in Dulles' first model of revelation. Indeed, a recent article in *New Blackfriars* has argued that revelation must be propositional.[72] The point of the argument breaks down, though, when one realises that one could replace the word "propositional" with the term "meaningful." The hidden assumption is that the only way in which meaning can be carried is through propositions. Remove this assump-tion and one is left with the more general statement that revelation is meaningful, which is hardly a theological breakthrough.

On the other hand, Lonergan would be the last person to reject the importance of linguistic meaning in the process of revelation. In his discussion of dogmatic development in *Way to Nicea*, he makes repeated comments about attending to the word of God, as expressed in Scripture and Church dogma, as true:

> ... if one separates the word from the truth, if one rejects proposi-tional truth in favour of some other kind of truth, then one is not attending to the word of God as true ... For at the root of these heresies lay the fact that their proponents paid insufficient attention to this particular aspect of God's word.[73]

Here, reference could be made to Lonergan's scathing review of Leslie Dewart's book, *The Future of Belief*, where Lonergan repeatedly criticises Dewart for his separation of "the word from truth", and the adoption of "some other kind of truth."[74]

Nevertheless, as can be seen from the discussion in this chapter, Lonergan does allow for the possibility of many other carriers of meaning, viz., intersubjective, artistic, symbolic, historical and incarnate meanings. While linguistic meanings have their proper place, ontological priority lies with incarnate meaning and intentional priority with artistic and symbolic meaning. Linguistic meaning lies between these two. On the one side, its veracity is a function of the authenticity of the incarnate meaning of the subject who authors it. On the other side, linguistic meaning may contain artistic and symbolic aspects. As Lonergan notes, "With Giambattista Vico, we hold for the priority of poetry."[75]

4.6.1 Revelation and Scripture

The most conspicuous example of linguistic meaning in the Christian tradition is to be found in the Scriptures. Linguistic meaning is a product of human speakers and authors. Inasmuch as these are touched by God's grace, and are progressed on the road to authenticity, inasmuch as the meanings they incarnate are God's meanings, to that extent what they write will be a further entry of God's meaning into human history. This is the basic notion of the inspiration of the Scriptures: such writings can truly be said to have both human and divine origin.[76] This position is clearly several steps removed from any naive notion of divine dictation which is found is some proponents of the propositional understanding of revelation. Again, as with incarnate and historical carriers of revelation, the ultimate ground for the inspiration of Scripture is to be found in a special providence flowing from divine transcendence.

An appeal to providence can also be made to address such questions as the much debated notion of the *sensus plenior*, the *excessus* of meaning found in scriptural texts.[77] While the primary meaning of texts is found in its relation to the intention of its author, other meanings can arise within a tradition of interpretation which go beyond those originally intended by the author.[78] These new meanings can become embedded within the tradition which is created by the originating revelatory events, in such a way that it would be difficult to remove them, despite their differing from the original intention of the author. What is at issue, then, is the authenticity of that tradition itself. Inasmuch as the tradition is itself authentic, the meanings it draws from its foundational documents will be authentic within the life of the community, even if distinct from the original inspired meaning intended by the authors of those documents. Indeed, this is precisely how the New Testament authors and early Church Fathers appropriated the Jewish Scriptures as sacred texts, finding in them constant prefigurings of the mystery of Christ.

4.6.2 Revelation and Systematic Theology

By linking revelation and the linguistic meanings found in the Scriptures, one can establish a connection between revelation and the functional specialty of interpretation. Through interpretation, the linguistic meanings of Scripture enter into, and are effective in, human history. Still, this is not the complete picture. For just as incarnate meaning can be related to dialectics and foundations, and historical meaning can be related to the specialties of history and doctrine, so in exploring linguistic meanings we need to attend not only to the specialty of interpretation, but also to the specialty of systematics.

Generally speaking, theologians might be slow to see any direct role for systematic theology in the ongoing process of revelation. Still, the possibility of such a connection should not be too quickly dismissed. Systematic theology marks a movement, away from commonsense and literary language, into the world of technical language with its systematic control of the meaning of terms. Thus Paul, Augustine and Aquinas all spoke of grace, but the relationship between the meaning of the term for Paul and Augustine and the meaning of the term for Aquinas, is like the relationship between commonsense apprehensions of heavy and light, and the scientifically controlled term, weight; or the relationship between commonsense apprehension of colour and scientifically controlled notion of wavelengths of light.

Systematic exigence demands, then, a movement out of the world of commonsense into a world where inquiry is pursued for its own sake, where logic and methods are formulated, where a tradition of learning is established, different branches distinguished, and specialties multiplied.[79]

Such a process, far from being inimical to the process of revelation, can be related to it in two ways. First, the achievements of systematic theology enter into the tradition in a vital way, and lead to the development of a post-systematic mode of expression. As Lonergan has observed, this post-systematic mode of expression can become the language of later doctrinal development, giving it a clarity and precision it would not otherwise enjoy. For example, the doctrinal decrees of the First Vatican Council are hardly intelligible outside the Thomistic framework which they presuppose.[80] Systematic theology can lead to doctrinal development by clarifying issues and making precise distinctions. Thus, it can assist the communication of divine meaning into the human situation.

Secondly, systematic theology relates to revelation – it emerges out of, and further promotes, a tradition of rationality which develops in response to revelation. Doran notes this role of systematic theology when he concludes that,

> ... systematic theology is a promotion of the being, and good systematic theology a promotion of the well-being, of meaning, and indeed of that meaning that is the outer word of God in history.[81]

Above I have argued that revelation demands the emergence of a critical realism, even a transcendental method, in order to turn around the longer cycle of decline caused by general bias. This demand is effected by the systematic exigence which seeks to understand revelation in a systematic manner. While I hope to illustrate this more fully in a later chapter, I would here draw attention to Augustine's efforts to understand the Trinity by means of a psychological analogy. These efforts represent a "turn to the subject" over a thousand years before Descartes and Kant; and the continuation of these efforts in the works of Aquinas and Lonergan have been largely instrumental in Lonergan's development of his transcendental method.

4.7 Concluding remarks on Lonergan's contribution

I hope that the above account is sufficient indication of the wealth of material from which a rich theology of revelation can be constructed. One aspect of the above account is the comprehensive sweep of its vision. It allows space for several other models present in the literature.

The emphasis on revelation as involving personal transformation through incarnate meaning subsumes Dulles' fifth model, of revelation as new consciousness. At the same time, it goes beyond the limits of the new consciousness model, by recognising the possibilities of a truly supernatural entry of the divine into human history, in the form of a searching Christology. Jesus is not only the revealer, the trans-formed subject who sees the world in a new way; he is also the revealed, an object of faith in his own right.

The emphasis on incarnate meaning also allows for Dulles' third model, of revelation as inner experience, especially given the place of religious experience in Lonergan's account of religion. However, his fuller account of the constitutive role of tradition in a historical com-munity can overcome the inherent individualism of the inner experience model. Also, Lonergan places far more emphasis on what the inner experience model considers secondary, that is, the written, often doctrinal expression of such experiences. Lonergan's emphasis on intellectual conversion does not allow him to dismiss these as quickly as proponents of the inner experience model usually do.

The recognition of historical carriers of meaning also allows for Dulles' second model, of revelation as history. Still, it overcomes the limits of the salvation history model with an emphasis on a universally efficacious providence, so that all history can be a carrier of divine meaning. This does not mean that the above account of history as a carrier of divine meaning is identical to Pannenberg's theology of revelation as universal history. Pannenberg's theology is marred by his account of human knowing. I shall deal with this more fully in the next chapter.

The recognition of literary carriers of meaning also allows for the first of Dulles' models, that of propositional revelation. Thus, the Scriptures and Church doctrines can be seen as true carriers of divine meaning into the human situation. Nonetheless, the above account is not bound by the hermeneutical naivety and conceptualism of the model, nor does it restrict revelation to such propositional forms. Hermeneutically, Lonergan demands a distinction between language and meaning, since the act of insight is preconceptual. Such a distinc-tion disallows any position which sees meaning as immediate in a text. A text is simply black marks on white paper until someone under-stands it. Interpretation is a necessary process in seeking the meaning of any text. Such a process of interpretation may require the reconstruction of the commonsense world of its author, particularly in the case of the Scriptures, if we are not the fall into fundamentalism.

The grounding of the above account in divine transcendence and a universally efficacious providence also allows for the fourth of Dulles' models, that of revelation as dialectic presence. The dialectic model stresses the otherness of God, in divine transcendence and incomprehensibility. Now, for Lonergan, the otherness of God does not place divinity beyond intelligibility; for God is conceived of as an act of infinite understanding.[82] There is an excess of intelligibility, more than can be comprehended by human reason, in the divine. By drawing attention to this excess of intelligibility, as opposed to the lack of it, the above account can avoid the incipient fideism of the dialectic model, particularly as found in the work of Karl Barth.

Finally, Lonergan's recognition of symbolic and artistic carriers of meaning allows for Dulles' own account of revelation as symbolic mediation. Yet, by its more precise analysis of the role of symbols and artistic expression, the above account is able to locate the symbolic aspects of revelation within a framework much larger than that given by Dulles.

I should remark that, whereas the various models given by Dulles simply appear as a coincidental manifold of competing models, the above account is able to integrate them coherently within a common framework. For Lonergan, revelation is the entry of divine meaning into the human situation. By a consideration of the various carriers of meanings we are able to both distinguish and relate the various models suggested by Dulles, in a way which integrates them into a common perspective. We are also able to locate the ontological priority and the intentional priority of each, in terms of which is first in itself, and which is first for us.

Revelation can be conceived of, then, as a hermeneutical process which has two phases: a healing, handing-on phase, and a creative, uncovering phase. The healing, handing-on phase has ontological priority. It begins with the transformation of incarnate meaning under the power of God's grace. This phase has tended to dominate the understanding of revelation within the Catholic tradition. What has most recently been discovered by theology is the creative, uncovering phase, arising from new historical studies, which Lonergan and others have sought to integrate into theology. Both phases are necessary, for, as Lonergan argues,

... just as the creative process, when unaccompanied by healing, is distorted and corrupted by bias, so too the healing process, when unaccompanied by creating, is a soul without a body.[83]

4.7.1 Differentiating features

At this stage one can ask, are there any specific features which differentiate the above conception of revelation from others in a significant way? In order to address this question, we turn own attention once more to Lonergan's account of human interiority, specifically his analysis of human judgment.[84] The constitutive role of judgment in human knowing enables him to escape from the incoherent realism which is a halfway house between idealism and empiricism, and to move into the critical realism which is the basis of his whole theological project.

If this is the case, we should expect two elements in the above account of revelation to stand out against other competing accounts.

The first of these elements has do to with the relationship between revelation and history. As Lonergan's exposition of the functional specialties makes clear, because history corresponds to the level of judgment, any theology of revelation based on *Method* should include revelation's relationship to history. The above account is not alone in seeing a relationship between history and revelation; for the work of Pannenberg also includes a reference to revelation as universal history. However, I will attempt to show in the next chapter that there are specific differences between what Lonergan means by history and what Pannenberg means by history.

The second of these elements has to do with the relationship between revelation, doctrine and culture. Again, *Method* identifies a correspondence between the level of judgment, the functional specialty of doctrines, and culture. "Doctrines express judgments of fact or value."[85] Similarly, in the scale of values, the level of culture correlates with the critical function of rational consciousness. I have already argued that *Method* contains an implicit understanding of revelation as initiating, sustaining and prolonging a tradition of rationality. Now, Lonergan is not alone in seeing a connection between revelation and culture. As I indicated in chapter one, George Lindbeck also makes such a connection. For Lindbeck, religions are primarily cultural linguistic systems which shape our experience, rather than arise out of that experience. Nonetheless, I will attempt to show in the next chapter that there are very significant differences between the approaches of these two authors to religious phenomenon.

4.8 Conclusion

To summarise: this chapter does not claim that Lonergan has developed an explicit theology of revelation. As I showed in the first chapter on this thesis, the topic of revelation hardly rates a mention, not only in Lonergan's writings, but even in the secondary literature dealing with him.

Nor do we claim that this is the theology of revelation Lonergan would have developed; for that is to enter a field of hypothetical speculation of dubious value.

Nonetheless, we do claim that any attempt to specify theological method logically correlates with an understanding of the nature of the theological object of revelation. Lonergan has clearly specified a theological method in his work, *Method in Theology*. This chapter has attempted to spell out this correlation by using the extensive intellectual framework Lonergan has given us. And so we have outlined an account of revelation congruent with his method. More specifically, it began with the concept of revelation as the entry of divine meaning into the human situation. It has connected this entry of meaning with the concept of carriers of meaning. These carriers were then correlated with the eight functional specialties identified in *Method*. This correlation allowed us to understand the process of revelation as a hermeneutical process of handing on and uncovering divine meaning made present in human history, primarily through its entry via incarnate meaning.

In its limited scope, this chapter has attempted to identify "what is going forward" in the conception of revelation in Lonergan's lifelong reflection on theological method. While such an account is grounded in Lonergan's writings, it need not claim to be "Lonergan's account of revelation", since, "in most cases, contemporaries do not know what is going forward." It is rather the task of the functional specialty of history which "involves a number of interlocking discoveries that bring to light the significant issues and operative factors" which may be unknown to the author himself.[86]

Hence, by attending to such developments in Lonergan's thought, this chapter has attempted to explicate the scope and richness of the notion of revelation operative in his writings. This has meant we were able to construct, in a reasonably rounded manner, Lonergan's theology of revelation, and to understand *Method* itself as congruent with such a sense of revelation. In so doing, I have also sought to show how this project subsumes various models of revelation proposed by Avery Dulles and others. In the next chapter, I shall take this process further, replacing the cursory comments of Chapter One with a more detailed comparison of the concept of revelation developed above with three key theologians, Karl Rahner, Wolfhart Pannenberg and George Lindbeck.

---

1. Lonergan, *Insight*, 661. This position stands in contrast with that of process philosophy which sees God as really related to, and hence affected by, creation.

2. Lonergan, *Insight*, 662.

3. Lonergan, *Insight*, 696. Following a classical metaphysics, evil is, for Lonergan, actually a non-occurrence, rather than an "occurrence". It is a failure to do what is intelligent, reasonable and responsible.

4. Lonergan, *Method*, 243.

5. Lonergan, *Way to Nicea*, 1, n.1.

6. Cf. B. Lonergan, *Philosophy of God, and Theology* (Philadelphia: The Westminster Press, 1973) 41: "Proof is never the fundamental thing. Proof always presupposes premises, and it presupposes premises accurately formulated within a horizon. You can never prove a horizon".

7. Lonergan, "Theology in its New Context", *Second Collection*, 62.

8. Lonergan, "New Context", 61.

9. Lonergan, "The Response of the Jesuit", 175.

10. Lonergan, *Method*, 73.

11. Lonergan, *Method*, 298.

12. Lonergan, *Method*, 116.

13. Lonergan, *Method*, 242.

14. Lonergan, *Method*, 284.

15. Lonergan, *Method*, 243.

16. Lonergan, *Method*, 298-9.

17. Note that the first index entry in *Method* for the term "tradition" occurs in relation to this discussion.

18. This is not to say that the community will not share other meanings and values derived from other sources. All such communities experience the problem of distinguishing their foundational meanings and values from those of other sources. For example, this is the main problem in the issue of circumcision in the early Christian communities.

19. Lonergan, *Method*, 73.

20. Lonergan, *Method*, 288.

21. "Religious effort towards authenticity through prayer and penance and religious love of all men shown in good deeds becomes an apostolate", *Method*, 119.

22. Lonergan, *Method*, 292.

23. Lonergan, "The Future of Christianity", 155.

24. Lonergan, "Mission and the Spirit", 32.

25. Lonergan, *Method*, 51.

26. This is distinct from the Enlightenment position that "man is the measure of all things". As MacIntyre has argued forcefully, the Enlighten-ment gradually abandoned any teleological account of human existence. It could no longer distinguish between "man as he is" and "man as he should be" (i.e. authentic), cf. *After Virtue* 2nd Ed. (Notre Dame: University of Notre Dame Press, 1984), 62ff. On the basis of Doran's work in *Theology and the Dialectics of History*, one could argue that the fundamental moral teleology in Lonergan's work is provided by the scale of values.

27. Lonergan, *Method*, 116.

28. This would undoubtedly have implications for the conscious life of such a person. In traditional theology, this would be discussed under the heading of the beatific vision. Here, we avoid the intellectualist assumptions of the tradition by focusing on question of value.

29. This statement presupposes an ontology of personhood which I will further develop in a Chapter 7.

30. Note that these three activities correlate with the second, third and fourth levels of intentional consciousness – the teacher stresses understanding, the prophet, truth, and the judge, moral evaluation.

31. It is interesting to note that Thomas Hughson is critical of Dulles' account of "Christ the Summit of Revelation" in *Models of Revelation*, 155ff, precisely because Dulles leaves no room for such self-understanding: "But apparently all of this is revelatory without the help of Christ's human mind interpreting himself in acts that Aquinas would have identified as judgments", cf. T. Hughson, "Dulles and Aquinas on Revelation", *The Thomist*, 52/3 (1988), 459.

32. Loneran, *Insight*, 734.

33. Rahner's programme has been taken up by D. Coffey, *Grace: The Gift of the Holy Spirit* (Sydney: Catholic Institute of Sydney, 1979), "The Incarnation of the Holy Spirit in Christ", *Theological Studies*, 45/3 (1983), 466-480, "A Proper Mission for the Holy Spirit", *Theological Studies*, 47/2 (1985), 227-250.

34. Cf. Lonergan, *De Verbo Incarnato*, 254-268.

35. Cf. K. Rahner, *Foundations to Christian Faith*, 295. See also J. McDermott, who argues that "given the religious context of Lonergan's conversions, the norm [of the good man] can be none other than the humanity of Christ, which is continued in His Body. No longer can one naively point,

like Aristotle, to the good man as the norm of virtue without identifying him", "Tensions", 129.

36. Lonergan's favourite example, taken from Aristotle, is the relationship between the phases of the moon and its sphericity. The phases are the *causa cognesendi* of the sphericity, while the sphericity is the *causa essendi* of the phases. Cf. "Christology Today", 79.

37. Cf. most notably, in Doran's essay, "Dramatic Artistry in the Third Stage of Meaning", *Lonergan Workshop*, Vol.2, F. Lawrence (ed) (Chico: Scholars Press, 1981), 147-200.

38. Doran states: "My position is simply this: the concern of existential intentionality – value, the good, real self-transcendence, being an originating value, a principle of benevolence and beneficence – links up with the psychic pattern of the dramatic subject. The success of the dramatic subject is ascertained in terms of his or her fulfilment of the purpose, direction, concern of the dramatic pattern - to make a work of art out of one's living. It is the authentic existential subject who is concomitantly a dramatic artist, and it is the unauthentic existential subject who is an *artiste manqué*, a failed artist ... Existential authenticity and dramatic art are respectively the intentional and psychic obverse and reverse of the same precious coin." *Theology*, 154.

39. Lonergan, *Method*, 243.

40. Doran argues: "Love is prior to all else, and prior to the word of tradition and belief ... there is a *vision* that proceeds from love and that causes the scales to drop from one's eyes, revealing values in their splendour and beauty ... The word of belief ... is itself emergent from the primordial *aesthetic* [emphasis added] enrapturing of the theological subject by the object of the unrestricted love to which one is awakened by that object itself", *Theology*, 164-5.

41. Lonergan, *Method*, 64.

42. Lonergan, *Method*, 66-67.

43. Lonergan, *Method*, 66.

44. Lonergan, *Method*, 245.

45. This, indeed, is the conclusion of Doran in his discussion of elemental symbols, found in dreams: "A symbol is sacramental, in that it gives what it symbolizes. It not only discloses but also transforms. A dream about healing is a healing dream. A dream about searching sets one searching. A dream about new life gives one new life. Psychic energy is itself transformed in the elemental symbols of our dreams. The dream symbolizes that transformation, which is in the direction of the meaning intended in the symbol itself", *Theology*, 288.

46. Cf. Lonergan, *Method*, 106.

47. See, for example, Hans Urs v. Balthasar, *The Glory of the Lord: A Theological Aesthetics*, Vol.1-7, (Edinburgh: T. & T. Clarke, 1982, 84, 86, 91, 91, and 89).

48. See, for example, J. B. Metz, *Faith in History and Society* (London: Burns & Oates, 1980), 163.

49. Saying that Lonergan's *Method* allows for these different concerns, is not to say that he fully exploits them. For example, many critics have expressed concern about Lonergan's handling of the symbolic, e.g. Braxton, "Bernard Lonergan's Hermeneutic of the Symbol", and Dulles, in his review of *Method* in *Theological Studies*, 33/3 (1972), 553-5. Doran concedes that, while Lonergan makes room for the symbolic, he "leaves others to explore [it] in explanatory fashion", *Psychic Conversion and Theological Foundations* (Lanham: University of America Press, 1980), 108. Lonergan also makes room for a full range of carriers of meaning, and so transcends the inherent limitations of a purely symbolic approach.

50. Lonergan, *Method*, 150.

51. Lonergan, *Method*, 73.

52. Cf. Loneran, *Insight*, 661ff, esp. the third and fourth corollary on 662, and the "nineteenth place" on 663.

53. Crowe has drawn attention to the parallels between Pannenberg's position on universal history and the notion of universal providence, cf. *Theology of the Christian Word*, 104-123. Note that Crowe does not commit himself to every detail of Pannenberg's project. He would not sit comfortably with empiricist elements in Pannenberg's position. Crowe traces a trajectory from the historical typologies of the early Church Fathers; through Aquinas' account of divine transcendence and efficacious providence; through the spirituality of de Caussade and his notion of abandonment to divine providence by which God speaks to us in every moment, every event; to conclude with Pannenberg's view of revelation as universal history. Crowe rounds off his discussion with the following comment: "In this view, then, the very realities of creation, seen as a whole and therefore necessarily incorporating the totality of history, are God's 'word' to us in some basic and primary sense. Then, all prophecy, all our traditions in doctrine, all our scriptures, are successive attempts, feeble and stammering but ever so precious, to understand, conceive, formulate, and express the inexhaustible meaning of this primary word", *Theology of the Christian Word*, 120.

54. Lonergan, *Method*, 319.

55. Lonergan, *Method*, 132.

56. Lonergan, *Method*, 311.

57. Lonergan, *Method*, 79.

58. Lonergan, *Method*, 118.

59. Lonergan, *Method*, 80.

60. Lonergan, *Method*, 110.

61. Lonergan, *Method*, 298.

62. Lonergan, *Method*, 298-9.

63. Lonergan, *Method*, 243.

64. Doran, *Theology*, 165.

65. While I have used terminology from the work of Alasdair MacIntyre, I do not think the notion is alien to Lonergan's work. Indeed, the concept of a tradition of rationality arises when one attends to the constitutive, communicative, cognitive and normative functions of meaning.

66. A. MacIntyre, *Whose Justice? Which Rationality?* (Notre Dame: University of Notre Dame Press, 1988), 350.

67. There are many similarities, but also key dissimilarities, between Lonergan and MacIntyre, both of whom claim allegiance to the Thomistic tradition. An exploration of this would take me beyond the bonds of this thesis. For a dialectic comparison of the two thinkers, see the article by M. Maxwell, "A Dialectical Encounter Between MacIntyre and Lonergan on the Thomistic Understanding of Rationality", *International Philosophical Quarterly*, XXXIII/4 (1993), 385-400.

68. Cf. B. Lonergan, *Caring About Meaning*, Lambert, P. et al. (eds), (Montreal: Thomas More Institute, 1982), 258. Liddy argues that this was the beginning of Lonergan's "intellectual conversion", *Transforming Light*, 114-119.

69. Lonergan, *Method*, 55.

70. Lonergan, *Insight*, 233. On the whole issue of the longer cycle of decline and its reversal, see *Insight*, 226-244.

71. Cf. Lonergan, *Insight*, 692: "The hopeless tangle of the social surd, of the impotence of common sense, of the endlessly multiplied philosophies is not merely a *cul-de-sac* for human progress; it is also a reign of sin".

72. J. Lamont, "The Nature of Revelation", *New Blackfriars*, 72/851 (1991), 335-345

73. Lonergan, *Way to Nicea*, 8.

74. Cf. Lonergan, "The Dehellenization of Dogma", 11ff.

75. Lonergan, *Method*, 73. Given what I have argued above, one would probably say that the type of priority referred to is in the intentional order.

76. Cf. *Dei Verbum*, Chap.3, no.11, in A. Flannery, *Vatican Council II: The Conciliar and Post Conciliar Document* (Northport: Costello, 1975), 756-7.

77. On the *sensus plenior*, see the article by R. Brown and Schneiders on "Hermeneutics" in *The New Jerome Biblical Commentary*, R. Brown et al. (eds), (Englewood, NJ: Prentice Hall, 1990), no.49-51. The article notes that the debate has shifted to a more general hermeneutical perspective, away from a particular focus on Scripture.

78. Though some modern hermeneutic theorists reject its importance, Ben Meyer has been a consistent advocate of maintaining the authorial intention as central to the meaning of texts, cf. his latest work, *Reality and Illusion in New Testament Scholarship* (Collegeville: Glazier, 1994), 94ff.

79. Lonergan, *Method*, 72.

80. T. Tekippe, "A response to Donald Keefe on Lonergan", *The Thomist*, 52/1 (1988), 88-95, makes this point in his response to the attack by Donald Keefe on Lonergan's work, "A Methodological Critique of Lonergan's Theological Method", *The Thomist*, 50/1 (1986), 28-65. Tekippe notes that Keefe fails "to understand how much that Council is based upon Thomas's thought, often following him almost distinction for distinction", 93.

81. Doran, *Theology*, 629.

82. Cf. Lonergan, *Insight*, 646ff.

83. Lonergan, "Healing and Creating in History", 107.

84. Even as strong a critic as J.P. Mackey concedes that Lonergan's position on judgment "is of lasting value", cf. "Divine Revelation and Lonergan's Transcendental Method in Theology", *Irish Theological Quarterly*, XL/1 (1973), 8.

85. Lonergan, *Method*, 132. Note that Dulles expresses concern about this correlation of doctrines with judgment in *Method*. Yet historically I would contend that it remains the best way to understand what the Church does when it proclaims a particular doctrine. It offers a judgment on interpretations present within the community. From the opposite direction, Thomas Hughson is critical, from a Thomistic perspective, of Dulles' own model of symbolic mediation because of its inadequate attention to the role of judgment, cf. Hughson, T., "Dulles and Aquinas on Revelation", esp. 458.

86. Lonergan, *Method*, 179.

CHAPTER FIVE: CLARIFICATION BY CONTRAST

In order to explicate further Lonergan's "account of revelation", I shall compare it with the work of three leading theologians. The three theologians chosen are Karl Rahner, Wolfhart Pannenberg and George Lindbeck. Each has written seriously in the area of revelation; each has been critical of various aspects of Lonergan's work; and, in the cases of Pannenberg and Lindbeck, their theologies highlight the areas of history and culture, respectively, which are also distinguishing features of Lonergan's account. The dialectical interplay between his account and theirs will add valuable clarification at the present stage of the analysis.

5.1 Rahner and Lonergan: alternative transcendental approaches[1]

Rahner and Lonergan are frequently mentioned in the same breath, largely because of their common origins in the movement which has been labelled "transcendental Thomism." Though both were influenced to some extent by the "founder" of the movement, Joseph Maréchal, each is a significantly independent thinker within that movement.[2] Both have had a critical impact upon modern Catholic theology, though in quite different ways. Rahner has generated an enormous body of work, touching upon just about every aspect of Catholic theology.[3] His writings have become the staple works of a generation of Catholic theologians, and many aspects of his work have become theological commonplaces: examples are his axiom on the immanent and economic Trinity, and his position on anonymous Christians. Lonergan, on the other hand, has produced relatively few works for general publication, but these few works have generated a large body of followers who have sought to apply Lonergan's approach to various aspects of Catholic theology. Whereas Rahner has set the Catholic theological agenda for the second half of the twentieth century, Lonergan has occasioned a movement, the fruits of which may not be apparent until the next century.

Still, both thinkers are influenced by their respective appropriations of the Thomist tradition; and out of this common heritage one can find both the common themes and the significant differences I now explore.

Both Rahner and Lonergan place their **transcendental anthropology** at the centre of their theological work. In both cases, this transcendental anthropology draws heavily on Thomist sources for its explication. Rahner's seminal study, *Spirit in the World,*[4] brings Aquinas into dialogue with Kant and Heidegger. In such a frame of reference, he works out an epistemology basic to his entire theological project. For Lonergan, this same grounding in Thomist sources occurred with his years of "reaching up to the mind of Aquinas", particularly in his *Verbum* articles. Here he utilised his own developing ideas on cognition to reappropriate Thomas' teaching on the procession of the Word. The fruits of this process were then brought into dialogue with modern philosophy and science in *Insight*.

For both theologians, the key to understanding the human subject is the notion of **self-transcendence**. Through knowing and loving, the human subject transcends itself to attain a fuller realisation of authentic existence. For both authors the clue to unpacking this dynamic process of self-transcendence is the structure of human questioning.

But there are differences. While Rahner speaks in general terms of knowing and loving, of intellect and will, Lonergan develops a much more precise account of human interiority. In the activity of knowing, Lonergan distinguishes three levels: empirical, intellectual and rational modes on intentional consciousness. Rahner's account of interiority is much less differentiated than that of Lonergan. While Lonergan does not contradict anything in Rahner's account, he does gives a far more nuanced treatment of intentional consciousness.[5]

The fruit of this more nuanced account of interiority is documented in the previous chapter in its treatment of the "carriers of meaning", applied to the theology of revelation. This is not to deny that Rahner's own theology of revelation, briefly presented in Chapter One of this thesis, contains most, if not all, of such elements. There are, indeed, certain obvious parallels. For Rahner understands the Incarnation as the "full and unsurpassable event of the historical objectification of God's self-communication to the world."[6] The Incarnation is the definitive entry of God into human history. This entry can be linked with "the horizon of a divinizing and divinized *a priori* subjectivity" which allows for God's entry into human history.[7] Similarly, Rahner understands revelation in terms of universal history: "the history of salvation and revelation is coexistent with the history of the world."[8] As with Pannenberg, universal history is the vehicle for revelation. Rahner also finds a place for doctrines: "we must not overlook the fact that this revelation, which closes and discloses the infinite, has the human word [i.e. dogma] as a constitutive element of its essence."[9] Further, Rahner has written on the theology of symbol and its role in the tasks of salvation and revelation in a way which parallels Lonergan's position.[10]

However, what Rahner does not do is to relate these various aspects of revelation in any systematic fashion. Indeed he is not able to do so, because his account of human interiority is too undifferentiated to be able to articulate the full scope of God's revealing action with the degree of precision that Lonergan's *Method* makes possible. Thus, while there are many parallels between the two approaches to revelation, I would argue that the account of revelation implicit in Lonergan's *Method* is more richly explanatory compared to Rahner's treatment of the same subjects.

One foundational problem in Rahner's approach is the incompleteness of the "turn to the subject." While Lonergan draws all his terms and relations from interiority, Rahner's approach remains basically metaphysical. This is not to say that Lonergan eschews metaphysics. Indeed his Latin works, in particular, operate out of a transformed Scholastic metaphysics. Nonetheless, Lonergan's metaphysics is grounded in his cognitional theory, not vice versa. Inasmuch as Rahner maintains a priority of metaphysics over cognitional theory, his metaphysics is not critically grounded with the radicality and precision characteristic of Lonergan.

I would like to illustrate the incomplete nature of Rahner's turn to the subject by reference to his treatment of the Trinitarian psychological analogy.

In his ground breaking work, *The Trinity*, Rahner concludes his study with a brief comparison of his approach to the classical "psychological doctrine of the Trinity."[11] Rahner embraces the broad lines of such an approach. He accepts that God is spirit and that there are precisely two spiritual activities, knowledge and love. Further, these activities can be seen as related to the two procession, of Word and Spirit, in God:

> We are allowed, then, to combine these two data and to connect, in a special and specific way, the intra-divine procession of the Logos from the Father with God's knowledge, and the procession of the Spirit from the Father through the Son with God's love.[12]

Despite this concession, Rahner shows no interest in a precise analysis of the psychological image, being content to treat the analogy in a rather general way. In fact, he is critical of any attempt to go beyond a rather general reference, for any such attempt must be "hypothetical":

> ... it postulates *from* the doctrine of the Trinity a model of human knowledge and love, which either remains questionable, or about which it is not clear that it can be more than a *model* of human knowledge as *finite*. And this model it applies again to God ... it becomes clear too that such a psychological theory of the Trinity has the character of what the other sciences call an "hypothesis."[13]

What is significant here is that Rahner backs away from the possibility of an account of human interiority which is anything more than a model or hypothesis. Hence, his turn to the subject is intrinsically incomplete. Certainly, at this point, he is in stark contrast with the intricate and detailed efforts of Lonergan to refine the Trinitarian psychological analogy, on the basis of human interiority.[14]

Moreover, Rahner has not explored the cultural significance of the psychological analogy. We may agree when he argues that the model of human knowledge and love is drawn from, or at least driven by, the doctrine of the Trinity. However, all this implies is that the doctrine of the Trinity has culturally elicited a turn to the subject in order that the doctrine be rendered analogously intelligible. As I have already argued in the previous chapter, part of the function of revelation is to establish a tradition of rationality with its own distinct cultural impact. Without a complete turn to the subject, as evidenced in the psychological analogy, Lonergan argues that it is impossible to heal the division between the world of theory and the world of common sense. This division generates the long cycle of decline and the possibility of the end of history.[15] Revelation seeks to redeem us from this decline.

A further point of comparison between these two theologians can be found in the notion of **divine self-communication**. Both Rahner and Lonergan speak of revelation as a divine self-communication, the self-giving of God to human history. For both, the Incarnation, in particular, is a real entry of the divine into that history. Thus, for both, revelation has a Trinitarian structure, given in Word and Spirit. The doctrine of the Trinity is not simply the content of revelation but a reflection on the very process of revelation itself.

Indeed, Rahner posits a very strong, even necessary, connection between the doctrine of the Trinity and God's self-communication in revelation:

> ... the differentiation of the self-communication of God in history (of truth) and spirit (of love) must belong to God "in himself", or otherwise this difference, which undoubtedly exists, would do away with God's *self*-communication.[16]

Here Rahner is closely following the Trinitarian approach of Karl Barth: God reveals the divine self through the Word, which is not other than God, and bestows that divine self through the Spirit, the Gift which is not other than God. Thus God's Word is not reduced to a merely human word – God is Revealer, the Revelation and the Revealedness.[17]

Lonergan follows basically the same structure. He extends *Method*'s distinction of the inner and an outer divine word,[18] in a more comprehensive statement in "Mission and the Spirit", where he argues:

> ... besides the visible mission of the Son there is the invisible mission of the Spirit. Besides *fides ex auditu*, there is *fides ex infusione*. The former mounts up the successive levels of experience, understanding, judging, deliberating. The latter descends from the gift of God's love through religious conversion to moral, and through religious and moral to intellectual conversion ... Without the visible mission of the Word, the gift of the Spirit is a being-in-love without a proper object; it remains simply an orientation to mystery that awaits its interpretation. Without the [in]visible mission of the Spirit, the Word enters into his own, but his own receive him not.[19]

Lonergan thus clearly ties the Trinitarian mission of Word and Spirit to the structure of revelation. He also identifies a healing movement "from above", whereby incarnate divine meaning enters human history, and a creative movement "from below", whereby we encounter that meaning in symbol, story and sacrament, as part of the structure of revelation.

Where Lonergan differs from Rahner is his elaboration of the category of meaning in order to clarify the nature of divine self-communication. For Lonergan, revelation is primarily the communication of divine meaning – more precisely, of meaning and value – into the human context. His more methodical account of the carriers of meaning allows, in general, for the development of a more systematic theology of revelation.

While the transcendental anthropology and the notion of divine self-communication are common elements between these two theologians, one area of difference lies in their respective treatments of the relationship between the divine and the creature. A basic component in Rahner's understanding of the human in relation to the divine is the category of **quasi-formal causality**. This category was initially introduced by Rahner to give a metaphysical account of the beatific vision, but was later extended to give accounts of the Incarnation and grace.[20] Lonergan, on the other hand, has not seen the need for such a metaphysical account, and has used the category of **contingent predication** to explain these diverse relationships. What is the significance of this difference?

Rahner's purpose is to overcome the limitations of classical accounts of divine communication given exclusively in terms of efficient causality. For Rahner, when God acts through efficient causality God creates that which is other than God. However, in grace and Incarnation, God is involved in a genuine *self*-communication to the creature. Efficient causality is insufficient to explain this. Rahner thus employs an analogy drawn from formal causality. Admittedly, in its Aristotelian meaning, to say that God is the formal cause of the creature would entail the destruction of the creaturely form, to say nothing of diminishing the ontological reality of God. To avoid any such implication, Rahner adopts the prefix "quasi", as a pointer to his analogical use of the term. It is "as if" the divine form were actuating human existence to its fullest possible potentiality.

Now, the use of such a theological analogy to explore the unique realism of the divine into human history has not been without its critics. Neo-Thomists, in particular, have drawn upon the Latin writings of Lonergan in their criticism of Rahner on this point.[21] For Lonergan sees no need for any metaphysical account of the beatific vision, the Incarnation or grace.[22] He prefers to speak of contingent predication, grounded in a universally efficacious divine providence, as I have previously described.

The problem is evident. Take the case of the Incarnation. The Chalcedonian categories of person and nature are heuristic, corresponding to the questions "who?" and "what?" respectively.[23] Chalcedon distinguishes between who Jesus is (the Logos, the second person of the Trinity) and what he is (human and divine). Formal causality deals with the communication of a form, which corresponds to the question "what?". If the divine form is communicated, Jesus ceases to be human. This is the Monophysite option. Rahner seeks to avoid this with the prefix, "quasi", but then is forced to argue that the divinity of Jesus is nothing other than the fullness of his humanity, a position which tends to the Nestorian extreme. His theological position then oscillates between these two unacceptable alternatives.[24]

The problem lies in Rahner's inadequate account of personhood. Classical Christology speaks not of a formal union, a union in natures, but of a hypostatic union, a union in person. Its concern is primarily with who Jesus is, not what he is.[25] By invoking the category of formal, or even of quasi-formal, causality, Rahner falls short of maintaining a clear distinction between person and nature. Consequently, he also runs the risk of compromising the divine transcendence. Such a compromise casts serious doubt on his ability to maintain an efficacious divine providence over all creation, and hence present revelation in terms of universal history.

On the other hand, while Lonergan's treatment of the notion of person in relation to his Christological writings awaits a fuller exploration, he does not compromise divine transcendence. The solution he offers to the problems of Incarnation, grace and beatific vision is a clear assertion of divine transcendence by means of the category of contingent predication. With such a strong position on divine transcendence, Lonergan can maintain an efficacious providence grounding a theology of revelation which encompasses universal history.

A further, and related, issue which distinguishes Lonergan and Rahner lies in their treatment of the origin of the religious orientation present within consciousness. Rahner's position is well-known. He locates the origin of our religious orientation in the **supernatural existential**. Lonergan, on the other hand, does not adopt this terminology. He prefers to speak of **religious conversion**. Is this simply a difference in terminology, or are there more serious issues at stake?

The notion of the supernatural existential is another essential component in Rahner's theological anthropology. The term *existential* is derived from the philosophy of Martin Heidegger. It designates "those components which were constitutive of human existence, that is, those features which were proper to and characteristic of a human existent."[26] A supernatural existential is a permanent constitutive feature of human existence, not as part of human "nature", but as part of the concrete historical situation in which humanity finds itself. It represents both a permanent offer of grace and a dynamic orientation within consciousness to the divine. Rahner insists that this existential is, in fact, both supernatural and universal. It is supernatural in that goes beyond any hypothetical state of "pure nature"; it is gift and grace from God, part of the divine self-communication, enabling us to receive God as God without reduction to some merely human event. But still it is universal. It is given freely to all, without compromising its status as gift. We could still be human without it, though what form such a humanity would take is not known to us.

This notion of the supernatural existential plays a central role in Rahner's theology of revelation. It is the basis of what Rahner calls "transcendental revelation", a universal revelation which grounds his concept of the "anonymous Christian." George Vass describes it as an intermediary principle between God and humanity which was designed to allow Rahner to,

> overcome the oddity of traditional extrinsicism and at the same time to preclude the dangerous tendency of the *nouvelle théologie* towards an intrinsicism of grace with the loss of the unexacted gratuitousness of God's gift to man.[27]

Rahner himself describes it as analogous to the Thomist notions of the light of faith and obediential potency.[28]

Although Lonergan's work has been interpreted as sympathetic to Rahner's notion of the "anonymous Christian",[29] he articulates no notion corresponding to Rahner's supernatural existential. Rather than speak of a *supernatural* orientation to the divine in human consciousness, Lonergan refers to the *natural* desire to see God, even though the fulfilment of this desire is supernatural.[30] He equates this natural desire with our human obediential potency. Though he also invokes the Thomist notion the light of faith, he does so in reference to the discussion of faith, in *Method*. There, faith is "knowledge born of religious love", in terms of Pascal's dictum that "the heart has reasons that reason does not know."[31] He explains:

> in acknowledging a faith that grounds belief we are acknowledging what would have been termed the *lumen gratiae* or *lumen fidei* or infused wisdom.[32]

But the category underpinning Lonergan's implicit account of revelation is religions conversion. It would seem, then, that the relevant issue becomes one of comparing and contrasting Rahner's notion of supernatural existential and Lonergan's notion of religious conversion.[33]

There are profound issues at stake here. They involve the whole debate about of the relationship between grace and nature. Both Lonergan and Rahner have made significant contributions to this discussion, especially in response to the controversy surrounding the *nouvelle théologie*.[34] For both, the problem lay in overcoming the "two storey" extrinsicist account of grace present in neo-Scholasticism. While it is not possible in this thesis to go into all the nuances of the debate, it is possible to distinguish between the positions of Rahner and Lonergan in terms of a analysis of divine transcendence.

Rahner's theology of the supernatural existential claims that grace is always and everywhere available. Grace is made available as a permanent offer to humanity through the supernatural existential. All that is required is our human response to that offer.[35] Lonergan's position on religious conversion implies that grace is offered at particular moments, in particular events and experiences. Further, he acknowledges what an older theology would have called "actual graces." These may prepare the subject for conversion so as not to create too great a psychological discontinuity.[36]

Thus, we have two positions: (1) grace as always and everywhere available, to which the human subject need only respond; and (2) grace as providentially available in particular situations and experiences, to which one will be called to respond, prior to which one is in a state of moral impotence.

It is difficult to see how the respective validity of these two positions might be distinguished empirically. Any particular concrete situation can be adequately accounted for by either stance. Nonetheless, there is clearly a formal distinction between them. Both theologies address the problem of the tension between the concrete mediation of grace and the universal offer of grace, as indicated by 1 Timothy 2:4. Rahner, it appears to me, cuts the tension by opting for the supernatural existential, and so makes the universal offer of grace part of the transcendental constitution of the human subject. Lonergan, on the other hand, maintains the tension between the two poles of concrete mediation and universal offer. Rather than locate the universal availability of grace in term of the transcendental constitution of the subject, Lonergan can tie the universal offer of grace to the agency of a universally efficacious providence.

What, then, does Rahner lose in cutting the tension between these two poles in favour of an "existential" availability of grace? The danger is that he promotes an individualistic understanding of the human subject and of human salvation, by neglecting the concrete mediation of grace. This is precisely the criticism made by his former student, Johann Baptist Metz. As Matthew Lamb has noted:

> for Metz, Rahner has paid too little attention ... to the problematic character of human experience, especially in its *intrinsically social and historical* dialectical dimensions.[37][emphasis added]

Metz suspects that the whole transcendental-idealist turn, initiated by Kant, extended by Hegel and adopted by Rahner, has failed to deal adequately with the social and historical dimensions of human existence.

For Lonergan, on the other hand, an efficacious providence can supply a sufficent guarantee that the offer of grace is universally available. Such a solution does not neglect, but requires a consideration of, the social and historical dimensions of human existence. It is precisely these which will be among the providential mediators of grace in our concrete human situation.

Fred Lawrence has asserted that Rahner is one of a number of modern theologians who has effectively compromised the divine transcendence in their theologies (along with Process theology and Edward Schillebeeckx).[38] Further, Stephen Duffy has noted that "Rahner can at times sound like an anonymous process theologian."[39]

The issues raised in the above material provide some evidence for such a concern with regard to Rahner's theology. By way of contrast, Lonergan's clear affirmation of divine transcendence, and of a corresponding universally efficacious providence, provide a solid basis for any theology of revelation. Without such a basis, Rahner is forced into the more *ad hoc* solutions provided by the category of quasi-formal causality and the notion of the supernatural existential.

More generally I would conclude that, after consideration of these four points of comparison, the account of revelation correlative to Lonergan's *Method* provides the elements of a more coherent theology of revelation than that explicitly developed by Rahner in his writings.

5.2 Pannenberg and Lonergan: Revelation as History

At the end of the last chapter, we suggested that Lonergan's emphasis on the constitutive role of judgment in human knowing implied a corresponding role for history in revelation. We also conceded that Lonergan is not alone in giving history a significant role in revelation. Wolfhart Pannenberg also gives history such a role. We shall now compare the approaches of these two thinkers.

Pannenberg is a leading German Protestant theologian of the second half of the twentieth century. His theology has developed out of an ongoing dialogue with other German Protestant theologians such a Friedrich Schleiermacher, Karl Barth and Rudolph Bultmann, as well as with a philosophical tradition based on Kant and Hegel. He also has an expert knowledge of the Scholastic past, particularly of Duns Scotus. Pannenberg has shown a strong interest in science and the humanities. He develops a theological position resolutely in accord with a contemporary world-view. Unlike many Protestants his theology has a strong philosophical, even metaphysical, content, responding to the same types of issues raised by the Process Philosophy of Alfred Whitehead. He is as much at home with abstruse metaphysical questions about the divine nature as he is with questions of Scriptural exegesis. As such he represents a formidable dialogue partner for comparison with the position so far outlined.[40]

In chapter one, we referred to Pannenberg's notion of revelation as universal history. This bears some similarity to the notion of a universally efficacious providence found in Lonergan's work.[41] Let me now attempt a brief exposition of Pannenberg's position, so as to point out the real differences between these two accounts of revelation. I will concentrate on history as a carrier of meaning, a notion which both theologians employ.

Pannenberg develops his position on revelation and history in response to the Enlightenment discovery of critical history.[42] Whereas Schleiermacher retreated from critical history into subjective religious experience, and while Barth and Cullman sought to protect revelation by positing a special "primordial" or "salvation" history, separate from the rest of history and immune from critical historical investigation, Pannenberg attempts to enlist critical history as a positive aid to faith:

> The conception of a redemptive history severed from ordinary his-
> tory ... in the sense of Barth's "primal history" is hardly acceptable
> on theological grounds, and is judged not to be so in the first
> instance because of historical presuppositions. It belongs to the full
> meaning of the Incarnation that God's redemptive deed took place
> within the universal correlative connections of human history and
> not in a ghetto of redemptive history, or in a primal history belong-
> ing to a dimension which is "oblique" to ordinary history.[43]

He greets "the critical rationality of the Enlightenment" with intellectual zest: "He asks no special favours for theology and makes an ally out of what appeared to be the most insidious enemy of all – critical history."[44] Something of his enthusiasm for critical history can be gauged from the following:

> Given the thesis that revelation is contained in a historical event of
> the past, and that there is no other mode of access to a past event
> than historical research, would it not be the case that the burden of
> proof that God had revealed himself in Jesus of Nazareth would fall
> upon the historian? This requirement ... can in fact hardly be
> avoided.[45]

In adopting critical history, however, he does not accept any posi-tivist understanding of history as an accumulation of "brute facts" separate from any interpretation. Rather, the meaning of events in-heres in those events; they are, in Lonergan's language, intrinsically meaningful. Hence, Pannenberg is more sympathetic to the Platonic idealism of the English historian R.G. Collingwood, than the neo-Kantian idealist separation of fact and meaning found in positivism:[46]

[Pannenberg] denies that such an absolute distinction between event and interpretation is valid. We can draw it abstractly; but we cannot apply it in practice. The meaning of events inheres in them. (This is crucial to his whole position). The 'brute facts' of positivist thought are pure abstractions. They do not exist concretely in the world. Facts are always experienced in a context in which they have significance.[47]

The universal history recovered by critical history is the indirect self-disclosure or revelation of God to humanity. It is indirect, for any notion of direct disclosure or communication as in theophanies, for example, is rejected as pagan and gnostic.[48] Because of this indirectness, a critical hermeneutic of history is needed to uncover revelation's true meaning.

Pannenberg's theology raises radical questions about the nature of faith. He rejects the idea that faith is somehow necessary in order to receive revelation: this would be the gnostic option – revelation would then be accessible only to initiates who have the right disposition. Thus, in the third of his seven theses on revelation, he states:

In distinction from special manifestations of deity, the historical revelation is open to anyone who has eyes to see. It has a universal character.[49]

Revelation, then, is accessible to historical research, to anyone "who has eyes to see", not only to those who have "the eyes of faith":

Nothing must mute the fact that all truth lies right before the eyes, that its appropriation is a natural consequence of the facts. There is no need for any additional perfection of man, as though he could not focus on the "supernatural" truth with his normal equipment for knowing.[50]

There is no place here for the Holy Spirit as a "supplementary condition or additional factor that the Christ events requires in order to be known as revelation".[51] Rather the Spirit inheres in the content of the Gospel itself:

The Spirit does not join itself to the gospel as something additional. It is rather the case that the proclaimed eschatological event and, proceeding from it, even the process of proclaiming the gospel is itself Spirit-filled. For this reason, the hearer receives a share in the

Spirit in attaining a share in the essential content of the Gospel, in relying upon what he has heard.[52]

If faith is not some special openness towards receiving revelation, how then does Pannenberg see it? Does not his reliance on critical history render faith superfluous? Here he draws on a classical Protestant distinction between knowledge of the content of faith (*notitia* with *assensus*) and faith as trust (*fiducia*). This trust provides the certainty of faith, even though critical history provides the content of faith:

> Faith is not something like a compensation of subjective conviction to make up for defective knowledge. If that were the case every advance in knowledge would certainly help to make faith superfluous. But faith is actually trust in God's promise, and this trust is not rendered superfluous by knowledge of this promise; on the contrary it is made possible by it for the first time.[53]

In summary, then, for Pannenberg revelation is objective, historical and publicly accessible. Revelation does not require faith to grasp its meaning, but only to trust in its promises. Finally, its revealed meanings are available primarily through critical historical methods.

We can sharpen our comparison between these two theologians by drawing upon Pannenberg's own response to Lonergan's writings. He was one of the contributors to the collection of papers, *Looking at Lonergan's Method*,[54] written in response to *Method in Theology*. Significantly, in this response, he shows particular interest in Lonergan's ideas on meaning and history.

He begins by observing that Lonergan's account of meaning is based on the intentionality of the subject, rather than "the objective content of a particular experience."[55] While he accepts that such an approach is "irreproachable" in itself, it is obviously not one he favours. Because he adopts such an understanding of meaning, Lonergan must separate the task of the exegete, who is concerned with meaning as intended by an author, from that of the historian, where no such intended human meaning may exist. For Pannenberg, however, historical events have their own objective meaning, apart from the intentionality of any human subject. Consequently, he is unhappy with the distinction between the functional specialties of interpretation (exegesis) and history. He writes:

The question is whether history and exegesis can be separated as neatly as [Lonergan] suggests. Is it not necessary to explore the historical context of the situation of the author's formulation of his text in order to interpret correctly the kind of intention which the author himself was expressing by his words? And is it not necessary, in addition, to explore also the historical conditions, why a given text meant to those who read it something other than the author intended?[56]

Pannenberg's epistemological stance can, on his own admission, be traced to his cognitional positions on experience, insight and reflection (judgment). Whereas Lonergan makes clear distinctions between experience, understanding and reflective judgement, Pannenberg prefers a more "*Gestalt*" approach, which emphasises the wholeness of the cognitional experience:

The sharp separation of understanding as attainment of insight from the data that are understood and from the reflective question as to the correctness of such understanding is not convincing.[57]

Hence, he is particularly critical of the distinction between understanding and reflection:

... reflection and the judgment based upon it concerning the relations between the asserted insight and its relevant data do not, however, transcend understanding, because they render explicit previous understanding and themselves express new understanding. The decisive point is that reflection in not something foreign to understanding, that on the contrary all understanding involves some degree of reflective awareness, and the process of reflection renders explicit the implications of previous understanding.[58]

Given this holistic sense of the activity of knowing, it is to be expected that Pannenberg would have problems with Lonergan's distinctions between the functional specialties of research, interpretation and history.

Pannenberg concludes his article by expressing concern about Lonergan's specialty of dialectics. In particular, he is concerned about the notion of dialectically opposed horizons for which the appropriate remedy is nothing less than a conversion. He suggests the problem:

One wonders how people who are imprisoned in such different horizons could communicate at all. It is certainly true that in many cases communication is extremely difficult. But Lonergan's theory of horizons would confine individuals to separate worlds except for some decision of conversion, which could scarcely be called rational any longer, because it lacks the possibility of motivation within a coherent horizon.[59]

To the degree that the constitution of meaning is located within the decision of conversion, Lonergan's position must appear to end in subjectivism and fideism, where faith is "a function of a more or less arbitrary subjective decision."[60]

To point to the contrast between these two theologians I would offer the following three points.

i) With regard to the intentionality of meaning, it is true that Lonergan stresses the constitutive acts of the subject with regard to meaning. However, particularly in *Insight*, Lonergan understands intelligibility, or meaning, to be intrinsic to reality. It has an objective status. What is more, "reality is completely intelligible", in principle. Such a position is the basis of his proof for the existence of God.[61] Subjectivity and objectivity are not incompatible polarities: "genuine objectivity is the fruit of authentic subjectivity."[62]

Further, although Lonergan does not explicitly speak of historical carriers of meaning, he does see history as meaningful. He speaks, for example, of historical understanding and historical judgement.[63] Most radically, the meaning of history emerges from the intentional act, not just of human subjects, but of the divine Subject, the transcendent author and provident Lord of history. The whole of history is expressive of divine meaning. Ultimately divine providence passes judgment of human history, through the progress and decline that history generates.[64] I would not see such a position as inimical to that of Pannenberg, for whom history is the indirect self-disclosure of God.

ii) Secondly, Pannenberg's approach to cognitional theory clearly cannot allow for the refined differentiation of consciousness which is fundamental to Lonergan's whole method. The former fuses what the latter distinguishes.[65] Admittedly, for Lonergan, there is always an interrelationship between the various levels of consciousness, as evidenced in the notion of sublation and in his treatment of the self-correcting process of learning (so prominent in *Insight*).[66] Just as data gives rise to insights, and insights demand judgment, so too judgments can give rise to new insights, and new insights can promote the search for new data. Nonetheless, sensation is not understanding; and understanding is not judgment. Hence, in his inability or unwillingness to differentiate the data of consciousness and the levels of conscious operations, Pannenberg' account does not escape the confusions endemic in philosophy and theology in the modern era.

Consider Pannenberg's treatment of fact and interpretation in history. Questions arise: Are the facts, in his sense, arrived at through the gathering of data? Or, are they the outcome of the balanced judgments of historians? If, indeed, the facts are available for "anyone with eyes to see", does this mean that Pannenberg is ascribing to the "principle of the empty head", so regularly rejected by modern hermeneutical theorists? More basically, is Pannenberg lapsing into a kind of naive empiricism? In contrast, Lonergan would argue that all that is available for "anyone with eyes to see" are data. These data must be questioned and understood, eventually to supply evidence for an absolute or probable judgment. It would seem that Pannenberg is constricted by a notion of objectivity narrowed down to the mere givenness of data. The authenticity of the subject is excluded from a judgment on the objective facts.[67]

iii) It would appear, then, that while both these theologians appreciate the importance of history in revelation, their respective meanings of history are quite different. For Pannenberg, history is a relatively undifferentiated amalgam of data, interpretations and judgments, in which any individual part can only be known when the whole is known. For Lonergan, history is known in the objective judgments of historians, where their objectivity is a fruit of their authenticity – that is, their fidelity to the transcendental precepts. This knowledge reaches its asymptotic limit in the divine knowledge which knows history "in its fixity and its unequivocal structures."[68]

From a Lonerganian perspective, Pannenberg lacks a coherent position on objectivity. While Pannenberg recognises that meaning is constitutive of reality, he is unhappy about the inevitable consequence of the human subject entering into the constitution of knowledge. For he wishes to recover an "objective" history without reference to the faith, or more generally, to the subjectivity of the investigator. As I have noted above, Pannenberg perceives any recourse to the faith of the investigator as a gnostic option. Revelation must be open "to anyone who has eyes to see." But Lonergan would consider such objectivity quite illusory.

As a consequence of his truncated conception of objectivity, Pannenberg necessarily has difficulties with Lonergan's functional specialty of dialectic. For dialectic focuses attention specifically on the subject's role in the constitution of knowledge. The judgments of historians are affected by a variety of factors. Because Lonergan can acknowledge a genuine perspectivism, as opposed to outright relativism,[69] he recognises differences which arise from differing perspectives. However, he also accounts for those radical differences which arise from dialectically opposed views on knowing, objectivity and reality. Such contradictory differences cannot be resolved by any appeal to historical data, but only by fundamental shifts within the historical investigator, through conversion.[70]

What is more, from different sides, serious theological doubts are being raised about the ideal of critical history that Pannenberg champions. Theologians with such diverse agendas as Elisabeth Schussler Fiorenza and Joseph Ratzinger have called into question the sufficiency of the "critical history" paradigm. For Fiorenza, critical history is good at finding what a text meant; but not what it now means for us.[71] Ratzinger has expressed fears that critical history does not do justice to the faith dimension of the texts it investigates.[72] While neither would necessarily want to necessarily abandon critical historical methodology, neither would see it as the complete solution to the problem of relating to the past. For both these critics there is the recognition of the role the subject plays in constituting knowledge. With Fiorenza, the question is how much maleness and patriarchy have distorted the results of so-called "objective" critical history. With Ratzinger, it is more a question of Enlightenment presupposition about what is possible and what is not possible in history; for example, the occurrence of miracles.

Feminist theologians, for instance, argue that there is a gap between a consciousness dominated by patriarchy and one which sees sexism as evil. Such a gap can only be bridged by some type of conversion experience.[73] True, Pannenberg does raise a significant question as to how rational such a process of conversion can be. If dialogue across dialectically opposed horizons is next to impossible, the process of conversion to the new horizon may not be rationally justified within the pre-existing horizon. Even for Lonergan, conversion is fundamentally a shift in values. These values are not apprehended by understanding but by the intentional response of feeling.[74] Is this a retreat, as Pannenberg suggests, into subjectivism, and ultimately into fideism? I shall consider this question in the next chapter. For the moment I note that Pannenberg's own retreat from the "turn to the subject" creates its own problems – not least, in a notion of objectivity which can exist without subjects.

It is clear that Pannenberg's criticism of Lonergan focuses entirely on the first phase of Lonergan's theological method: research, interpretation, history and dialectic. There is no normative, healing phase in operation after conversion.[75] Given Pannenberg's rejection of an independent role for the Holy Spirit in transforming the subject, in order to receive historically mediated revelation, we find it is small wonder that Pannenberg has little to say about this phase. It would scarcely be intelligible within his theological framework.

To conclude, let me cite the following words from the introduction to *Insight*, where Lonergan claims that,

> there are two quite different realisms, that there is an incoherent realism, half animal and half human, that poses as a half-way house between materialism and idealism and, on the other hand, that there is an intelligent and reasonable realism between which and materialism the half-way house is idealism.[76]

One may suggest, then, that Pannenberg's position is caught in such a half-way house of incoherent realism, in his efforts to straddle the alternatives of materialism and idealism. Because he maintains an empiricist notion of objectivity, while holding a more idealist position on the constitutive role of meaning in historical events, judgments simply do not play a constitutive role in knowledge; they merely make explicit what is implicit in understanding. When the constitutive and distinct role of judgment in human knowing is not given its due, there is no escape from this half-way house between empiricism and idealism. Pannenberg has no way of resolving the tension between the already-out-there-now reality of empiricism, and the world mediated by meaning incompletely grasped by idealism.

In contrast, Lonergan resolves this tension through a critical realism which acknowledges the constitutive role of the subject in knowing. As a consequence, the revelatory history that Lonergan's *Method* envisages is not available to "anyone with eyes to see", but is known in the balanced judgments of authentic, and faith-filled, human subjects.

5.3 Lindbeck and Lonergan: Revelation and Culture

George Lindbeck, Pitkin Professor of Historical Theology at Yale University, is influenced by linguistic philosophy, particularly the work of Wittgenstein, and as well by the more contemporary approaches to the philosophy of science, especially the work of Thomas Kuhn. Theologically his ecumenical range includes Catholic theologians, such as Lonergan and Rahner, and Protestant theologians, such as Schleiermacher, Barth and Tillich. Over the years he has written extensively on the question of doctrines and creeds, especially in an ecumenical context. In 1984 he published a major contribution to this issue with his book, *The Nature of Doctrine: Religion and Theology in a Post-Liberal Age*, the slender size of which belies its enormous influence. I would like now to subject it to a more detailed analysis in light of the previous chapter, since Lonergan's *Method in Theology* is so obvious a point of reference for him; and also because both he and Lonergan place such importance in the role of a cultural tradition in religion.

I will make my analysis under four headings, the first of which is:

a) Doctrines

Lindbeck sets out to contrast three different approaches to the significance and role of religious doctrines.

The first is "propositionalist", for it,

> emphasizes the cognitive aspects of religion and stresses the ways in which church doctrines function as informative propositions or truth claims about objective realities ... This was the approach of traditional orthodoxies (as well as of many heterodoxies).[77]

For this approach, "if a doctrine is once true, it is always true, and if it is once false, it is always false."[78] On this basis, ecumenical dialogue is inherently conflictual, since "agreement can be reached only if one or both sides abandon their earlier positions."[79] He contrasts this propositional approach with what he sees as the dominant alternative, the "experiential-expressive" approach, a key exponent being the liberal Protestant theologian, Friedrich Schleiermacher. This latter differs from the propositional understanding of doctrines since, it interprets doctrine as noninformative and nondiscursive symbols of inner feelings, attitudes, or existential orientations. This approach highlights the resemblances of religions to aesthetic enterprises.[80]

In the experiential-expressivist understanding, doctrinal differences are of lesser significance:

> They are not crucial for religious agreement or disagreement, because these are constituted by harmony or conflict in underlying feelings, attitudes, existential orientations, or practices, rather than what happens on the level of symbolic (including doctrinal) objectifications. There is thus at least the logical possibility that a Buddhist and a Christian might have basically the same faith, although expressed differently.[81]

Lindbeck concedes that some approaches attempt to combine both dimensions of the propositional and the experiential-expressive. However,

> even at their best, as in Rahner and Lonergan, they resort to complicated intellectual gymnastics and to that extent are unpersuasive.[82]

As an alternative, Lindbeck seeks to develop what he calls a "cultural-linguistic" model of doctrine. Doctrines are not statements of truth about divine realities – as in the propositional approach; nor are they symbolic expressions of inner experiences – as in the experiential-expressive approach. Rather, they are rules and protocols designed to regulate the religious practice of a particular community. Such doctrines become "communally authoritative rules of discourse, attitude and action."[83] Such a model, Lindbeck believes, is much more conducive to ecumenical dialogue:

> ... to the degree that doctrines function as rules ... there is no logical problem in understanding how historically opposed positions can in some, even if not all, cases be reconciled while remaining in themselves unchanged. Contrary to what happens when doctrines are constructed as propositions or expressive symbols, doctrinal reconciliation without capitulation is a coherent notion.[84]

Lindbeck admits that, though such an model of doctrines may seem strange, there is nonetheless some impressive interdisciplinary scholarly support for it: "on the cultural side [from] Marx, Weber, and

Durkheim, and on the linguistic side [from] Wittgenstein"[85], as well as from more recent authors such as the sociologists of religion, Thomas Luckmann and Peter Berger. Despite the Kantian "turn to the subject" at the beginning of the modern era, the recent trend is moving against the experiential-expressive approach:

> [It] has lost ground everywhere except in most theological schools and departments of religious studies ... Historians, anthropologists, sociologists, and philosophers ... seem increasingly to find the cultural-linguistic approaches congenial.[86]

On this account of doctrine, religions are cultural-linguistic systems or languages. People become "religious" by entering into the religious culture and learning the religious language. These, in turn, are regulated by doctrines, much as grammar regulates ordinary language. By entering into a religious culture, people have certain experiences which they then interpret as religious experiences. Religion,

> ... functions somewhat like a Kantian *a priori*, although in this case the *a priori* is a set a acquired skills that could be different. It is not primarily an array of beliefs about the true and the good ... or a symbolism expressive of basic attitudes, feelings or sentiment ... Rather, it is similar to an idiom that makes possible the description of realities, the formulation of beliefs, and the experiencing of inner attitudes, feelings, and sentiments. Like a culture or language, it is a communal phenomenon that shapes the subjectivities of individuals rather than being primarily a manifestation of those subjectivities. It comprises a vocabulary of discursive and nondiscursive symbols together with a distinctive logic or grammar in terms of which this vocabulary can be deployed. Lastly, just as a language ... is correlated with a form of life, and just as a culture has both cognitive and behavioural dimensions, so it is also in the case of a religious tradition. Its doctrines, cosmic stories or myths, and ethical directives are integrally related to the rituals it practices, the sentiments or experiences it evokes, the actions it recommends, and the institutional forms it develops.[87]

This rather long quotation spells out Lindbeck's basic programme with regard to religion and the role of doctrines within religion.

Having established Lindbeck's basic framework we can move to our second point.

b) Lonergan's experiential-expressivism

As I already mentioned, Lindbeck takes Lonergan as one of his major dialogue partners in his discussion.[88] Although he recognises that Lonergan does not fall neatly into either the propositional or expe-riential-expressive categories, he uses Lonergan's position in reference to both.

Interpreting Lonergan as a representative of the experiential-expressive account of religion, Lindbeck summarises Lonergan's "theory of religion" under five theses:

> (1) Different religions are diverse expressions or objectifications of a common core experience. It is this which identifies them as relig-ious. (2) The experience, while conscious, may be unknown on the level of self-conscious reflection. (3) It is present in all human be-ings. (4) In most religions, the experience is the source and norm of objectification: it is by reference to the experience that their ade-quacy or lack of adequacy is to be judged ... A fifth point ... characterizes the primordial experience as "God's gift of love" or, when fully present, as "the dynamic state of being in love without restrictions" and "without object."[89]

He draws attention to Lonergan's use of the work of Friedrick Heiler, noting that it provides some evidence that Lonergan's theory has some relevance to world religions. He suggests that Lonergan has theological reasons for affirming the underlying unity of religious experience, throughout world religions. It can ground the possibility of universal salvation, much as does Rahner's theory of anonymous Christianity. Lonergan locates religious experience as "alone among inner nonsensory experiences [which] seems to be prior to all concep-tualization or cognition."[90]

Such an assertion causes grave problems:

> Because this core experience is said to be common to a wide diver-sity of religions, it is difficult or impossible to specify its distinctive features, and yet, unless this is done, the assertion of commonality becomes logically and empirically vacuous.[91]

In the light of the linguistic philosophy of Wittgenstein, Lindbeck questions an appeal to inner experience. He prefers to employ Ockham's razor to eliminate any discussion of inner states. Using the "classical medieval distinction between first and second intentions", he distinguishes between "the first intention ... whereby we grasp objects ... [and] the second intention [which] is the reflective act of grasping or reflecting on first formal intentions."[92] Only in the second act do subjects attend to their own activity, while, in the first act, the focus is on the object. Though he does not deny the existence of such a first act, he is convinced that we have no experience of it as our act, for the focus is entirely on the object. Nor should we assume that such first acts are "somehow preverbal or linguistically unstructured."[93] Applying this to so-called religious experiences, he argues that:

> they can be construed as by-products of linguistically or conceptually structured cognitive activities of which we are not directly aware because they are first intentional. The sense of the holy of which Rudolf Otto speaks can be construed as the tacit or unthematic awareness of applying a culturally acquired concept of the holy in a given situation.[94]

At his most succinct, Lindbeck states:

> affective experiences (in which would be included a sense of the holy or of absolute dependence) always depend on prior cognition of objects, and the objects available to us in this life are all in some fashion constructed out of ... conceptually or linguistically structured experience.[95]

Then, in an extensive footnote, he surmises that this position separates his account from that of Lonergan. Their opposition is not philosophical, but theological:

> ... [Lonergan] seems to have only theological reasons for rejecting the thesis of this present book that intersubjective communicative systems are the source rather than the product of distinctively human experience, whether religious or nonreligious.[96]

Admittedly, Lindbeck is correct in identifying the key issue as one of the character of internal or conscious acts. Lonergan has always maintained the nonlinguistic and preconceptual nature of specific conscious acts (not just religious experience). For example, Lonergan has consistently held that the act of understanding, or insight, is preconceptual. This position has separated him from a conceptualist version of the Scholastic tradition. Consequently, his recovery of the authentic intellectualism of medieval Scholasticism enabled him to appreciate the significance of Thomas' teaching on intelligible emanations in the trinitarian psychological analogy. On this basis, there **are** theological grounds for the opposition between Lonergan and Lindbeck, more radically different, perhaps, than the latter imagines.[97]

Still, it would be quite misleading to confine these difference to theological considerations. Lindbeck has found Lonergan's account of consciousness unacceptable: the "first intention" of the subject is focussed on the object, not the subject. Hence, the subject, in itself, is not accessible to investigation. Such a conviction is clean contrary to Lonergan's whole generalised empirical method, not only to his account of religious experience. It would seem that Lindbeck reduces consciousness to a "black box", the only clear products of which are concepts. The rest is simply inaccessible. The already cited statement illustrates the difficulty:

> Because this core experience is said to be common to a wide diversity of religions, it is difficult or impossible to specify its distinctive features, and yet, unless this is done, the assertion of commonality becomes logically and empirically vacuous.[98]

Now, if the word "religions" were to be replaced by the phrase "cognitional theories", so that one were now talking about a diversity of "cognitional theories", Lindbeck's argument would then appear to deny the possibility of any account of cognitional operations. The argument would be as follows. These theories are also built on core experiences, that is, our common experiences of knowing. They are also prone to a diversity of expression, as witnessed by the diversity of philosophical positions on knowing. They reflect what Lonergan refers to as "the polymorphism of human consciousness." Hence, on Lindbeck's analysis, a philosophical account of cognitional activities would be just as vacuous as a consideration of religious experience based on inner experience.

On the other hand, if Lindbeck is correct in his assertion that there is no prelinguistic conscious cognitional activity, then the rest of his thesis follows logically. Cultural-linguistic systems do determine inner experience. Hence, different religions, as examples of cultural-linguistic systems, are incommensurable. This stance is a form of conceptualism, but one cut off from the classicist assumptions of a previous era. A previous classicist culture held for the normativity of its own particular cultural milieu. Lindbeck holds, on the other hand, that no culture and no religion is normative because there are no norms shared by incommensurable systems. Because metaphysics is impossible, there are no metaphysical issues to be debated. The only truths are intrasystemic. Judgments are true only within the system. The rules of a particular "language game" specify what can and cannot be done within that game.

The issue becomes, in the end, one of fact. Lindbeck asserts that, in the initial cognitional act, the "first intention", the focus is on the object, not on the subject. The subject has no direct access to this act. Lonergan in fact agrees that the focus is primarily on the cognitional object. However, he disagrees that the problem of introspection is one of "looking at the looker." Rather, he contends that subjects experience themselves precisely as subjects in the very act of focussing on the object. Thus, consciousness is not self-knowledge; it is self-presence. The self is experienced , "in action" as it were, as the conscious subject of cognitional activity.[99] Only by objectifying the subject-as-subject does it become possible to overcome the relativism inherent in Lindbeck's conceptualist programme. Lonergan's brief summary is relevant here:

> The argument is: that the prior is not object as object or subject as object; there only remains subject as subject, and this subject as subject is both reality and discoverable through consciousness. The argument does not prove that in the subject as subject we shall find the evidence, norms, invariants and principles for a critique of horizons; it proves that unless we find it there, we shall not find it at all.[100]

It would seem that both Lindbeck and Lonergan would agree with that conclusion: Lindbeck claims that such evidence, norms, invariants and principles cannot be found; Lonergan claims to have found them.

c) Lonergan's "Propositionalism"

The difference between these two thinkers can be further clarified at another extreme of contrast. In Lindbeck's opinion, Lonergan is not only too naively experiential; he is also too propositionalist in his approach to doctrine. While Lindbeck considers Lonergan mainly under the category of experiential-expressive, he also discerns a certain combination of elements in *Method* which he considers to favour a propositional account of doctrine.[101]

First of all, he connects Lonergan to a correspondence theory of knowing based on propositions. Here Lindbeck's reference to Lonergan is vague, which is surprising, given Lonergan's own strong explicit clarification of such matters.[102] He concedes that Lonergan overcomes some of the difficulties associated with traditional propositional accounts of doctrines, "by distinguishing between what a doctrine affirms ontologically and the diverse conceptualities or formulations in which the affirmation can be expressed."[103] However, despite Lonergan's nuanced discussion of doctrinal development and diversity of expression, Lindbeck gives little attention to this context.[104]

More to the point, Lindbeck draws some parallels between his own cultural-linguistic model of doctrines and Lonergan's account of the doctrinal development leading up to Nicea. On Lindbeck's account, doctrines are primarily regulative; they provide the grammar of faith, controlling what can and cannot be said about God. As one reviewer noted, "all this sounds so much like Lonergan that one wonders why ... he is numbered among the experiential-expressivists."[105] In Lonergan's treatment of the significance of *homoousios* in the doctrine of Nicea, he follows Athanasius. The meaning of the *homoousios* can be articulated in the rule: "what is true of the Father is true of the Son, except that the Son is not the Father ...." As such, the *homoousios* is a second order statement. It is a proposition about propositions, regulating what can be said about the Father and the Son. Indeed, Lindbeck refers to Lonergan's studies on the matter and finds his position persuasive.[106]

Despite these similarities, there are marked differences. While Lonergan grasps the Nicene development of the *homoousios* as regulative, he recognises that there is more at stake than a simple regulation of discourse. For the propositions of dogma have ontological reference. The point of the doctrinal development leading up to Nicea is not just regulation of God-talk. It is the refinement of our ontological conceptualisations in order to transcend the images of Stoic materialism found in Tertullian, and the unrestrained neo-Platonic idealism of Origen, in the direction of the dogmatic realism of Anthanasius. For Lonergan, being and truth are one. True propositions have ontological significance. If Athanasius' rule is true, then it has ontological import.

For Lindbeck, however, a truth claim is always within a system: "doctrines qua doctrine ... are to be construed as second order [propositions]: they make ... intrasystematic rather than ontological truth claims."[107]   Such rules have no further ontological reference point; or, if they do, we have no way of knowing about it. Now, while such an ontological diffidence may suit the needs of ecumenical dialogue, the price to be paid is high: the radical alteration of the traditional understanding of what Christian truth claims mean.

Charles Hefling pinpoints the problem here.[108]   In attempting to develop an account of doctrine which is neutral in regard to the truth claims of different religions, Lindbeck has adopted a philosophical position which, either philosophically or theologically, is far from neutral.   As we saw above, Lindbeck compares his position with that of Kant; and clearly the metaphysical results are the same.   The ontological realm consists in noumena beyond our reach, not unlike the "first intentional" acts of the subject.   The function of doctrines is not unlike Kant's postulates of practical reason.   We must act as if they are true.   They regulate our behaviour.   But ultimately we cannot know whether they are true or not.   Now, this is hardly a philosophically neutral stance.   It is but one among a diversity of philosophical options, reflecting the polymorphism of human consciousness.

Moreover, such a option is not theologically neutral.   It is classically Lutheran in its separation of faith from reason, a position at odds with the Catholic tradition.   Thus, Lindbeck has made his own theological options which cannot claim to be ecumenically neutral.

d) Lonergan and the Cultural-Linguistic Approach

I have indicated how Lindbeck deals with Lonergan under the headings of experiential-expressive and propositionalist.   Though Lindbeck finds certain similarities between himself and Lonergan on the role of doctrine, it is surprising that he fails to draw attention to the wealth of material in Lonergan's writings which could have placed Lonergan under the heading of the cultural-linguistic approach. Here I would make three comments.

i) First, there is the matter of Lonergan's insistence, in both *Method* and *Insight*, on the importance of belief.   Here Lonergan is countering the Enlightenment "prejudice against prejudice" which would call into question any acquired belief and any claim to the authority of a tradition. Rather than urging on us the systematic doubt of Descartes, Lonergan prefers the approach of John Henry Newman,

> who remarked, apropos of Descartes' methodic doubt, that it would be better to believe everything than to doubt everything. For universal doubt leaves one with no basis for advance, while universal belief may contain some truth that in time may gradually drive out the errors.[109]

Indeed, in *Insight*, Lonergan proposes a radical solution to the problem of false belief. As a strategy, he adopts a personal "hermeneutic of suspicion" to speed up the process by which the truth "may gradually drive out the errors."[110]

Still, it is not just a matter of driving out false belief. For Lonergan, belief is not the imposition of an arbitrary external authority. Rather, it is a basic principle of human progress, by which human knowledge and wisdom may increase and pass from one generation to the next. Lonergan is insistent on this aspect of belief, not only in a religious context, but also in the scientific context. Here Lonergan is attacking the Enlightenment position in its stronghold. For the scientific peoples of the seventeenth and eighteenth centuries saw the rejection of traditional beliefs as pivotal. Although Enlightenment science was opposed to belief, Lonergan's analysis of belief makes it clear just how dependent even science is upon a tradition of beliefs, if it is to advance as science. The point is that believing is a reasonable, responsible act of the self-transcending subject. Such believing is grounded partly in an evaluation of the trustworthiness of the person believed, and partly in an evaluation of the importance of belief itself in human progress.[111]

ii) Secondly, there is the role of tradition in Lonergan's writings. This is, of course, not completely separate from Lonergan's treatment of belief. Tradition is best understood as the full extension of belief into its social and cultural-historical context. Lonergan's discussion of tradition coincides with his discussion of the constitutive and communicative functions of meaning. Human community is grounded in common meanings (constitutive meaning), and prolonged by the communication of meaning. The process of grounding and prolonging community constitutes a tradition. Granted that Lonergan makes no explicit mention of belief in his discussion of tradition, still belief clearly plays a key role in creating the fields of common meanings and values as these function in the progress of traditions:

> As it is only within communities that men are conceived and born and reared, so too it is only with respect to the available common meanings that the individual grows in experience, understanding, judgment, and so comes to find out for himself that he has to decide for himself what he is to make of himself.[112]

This is not dissimilar to the understanding of the cultural role of religion developed by Lindbeck. A tradition forms those who enter into it, shaping their whole consciousness. Not only the tradition, but even language, itself the product of a tradition, plays such a shaping role:

> So it is that conscious intentionality develops in and is moulded by its mother tongue. It is not merely that we learn the names of what we see but also that we can attend to and talk about the things we can name. The available language, then, takes the lead.[113]

These are clearly statements which lend support to the cultural-linguistic account of religion that Lindbeck is developing, and to which he makes no reference.

iii) A third element akin to Lindbeck's treatment of doctrines is Lonergan's understanding of transcendental method as set within a Western tradition of intellectual inquiry. The most significant figures in this tradition are undoubtedly Aristotle and Aquinas, though Plato, Augustine and, more recently, John Henry Newman all make a distinctive contribution. Lonergan presents his method as one instance of the modern philosophical "turn to the subject", with its beginnings in Descartes, and its developments in Hume, Kant, Hegel, Kierkegaard, existentialism and phenomenology, respectively. Lonergan locates his own work at the crucial point of the emergence of a third stage of meaning, which is to be methodologically grounded in interiority. Only in such a methodological foundation can the division between the competing claims of common sense and the systematic meaning of science be radically reconciled.[114]

From these three indications it may well be judged that there is much that Lindbeck could have drawn on, had he sought to portray Lonergan's work as related to the cultural-linguistic model. However, it is clear that Lonergan's position does not accept the conceptualist assumptions inherent in Lindbeck's account. What is more, a profound challenge to Lindbeck's position is implied.

Because he rejects these conceptualist assumptions, Lonergan speaks, not only of the minor unauthenticity of a subject with respect to his or her tradition. He can also recognise the possibility of a major unauthenticity within the tradition itself:

> The chair was still the chair of Moses, but it was occupied by the scribes and Pharisees. The theology was still scholastic, but the scholasticism was decadent ... So the unauthenticity of individuals becomes the unauthenticity of a tradition. Then, in the measure a subject takes the tradition, as it exists, for his standard, in that measure he can do no more than authentically realize unauthenticity.[115]

Hence, there are norms which transcend every cultural-linguistic context, inherent as they are within the subject itself. These norms provide a basis for a critique of all traditions, something Lindbeck cannot achieve. While Lonergan can acknowledge that the explication of these norms is itself the achievement of a tradition of inquiry, still these norms operate spontaneously in every human being. If this were not so, no tradition would ever have been able to produce its own critics:

> Then, persons, brought up in an unauthentic tradition, can become authentic human beings and authentic Christians only by purifying their tradition.[116]

Lonergan can also account for religious novelty and change in a more adequate manner. For he can acknowledge religious experiences which go beyond the resources of a presently constituted cultural-linguistic horizon, so as not to be contained by it.

To conclude our comparison, from Lonergan's perspective, Lindbeck's programme of reformulating religion in terms of cultural-linguistic analysis falls under the weight of its own conceptualist assumptions. While Lindbeck has highlighted the importance of religious tradition in shaping our religious consciousness, his conceptualist assumptions have trapped the subject within the horizon created by that tradition. Even though Lindbeck has freed himself from the classicist variant of conceptualism, which would impose Western consciousness as normative for all humanity, the price he pays is a complete relativism. Incommensurable cultural-linguistic religious systems are left to vie with one another for the loyalties of potential adherents who are either born into a particular system, or make an arbitrary choice to move from one to another.

On his part, Lonergan certainly recognises the importance of a religious tradition in shaping our religious consciousness. But, precisely because he is freed from conceptualist misunderstandings, he finds in consciousness a real source of novelty and change. Out of the preconceptual experiences of the authentic subject, the subject is both constituted and rendered creative in transforming the world. For, in the consciousness of the subject, are experienced the norms, invariant structures and principles fundamental for a critique of any and all horizons, cultural-linguistic systems or religions. At the same time, Lonergan can maintain a role for doctrines which is more in keeping with the place and value generally accorded them in the Christian tradition. He is not forced to strip them of all ontological reference as is the case with Lindbeck.

Even if Lindbeck finds Lonergan's "intellectual gymnastics" unpersuasive, Lonergan's implied theology of revelation, and his explicit articulation of religious experience in general, are demonstrably more comprehensively explanatory than the corresponding analyses given by Lindbeck. *Method* encompasses all the gains *The Nature of Doctrine* seeks, but without the confusions and limitations in which Lindbeck is trapped.

5.4 Conclusion

I have sought to clarify Lonergan's account of revelation by contrasting it with corresponding treatments of this theme in the writings of Karl Rahner, Wolfhart Pannenberg, and George Lindbeck. Of these, Rahner obviously comes closest to Lonergan's overall position. Though there is a family resemblance between these two, and many elements of a common tradition, Lonergan's more nuanced account of human interiority allows, I have argued, for a more nuanced theology of revelation compared to that of Rahner.

Pannenberg and Lindbeck both attack fundamental aspects of Lonergan's method. Pannenberg's "Gestalt" approach to cognitional activity in human consciousness means that he fuses what Lonergan distinguishes. Thus, while both he and Lonergan stress the significance of universal history, what each means by universal history is not the same: unlike Pannenberg, Lonergan clearly differentiates the givenness of historical data from the objectively given judgments of authentic subjects on historical issues. Finally, where Lindbeck sees consciousness as a black box from which emerge our religious concepts, he rejects any possibility of a method based on interiority; and so makes a direct assault in Lonergan's approach. But Lonergan's overall treatment of the issues contains all the gains Lindbeck wants to achieve through his cultural-linguistic approach. At the same time, Lonergan does not fall into the unintentional relativism which inevitably follows on the path Lindbeck has taken.

This dialectical exercise could, of course, be extended indefinitely into other contributions to the theology of revelation. But by restricting my analysis of Lonergan to these three key figures, the clarification necessary to the limited scope of this thesis is, I hope, substantially achieved.

---

1. For a more sympathetic comparison, see M. O'Callaghan, "Rahner and Lonergan on Foundational Theology", in M. Lamb (ed.), *Creativity and Method: Essays in Honor of Bernard Lonergan S.J.* (Milwaukee: Marquette University Press, 1981), 123-140, and his *Unity in Theology: Lonergan's Framework for Theology in Its New Context* (Washington: University Press of America, 1980), esp. 469ff. Also see W. Dych, "Method in Theology According to Karl Rahner", in *Theology and Discovery: Essays in Honor of Karl Rahner, S.J.*, William J Kelly (ed.) (Milwaukee: Marquette University Press, 1980), 39-53.
2. Note Lonergan's own comments with regard to the influence of Maréchal via Stephanou, Cf. F. Crowe, *Lonergan*, 39.
3. One need only consider the vast array of topics covered in the multi-volume *Theological Investigations*.
4. K. Rahner, *Spirit in the World* (London: Sheed and Word, 1968).
5. I note, also, that Lonergan's precise account of the operation of bias within consciousness has no clear parallel in Rahner.
6. K. Rahner, *Foundations of Christian Faith* (NY: Crossroad, 1982), 157.
7. Rahner, *Foundations*, 150.
8. Rahner, *Foundations*, 153.
9. Rahner, "Considerations on the Development of Dogma", *Theological Investigations*, Vol.4 (London: Darton, Longman and Todd, 1966), 10.
10. Rahner, "Consideration on Development", 245.
11. K. Rahner, *The Trinity* (London: Burns & Oates, 1970), 115.
12. Rahner, *Trinity*, 116.
13. Rahner, *Trinity*, 117-8. Also, in more muted form, see Rahner's *Foundations*, 135-6.

14. Cf. Lonergan, *Verbum,* and later in his Latin work, *De Deo Trino II: Pars Systematica* (Rome: Gregorian University, 1964).

15. See, for example, Doran, *Theology,* 459.

16. Rahner, *Trinity,* 99-100.

17. K. Barth, *Church Dogmatics,* Vol.1, Part 1 (Edinburgh: T. & T. Clarke, 1975), 339. See also the account of Barth's theology in J. O'Donnell, *The Mystery of the Triune God* (London: Sheed and Ward, 1988), 18-24.

18. Lonergan, *Method,* 113.

19. Lonergan, "Mission and the Spirit", 32. The text actually concludes with the phrase "*visible* mission of the Spirit", but this is clearly a misprint. Also, note the trinitarian structure to revelation posited in the paper, "The Response of the Jesuit as Priest and Apostle in the Modern World", *Second Collection,* esp. 174-5.

20. See D. Coffey, *Grace: The Gift of the Holy Spirit* (Sydney: Catholic Institute of Sydney, 1979), 56ff, for a brief history of Rahner's use of this category.

21. See, for example, G. Mansini, "Quasi-Formal Causality and 'Change in the Other': A Note on Karl Rahner's Christology", *The Thomist,* 52/2, (1988), 293-306.

22. Cf. Lonergan, *Insight,* 734.

23. Cf. my paper, "The Transcultural Significance of the Council of Chalcedon", *Australasian Catholic Record,* LXX/3 (1993), 322-332. Also, D. Helminiak, *The Same Jesus: A Contemporary Christology* (Chicago: Loyola University Press, 1986), 133ff.

24. This is not to deny the orthodoxy of Rahner's faith, but more to question the inadequacy of his philosophical tools to deal with the issue. For an interesting comparision between Rahner and Lonergan on Christology, see R. Moloney, "The Mind of Christ in Transcendental Theology: Rahner, Lonergan and Crowe", *The Heythrop Journal,* XXV/3 (1984), 288-300.

25. For example, this is the question Jesus addresses to his disciples at Caesarea Philippi, "*Who* do you say that I am?", Mt 16:15.

26. W. Dych, *Karl Rahner* (London: Geoffrey Chapman, 1992), 36.

27. G. Vass, *The Mystery of Man and the Foundations of a Theological System: Understanding Karl Rahner,* Vol.2 (London: Sheed & Ward, 1985), 67.

28. Cf. Rahner, *Foundations,* 148-151. Rahner states that "there corres-ponds to the objective supernaturality of a revealed proposition a divine and subjective principle for hearing this proposition". This is his notion of the supernatural existential or grace's "light of faith", 150.

29. Cf. G. Lindbeck, *Nature of Doctrine,* 56-57. Certainly Lonergan's later writings are open to the possibility of salvation outside Christianity, though he does not use Rahner's terminology of "anonymous Christian".

30. Cf. B. Lonergan, "The Natural Desire to See God", *Collection,* 84-95.

31. Lonergan, *Method*, 115.

32. Lonergan, *Method*, 123.

33. Lonergan himself makes the connection in the recently published article, "Philosophy and the Religious Phenomenon", *Method: Journal of Lonergan Studies*, 12/2 (1994), 125-146. He draws a parallel between his notion of "being in love in an unrestricted manner" and Rahner's notion of the supernatural existential, 136. Crowe claims that, as far as he knows, this is Lonergan's only reference to Rahner's notion of the supernatural existential, cf. 145, note.f.

34. For an excellent account of the different positions on the grace-nature distinction arising out of this debate, see S. Duffy, *The Graced Horizon: Nature and Grace in Modern Catholic Thought* (Willmington: Glazier, 1992). For a detailed analysis of Lonergan's position, and his role in this debate, see J.M. Stebbins, *The Divine Initiative: Grace, World Order, and Human Freedom in the Early Writings of Bernard Lonergan* (Toronto: Toronto University Press, 1995), esp. 142ff.

35. Cf. Rahner, *Foundations*, 126-128. Rahner notes that the supernatural existential is present either "in the mode of acceptance [or] in the mode of rejection", 128.

36. Lonergan, *Method*, 107.

37. M. Lamb, *Solidarity with Victims*, (NY: Crossroad, 1982), 126.

38. F. Lawrence, "Method and Theology as Hermeneutical", *Creativity and Method*, 92. I do not mean to suggest that Lawrence could not support his statement, simply that he does not in this context.

39. S. Duffy, *The Dynamics of Grace: Perspectives in Theological Anthropology* (Willmington: Glazier, 1993), 340.

40. For a sympathetic comparison between Pannenberg and Lonergan see M. O'Callaghan, *Unity in Theology*, esp. 465ff.

41. Especially if this is related to revelation in the manner suggested by Crowe in *Theology of the Christian Word*.

42. Cf. A. Galloway, *Wolfhart Pannenberg*, (London: George Allen and Unwin, 1973), 36.

43. W. Pannenberg, *Basic Questions in Theology* (London: SCM Press, 1970), Vol.1, 41-2.

44. Galloway, *Pannenberg*, 36.

45. Pannenberg, *Basic Questions*, Vol.1, 66.

46. Pannenberg, *Basic Questions*, Vol.1, 70ff.

47. Galloway, *Pannenberg*, 38. In this regard his position is similar to that of Schillebeeckx, cf. *Christ*, 31ff. For a critique of Schillebeeckx, see my paper "Schillebeeckx's Philosophical Prolegomenon: A Dialectical Analysis", *Australian Lonergan Workshop*, (Lanham: University Press of America, 1993), 69-78.

48. Cf. Galloway, *Pannenberg*, 51.

49. W. Pannenberg, "Dogmatic Theses on the Doctrine of Revelation", *Revelation as History*, W. Pannenberg, et al., (London: Macmillan, 1968), 135.

50. Pannenberg, *Revelation as History*, 136.

51. E.F. Tupper, *The Theology of Wolfhart Pannenberg*, (London: SCM Press, 1974), 123.

52. Pannenberg, *Basic Questions*, (London: SCM Press, 1971) Vol.2, 34, n.11.

53. Pannenberg, *Basic Questions*, Vol.2, 64-5. See also the essay in Vol.3, "Faith and Reason", where, by reason, Pannenberg means "historical reason."

54. P. Corcoran (ed.), *Looking at Lonergan's Method* (Dublin: Talbot Press, 1975).

55. W. Pannenberg, "History and Meaning in Bernard Lonergan's Approach to Theological Method", in *Looking at Lonergan's Method*, 88-100, esp. 89-90.

56. Pannenberg, "History and Meaning", 91.

57. Pannenberg, "History and Meaning", 92.

58. Pannenberg, "History and Meaning", 95.

59. Pannenberg, "History and Meaning", 97.

60. Pannenberg, "History and Meaning", 98.

61. Lonergan's summary argument is as follows: "If reality is completely intelligible, God exists. But reality is completely intelligible. Therefore God exists." Cf. *Insight*, 672.

62. Lonergan, *Method*, 292.

63. Cf. Lonergan, *Method*, 229ff, where Lonergan speaks the similarities and differences between historical and scientific understanding.

64. Cf. Lonergan, *Method*, 80, "... history and, ultimately, divine providence pass judgment on traditions."

65. The same compression of consciousness is evidenced in the writings of Schillebeeckx considered in Chapter 1 of this thesis.

66. Cf. Lonergan, *Insight*, 174ff.

67. Here Pannenberg differs from the otherwise similar account of Schillebeeckx, who clearly recognises the constitutive role of the subject in the process of knowing.

68. Lonergan, *Method*, 218.

69. Cf. Lonergan, *Method*, 214-220.

70. Lonergan, *Method*, 224.

71. E. Schussler Fiorenza, *Bread, not Stone* (Boston; Beacon Press, 1984) 32: "... biblical interpretation cannot limit itself to working out what the author meant; it must also critically elaborate what the theological significance of the text is for today".

72. J. Ratzinger, "Foundations and Approaches of Biblical Exegesis", *Origins*, 17/35 (1988), Feb 11. He identifies as a central problem the need to

find "a better synthesis between historical and theological methods, between higher criticism and church doctrine". Further: "a truly pervasive understanding of this whole problem has yet to be found which takes into account both the undeniable insights uncovered by historical method, while at the same time overcoming its limitations", 596.

73. See, for example, R. Reuther, *Sexism and God-Talk: Toward a Feminist Theology* (Boston: Beacon Press, 1993), 159ff.

74. Cf. Lonergan, *Method*, 245: "Now the apprehension of values and disvalues is the task not of understanding but of intentional response."

75. The more detailed study by O'Callaghan agrees with this analysis: "The difference between Pannenberg and Lonergan ... lies in the fact that Pannenberg has chosen to concentrate on the function of theology *in oratione obliqua*, while Lonergan would draw attention to the additional function of theology as praxis – *in oratione recta*. Pannenberg conceives of theology as an evaluative mediation of the past into the present; Lonergan ... would ask as well for a theology that critically mediates the present into the future", *Unity in Theology*, 467.

76. Lonergan, *Insight*, xxviii.

77. G. Lindbeck, *The Nature of Doctrine*, 16.

78. Lindbeck, *Nature of Doctrine*, 16.

79. Lindbeck, *Nature of Doctrine*, 16

80. Lindbeck, *Nature of Doctrine*, 16.

81. Lindbeck, *Nature of Doctrine*, 17.

82. Lindbeck, *Nature of Doctrine*, 17.

83. Lindbeck, *Nature of Doctrine*, 18.

84. Lindbeck, *Nature of Doctrine*, 18

85. Lindbeck, *Nature of Doctrine*, 20.

86. Lindbeck, *Nature of Doctrine*, 25.

87. Lindbeck, *Nature of Doctrine*, 33.

88. This is partly circumstance. Lindbeck's book arose from the 1974 St Michael's Lecture at Gonzaga University. Lonergan had given the previous lecture, published as *Doctrinal Pluralism* (Milwaukee: Marquette University Press, 1971) which recapitulates much of his position developed in *Method*. One of the conditions imposed on the invited lecturer is that he respond to issues raised by the previous lecturer.

89. Lindbeck, *Nature of Doctrine*, 31.

90. Lindbeck, *Nature of Doctrine*, 32.

91. Lindbeck, *Nature of Doctrine*, 32.

92. Lindbeck, *Nature of Doctrine*, 38.

93. Lindbeck, *Nature of Doctrine*, 38.

94. Lindbeck, *Nature of Doctrine*, 38.

95. Lindbeck, *Nature of Doctrine*, 39.

96. Lindbeck, *Nature of Doctrine*, 44, n.18.

97. It seems more likely that Lindbeck has in mind the problem of salvation for non-Christians, a point he refers to elsewhere, cf. *Nature of Doctrine*, 56-7. Lindbeck shows no familiarity with Lonergan's trinitarian investigations.

98. Lindbeck, *Nature of Doctrine*, 32.

99. For a succinct account of the problem of consciousness, see Lonergan's essay, "Christ as Subject: A reply", *Collection*, esp. 175ff.

100. B. Lonergan, notes on "Existentialism", from lectures given at Boston College, July, 1957.

101. See, for example, Lindbeck, *Nature of Doctrine*, 105, where Lindbeck refers to "contemporary propositionalism represented by someone like Lonergan".

102. Lindbeck, *Nature of Doctrine*, 51. On the correspondence theory of truth, see B. Lonergan, "The Dehellenization of Dogma", *Second Collection*, 13ff.

103. Lindbeck, *Nature of Doctrine*, 80.

104. For example, in Lindbeck's chapter, "Theories of Doctrine", *Nature of Doctrine*, Lonergan only receives one brief mention in the text, together with three footnote references.

105. C. Hefling, "Turning Liberalism Inside-Out", *Method: Journal of Lonergan Studies*, 3/2 (1985), 58.

106. Lindbeck, *Nature of Doctrine*, 94.

107. Lindbeck, *Nature of Doctrine*, 80.

108. Hefling, "Turning Liberalism Inside-Out", 58.

109. Lonergan, *Method*, 223.

110. Cf. Lonergan, *Insight*, 713-718.

111. See Lonergan's account of the act of believing in both *Insight*, 703ff, and *Method*, 41ff. There is no major difference between these two accounts.

112. Cf. Lonergan, *Method*, 79.

113. Lonergan, *Method*, 71.

114. Lonergan, *Method*, 96ff.

115. Lonergan, *Method*, 80.

116. Lonergan, *Method*, 299.

CHAPTER SIX:
ADDRESSING THE CRITICS

In the previous chapter, I sought to clarify the position on revelation developed in Chapter 3 by contrasting it with that of three major theologians. My task was assisted by the fact that all three of these theologians engaged in some dialogue with Lonergan's work. In this chapter, I would like to turn my attention to a special problem which has arisen in the work of a number of other theologians who have been critical of *Method*. From two dialectically opposed extremes, it has been interpreted as either excessively rationalistic, or too affectively fideist – and sometimes even as both.

Either these critics are missing something, or there are deep internal contradictions present in it. Lonergan's project, I would argue, admits tensions, but not contradictions, in this regard. But, to take up the precise issues, I shall consider the critics in detail.

6.1 Is *Method* excessively rationalistic?

a) A question of Adequacy – Tony Kelly

In the paper, "Is Lonergan's *Method* Adequate to Christian Mystery?",[1] which appeared three years after the publication of *Method*, Tony Kelly provides an appreciative criticism of Lonergan's approach.

Kelly begins by citing Tertullian's question, "What has Athens to do with Jerusalem?" What is the relationship, Kelly is asking, between philosophy and theology, between the eros of the mind and God's grace, between "the general impulse towards self-transcendence [and] activity of the Spirit of Christ"?[2] More concretely, how valid is the distinction Lonergan draws between his theological method, grounded in his transcendental anthropology, and the actual content of theology? With greater precision Kelly asks, "Why should Christ make any difference to theological method?":

> And here precisely is my question: how does this theological method take faith in Christ into its inner vitality? How is Lonergan's *Method* alive to the unique, the original, the absolute element in Christian faith.[3]

Is Lonergan's method a function of Christian faith, or does it "see faith as any faith, a mere range of data that theology will dispassionately survey in the light of method" determined on the basis of a transcendental *a priori*? In his own way, Kelly is posing the question of the relationship between faith and reason with regard to Lonergan's method. As the direction of his questions indicate, he is clearly concerned that Lonergan falters in the direction of rationalism. As he puts it:

> The subject matter should command the nature of the method, and certainly we must be alert against the possibility of allowing a prior method to delineate the subject matter independently.[4]

To emphasise the point, he cites von Balthasar:

> Christianity is destroyed if it lets itself be reduced to transcendental presuppositions on man's self-understanding whether in thought or in life, in knowledge or in action.[5]

Kelly then proceeds to analyse Lonergan's treatment of what is specific to Christian faith. In this connection, he considers particularly Lonergan's model of inner and outer words. The inner word is the gift of God's love, poured into our hearts. The outer word is born by a religious tradition, and, indeed, may be the entrance of the word of God himself into human history. However, once this issue is raised, Kelly considers that Lonergan backs away from it, by retreating to a methodological issue, to the detriment of the theological. As Lonergan writes: "To the theologians we must leave them."[6] It is here that Kelly takes Lonergan to task:

The methodologist does not feel constrained to leave to theologians the rather momentous questions concerning the nature of grace, the universality of its occurrence, the significance of world religions; yet, he hands back to theologians the specifics of Christian experience as outside the concerns of method. What is specific does not determine the method, neither as a ground, a scope, or style of exploration. The method is in possession independent of what is absolute or unique in the field of investigation.[7]

Thus, while Lonergan admits into the heart of theology the question of religious experience and conversion, the occurrence of conversion is spoken of in three modalities, namely, the religious, moral and intellectual. But where, in such an event, is there the specifically Christian mode of conversion, that is, conversion to Christ?

... if the theologian is indeed converted to Christ, I would be inclined to think that the Mystery of Christ would enter into the fundamental vitality of methodology.[8]

But instead, Kelly finds only as "awkward exteriority" in dealing with the Christ event, and belated assurances concerning the "interpersonal, intersubjective component" of such a conversion. He proceeds to argue:

... if such an experience is notably one of intersubjectivity with Christ, it would appear that a good deal more is demanded of theological method than the model of self-transcendence.[9]

The end result is that Kelly finds the Christian component in Lonergan's profound methodological discussions to be "almost an afterthought."

Kelly concludes his analysis of Lonergan method with two notes, one on the notion of mystery, as exemplified in the work of Rahner, the other on aesthetics, as exemplified in the work of von Balthasar. In the light of his earlier comments, Kelly prefers the approach of Rahner who places mystery, not method, as fundamental to theology. For Rahner, claims Kelly, "the *a priori* of method is always in the light of the *a posteriori* of Mystery."[10] Lonergan's *Method*, on the other hand "tends to repulse mystery to its final impregnable outpost within the divinity, so aggressive is its scientific onrush."[11]

Kelly also draws attention to the approach of von Balthasar, who, in emphasising the glory of revelation, draws attention to the startling originality of the Word of God which cannot be anticipated through some transcendental deduction:

> It is the self-validating splendor like that of a great work of art that does not fulfil any need primarily but rather provokes the exigence to reorganize our cosmological and anthropological knowledge for the purposes of being truly open to the radiant form of the Word. Accordingly, aesthetics must enter into the very heart of theology ...[12]

Von Balthasar thus distinguishes between a "religious *a priori*", which arises from the self-transcendence of the human spirit, and the "theological *a priori*":

> This comes as a surprise to the human spirit. It is a "shock", overwhelming man with an offer of intimacy with God ... We would say, then, that the glory of revelation, as such a surprise and shock and even a scandal to man "transcends" our experience of transcendence.[13]

Again we see here a concern that method not be such as to restrict proper attention to its object. Revelation, claims Kelly, can go beyond our transcendental anticipations. It can appear as folly to our human wisdom. "It might well elude what we call transcendental and dislocate what we take to be methodological."[14]

Kelly concludes his article with some comments of the place Lonergan gives to conversion in theological method. Kelly freely admits the likelihood of his own lack of conversion, be it intellectual, moral or religious. Rather than regard conversion as foundational, Kelly prefers,

> to regard theology as primarily an intelligent "ministry of the Word" originating, even as one thinks theologically, from a receptivity and responsiveness to the "datum" of God's communication in Christ, mediated to me in the life, communion, and mission of the Church. I prefer this to the elitist standpoint of my own conversion.[15]

Consequently Kelly sees his article as providing a wholesome critique of Lonergan's *Method.* He does not seek to reject Lonergan's overall approach but raises critical questions about the adequacy of the model Lonergan has developed to account for the Christian mystery.

b) A question of Separation – Terrence Reynolds: "Method Divorced from Content."

Some sixteen years after the publication of Kelly's article, his analysis was amplified by Terrence Reynolds in his article "Method Divorced from Content in Theology: An Assessment of Lonergan's *Method in Theology*."[16]   Reynold's also refers to similar criticisms levelled at Lonergan's project by Avery Dulles and Maurice Wiles, but here I shall focus on his comments on Kelly's article.

With Kelly, Reynold's raises the issue of whether and to what extent it is possible to divorce theological method from explicit reference to the specific content of theology, particularly in a Christian context. However, rather than focus on the Christological issue, Reynolds is more concerned with the question of a theology of grace.   Reynolds sees Lonergan as engaged in a project of developing a theological method which is philosophically sound, yet sufficiently acceptable to a "Roman Catholic audience."   The key issue, which he picks up from Kelly, is the relationship between the human drive to self-transcendence and the operation of grace.   Reynolds holds that Lonergan maintains "that this inclination of self-transcendence towards religious awareness ... is propelled by a form of grace."[17]   Yet this appeal to grace produces a dilemma.   It cannot be used to ground special insights unavailable to the ungraced, or "the universality of the method would immediately collapse."   On the other hand, if the appeal to grace disregards the particularity of the Christian experience, "it will do an injustice to the notion of grace as it has traditionally been understood within the Church."[18] Reynolds claims that Lonergan could have satisfied Kelly's objection by the development of a theology of grace along, say, the lines of Rahner's theology of grace.   However, such an approach would have undermined the nature of Lonergan's project:

> If Lonergan were to graft his methodology onto a constructive approach such as that, he would have be enmeshed in a rather hopeless contradiction of intentions.   After promoting a neutral method based upon philosophical inquiry, if Lonergan were to lapse into theological formulations of a neo-orthodox character, he would

thoroughly erode his claim to objectivity and lay waste his methodological programme.[19]

Thus, Reynolds finds that Kelly's criticisms, in this regard, are unfounded and that he has displayed a certain insensitivity to Lonergan's programme. However, he acknowledges that Kelly has put his finger on a basic difficulty with Lonergan's approach, namely, the disjunction between method and content:

> Lonergan may have escaped the Scylla of Rahner's "neo-orthodoxy" but has fallen prey to the Charybdis of an implicit Christian theology devoid of its central mystery.[20]

Reynolds concludes that Lonergan's attempt to separate method from its content is ill-conceived and unconvincing.

Kelly's criticisms of Lonergan's *Method* are, in many ways, truly perceptive, especially in the ways in which they anticipate the extension of Lonergan's methodology as they would later occur in the work of Robert Doran.[21] Where Kelly questions the lack of a specifically Christian conversion, Doran has sought to explicate the features of a specifically Christian conversion with what he will identify as a soteriological differentiation of consciousness.[22] Again, where Kelly notes the lack of an aesthetic dimension to Lonergan's work, Doran explicates a specifically psychic dimension to conversion, associated with the transcendental of the beautiful.[23] Further, where Kelly questions the relationship between the eros towards self-transcendence within human consciousness and the divine gift of grace, Doran analyses this relationship in terms of the healing and creative vectors within consciousness.[24] I would contend that this theme, developed more fully in Lonergan's post-*Method* writings, overcomes Kelly's concern that Lonergan confuses self-transcendence and grace. For his part, Doran is seeking to identify and develop positions in Lonergan's work which were less than completely dealt with.

Yet Kelly's own analysis suffers from an internal unresolved tension, reflecting the taut balance present in Lonergan's stance. The tension can be identified in Kelly's dual stance: on the one hand, he is critical of Lonergan's invocation of conversion as central to theology, a move Kelly labels as "elitist"; on the other hand, he wants a specifically *Christian* foundation to the methodological issues raised by

Lonergan. To ask for such a foundation is clearly to seek a theological method based on conversion, a specifically Christian conversion. One has to ask why Lonergan's invocation of religious, moral and intellectual conversion is elitist, yet Kelly's implicit requirement of Christian conversion is not? Clearly there is a tension here in Kelly's analysis, a tension which replicates the long standing tension between faith and reason. Kelly, indeed, invokes the name of Karl Barth, which indicates his concern that Lonergan has placed too much emphasis on reason at the expense of faith.

Reynolds takes the matter even further with, what I would claim, is a serious misreading of Lonergan's work. Reynolds understands Lonergan as trying to provide "a neutral method based upon philosophical inquiry":[25]

> Standing at the intersection of method and theology, Lonergan attempts to harmonize these seemingly disparate options in a manner which preserves the philosophical integrity of his system and at the same time presents a treatment of grace suitable to his Roman Catholic audience.[26]

Reynolds sees Lonergan as separating method from content, with the method arising from a purely philosophical process. Yet such a separation is not, I would argue, inherent in Lonergan's thought. Indeed, as I have previously noted, much, if not all, of what Lonergan develops in the first five chapters of *Method*, could be subsumed in the *theological* functional specialty of foundations. While Lonergan distinguishes between theology and methodology, it is not clear that he separates them.

Clearly, then, despite Lonergan's insistence on the role of conversion, both Reynolds and Kelly are taking Lonergan's method as in some way moving towards rationalism. The concern is that *Method* is grounded in a purely anthropological, transcendental or philosophical option. Both want closer reference to the content of Christian faith, but neither addresses, in their brief analyses, how this can be done without facing the converse problem of fideism.[27] Is there a way out of this dilemma?

The solution, I would suggest, lies in attending to the role of revelation in establishing a tradition of rationality. I would suggest that both Kelly and Reynolds are caught in a-historical, classicists assumptions about the nature of human rationality. As a consequence, both are in danger of removing Lonergan's transcendental analysis of human subjectivity from its deep roots within the Christian tradition; Reynolds far more so than Kelly. Admittedly, the references in *Method* are not prominent, but they are explicit. Lonergan perceives, for example, the causal connection between religious conversion, the place of tradition and the beliefs "which are the seeds of intellectual conversion."[28] Further, he identifies part of the "normative function" of doctrine to be the promotion of religious, moral *and* intellectual conversion.[29] However, in his paper "The Origins of Christian Realism", delivered immediately after the publication of *Method*,[30] Lonergan argues forcefully that Christian revelation demands the emergence of at least a dogmatic realism. Picking up these clues, Doran suggests that:

> Perhaps only a Christian theologian could have articulated critical realism, for only within the horizon informing such a theologian's tradition are the objects of intentional consciousness so obviously such as to require the understanding of analogous insight and the assent of unconditioned judgment as the exclusive medium of their truth.[31]

Doran goes on to state that in fact there is a definite doctrinal component in the objectification of foundations presented in *Method*, but he asks why that should cause a problem. He sees no real problem so long as we refer to the concrete situation of the conversion process:

> The religious conversion of the subject already within a long tradition will inescapably, and more or less proximately and foundationally, entail a doctrinal commitment, and an opposition to that constituent of foundations reveals a disproportion to the theological object that can only be termed a less than complete attunement through religious conversion.[32]

What both Reynolds and Kelly have done is to make of Lonergan's discussion of conversion an abstraction. They have, I would suggest, removed it from any concrete historical context. This is not the position of Lonergan, who conceives of conversion concretely; hence in relationship to a religious tradition. He writes:

> First there is the gift of God's love. Next, the eye of love reveals values in their splendour, while the strength of this love brings about

there realization, and that is moral conversion. Finally, *among the values discerned by the eye of love is the value of believing the truths taught by the religious tradition, and in such tradition and beliefs are the seeds of intellectual conversion.*[33] [emphasis added]

Once we move from the abstract conception of conversion to the more concrete conception envisaged by Lonergan, it is no longer possible to see his approach as reductively rationalistic. For the "seeds of intellectual conversion", which are the basis for his analysis of interiority, are to be found in a tradition of enquiry initiated by revelation. In other words, the tradition of reason arises out of the "truths taught by the religious tradition." In terms of such a tradition of rationality, the objections raised by Kelly and Reynolds can be faced and answered, even if they necessitate a development along the lines of Doran's suggestions.

c) A Question of Foundations – Donald Keefe: "A Methodological Critique of Lonergan's Theological Method."[34]

In 1988 Donald Keefe published a critique of Lonergan's *Method*, far more radical than the above instances. He, too, has problems with a theological method developed without reference to what is specific to Christian theology, namely, to the historical revelation of Jesus Christ. He claims that,

> Theological method is such only in this concrete posture of conversion to the historical revelation in the historical Church: it can no more prescind from the concreteness and particularity of this conversion than it can from the conversion itself ... it must begin and end with the concreteness of the Christian conversion to the explicitly Christian faith; a dehistoricized method of theology is immediately and irredeemably autonomous, incapable of that reflection upon the historical faith which Lonergan's method intends.[35]

Keefe argues that,

> Theology cannot construct its own beginning point; that is given in the revelation, the Christ, and there is no other base upon which theological method can stand.[36]

Keefe goes further than either Kelly or Reynolds in understanding Lonergan's position as inescapably rationalistic: an autonomous self-validating reason determines the *a priori* structure of theology with the "religious part" tacked on as an extrinsic factor.

According to Keefe, the problem lies in the way grace is separated from nature. Grace is considered as accidental to the human substance; *gratia Christi* is separated from the gratuity of creation. Such theology forgets the fallenness of human reason in favour of its autonomy. Thus, for Keefe, the starting point of theology should not be the unrestricted dynamism of human consciousness, which he calls "cosmological consciousness." Rather, it should be conscience affected by "guilt and alienation." This starting point leads to a conscious experience of "intrinsic contradiction" between sin and grace, rather than the harmonious "integration" of consciousness, as posited by Lonergan:

> The ultimate problem which Lonergan's treatment of the unity of consciousness fails to solve is that of harmonizing the cosmological and the Christian consciousness. Nor is this failure strange: the problem is a false one, without solution. The cosmological consciousness is that from which one is converted: it is the standing alternative to Christianity, and any failure in Christianity reverts to it. Here, the failure is that of Lonergan's cognitional analysis, which makes cosmological anthropology normative for the theological enterprise.[37]

More generally, Keefe is targeting not just Lonergan, but the whole Thomistic tradition. It has failed to produce a coherent theology of grace. In such a supposed history of failure, Lonergan's theological method is "no more than a restatement of the merely nominal continuum between grace and nature by which the Thomists old and new have avoided the systematic problem" of accounting for God's action in human history.[38] Keefe's solution to this "systematic problem" is to abolish the distinction between grace and nature. His theological starting point is that the *gratia Christi* is nothing other than creation itself. As such, grace is universally accessible within consciousness through an *interior instinctus*. On this reading, "the universally given eros of the mind is also our concrete involvement in the supernatural."[39] This implies a "Christocentrism of human intentionality", something which Lonergan's transcendental method excludes "without discussion."[40]

Keefe has a number of other criticisms of Lonergan's approach, which may be summarised as follows: i) Lonergan undercuts the value of revealed doctrine and the authoritative teaching of the Church, replacing it with the views of academic theologians; ii) Lonergan's appeal to conversion is elitist; iii) Lonergan misreads the intention of Vatican I on the natural knowledge of God; iv) Lonergan does not pay enough attention to the problem of fallenness and its implications for consciousness. However, rather than consider these separately, it is clear that these points all cluster around what is Keefe's central criticism, that Lonergan errs in maintaining the distinction between grace and nature.

Now, it is very obvious that the distinction between grace and nature runs as a constant thread, not only through *Method*, but through all Lonergan's writings. Surely, Keefe is correct in observing this matter. It is also clear that there are profound difficulties in giving a coherent account of how grace can be universally accessible within the framework of the distinction between grace and nature. Theology is constrained to balance, in some way, the accessibility of grace with its concrete mediation. In this regard, Rahner's theology of the supernatural existential is similar to Keefe's implied position, even if Rahner is always careful to maintain the distinction between grace and nature, a distinction to which Keefe is opposed. Lonergan, on the other hand, speaks of a *natural* eros of the mind for God and a supernatural fulfilment of that desire.[41] For him, the solution to the problem of the universal accessibility to grace must then be found in divine providence, as we mentioned in Chapter 4.[42]

However, Keefe's solution to the problem raises questions which must be seriously addressed by any Catholic theologian. Terry Tekippe, for example, defends Lonergan against Keefe's attack, suggesting that this latter's treatment of grace and nature is more akin to the classical Protestant-Lutheran tradition on this issue.[43] To identify this kinship is not, of course, to dismiss Keefe's position, but it does identify significant tensions within it. How does Keefe maintain a position which recognises the authority of Catholic Church teaching (note his criticism above of Lonergan, in this regard), yet which finds him adopting a Protestant-Lutheran stance on the theology of grace? This is all the more problematic given that Vatican I, and the more recent encyclical, *Humani Generis*, see the distinction between grace and nature as part of Catholic teaching?

The problem lies in Keefe's reading of the Christian intellectual tradition. He detects a conflict between two types of consciousness, the "cosmological" and "Christian."[44] Cosmological consciousness takes its stand on the natural eros of the mind, whereas Christian consciousness is dominated by the issues of alienation and guilt. Christians fail, he states, whenever they revert to cosmological consciousness. These two types of consciousness are, according to Keefe, diametrically opposed. In Christian consciousness we recognise the contradictions within ourselves – the *simul justus et peccator*, which expresses both our basic alienation and our dependence upon Christ. Cosmological consciousness, on the other hand, represents "self-salvation", through the autonomy of the mind. Such a consciousness fails because it barricades itself against the destructive effects of sin. Christian tradition is thus a dialectic conflict between these two forms of consciousness. On this reading Thomism in general, and Lonergan in particular, represent a falling away from a genuine Christian consciousness.

While this is one reading of the history of Christian thought, one is entitled to ask whether it really does justice to that history. Does it not present history as really worse than it was? May there not be an alternative reading which would put that same history in a completely different light? Such an alternative reading is made possible by the position I have been seeking to develop throughout this thesis; namely, that revelation establishes its own tradition of rationality.

As a starting point, we could agree with Keefe that the basic experience within consciousness is one of alienation and guilt. He has stated that an emphasis on fallenness is "curiously absent" from Lonergan's anthropology.[45] But here we note that Lonergan has explicated intellectual, volitional and psychic components in the experience of moral impotence within consciousness. Further, he has catalogued the effects of dramatic, individual, group and general bias. Consequently, he can hardly be indicted of having a naive or unproblematic account of "unthematic consciousness."[46] Even more specifically, Lonergan identifies the polymorphism of human consciousness, registered in the cacophony of desires and impulses affecting the human person. As a result, the philosophical task, in his view, is one of clarifying this compact polymorphic fact, by distinguishing and relating the various desires in an overall account of human authenticity and progress. Hindering the clarification of the compact manifold of consciousness are the various biases detectable within such awareness. In this regard, the multiplicity of philosophical accounts is not simply regrettable. More threateningly, such contradictory multiplicity is an instance of the "reign of sin" in human history.[47]

If this is in fact the case, then the clarification of the polymorphism of human consciousness is an aspect of overcoming the "reign of sin." Indeed, it is a manifestation of the work of grace in human history. As a consequence, revelation can be seen as establishing a "tradition of rationality" whose task it is to clarify that polymorphism; to identify its biases, its invariant structures and its self-transcending dynamics. The Christian tradition, including Thomism, has indeed played a vital role in this process of clarification. For example, in his essay, "The Origins of Christian Realism", Lonergan identifies the ways in which dogmatic developments, culminating in the Councils of Nicea and Chalcedon, clarify the distinctions between the empirical, intellectual and rational levels of intentional consciousness. In a similar vein, Alasdair MacIntyre, in his major study, *Whose Justice? Which Rationality?*, credits Augustine with the "invention? Or discovery" of the concept of "free will", in order to give a Christian account of sin.[48] We could also draw attention to the Augustinian theology of grace and the Augustinian-Thomistic Trinitarian psychological analogies, which provide further examples of how revelation forces clarification of the nature of human consciousness. I shall expand more fully on this issue in the next chapter. However, the above remarks are sufficient indication of how the Christian intellectual tradition can be read in quite a different light from that proposed by Keefe.

At the root, we have a conflict between different accounts of that polymorphic consciousness. Keefe adopts a position based on Augustinian "divine illumination" as the basis for cognitional acts. This is the correlate within consciousness of his position that the eros of the mind is itself a participation in the grace of Christ. Lonergan, on the other hand, sees the same eros as natural, clearly clouded by sin, but capable of restoration and fulfilment by grace. Thus, Lonergan speaks of a natural desire to see God, but only of a supernatural fulfilment of that desire.

Recently, MacIntyre has identified major problems associated with the Augustinian position which Keefe proposes. In particular, he singles out for criticism Augustine's account of divine illumination as the basis for cognitional activity:

Augustine had agreed with Plotinus in denying that the human mind possesses within itself, as part of its own nature, an active principle which effects understanding. Hence all understanding requires divine illumination ... But Augustine also held that due to sin deriving from Adam's fall human beings in a state of nature could not see or benefit from that light. Only by the grace afforded by our redemption is illumination restored. Hence it seems to follow that human being in a state of nature must lack understanding altogether. And plainly, they do not, something which Augustine himself recognizes time and again. So there is an apparent contradiction at the heart of the Augustinian account of knowledge.[49]

MacIntyre sees the Thomistic account of cognition as providing a rationally superior account of knowledge by eliminating this contradiction.

Tekippe comes to a similar conclusion in his response to Keefe:

There is another implication to the collapse of grace into nature, so that grace is of the substance of the human: if a person falls from grace, then he or she also falls from human nature.[50]

At such an extreme, those who are excluded from grace are not only excluded from understanding, as Augustine's position implies; they are also excluded from human nature, from human dignity, perhaps even from human society. The socio-political consequences of such a position would, indeed, be grave. In a world in which millions of people are struggling for the recognition of their human dignity, Keefe's proposal would threaten to cast the unrepentant into the role of non-persons; their very humanity would be called into question. In face of such dire consequences, it is hard to imagine that Keefe has considered all the difficulties inherent in his proposal.

Keefe is surely correct in rejecting the static conceptualist distortion which contaminated the Thomistic tradition, for it did lead to an extrinsicist account of the relationship between grace and nature. He is mistaken, however, in locating Lonergan within that same contaminated tradition. For Lonergan does not stand for the total autonomy of the human mind, even though he affirms its relative autonomy. And it is only *relative* autonomy. The distortions of bias, and the resulting moral impotence, demand grace if the mind is to be free to be itself. Nonetheless, it is a genuine relative *autonomy*. That autonomy can be evidenced by the progress of the natural sciences, developing independent of any reference to God or grace. Even sinful people can do mathematics! Finally, there are no grounds for thinking that Lonergan gives a static account of the relationship between grace and nature. Tekippe suggests, in fact, that Keefe has missed entirely the dynamic and finalistic sweep of Lonergan's approach.[51]

In conclusion, Keefe' criticisms do not effectively engage Lonergan's work, because of such fundamental misinterpretations. He has placed Lonergan within a tradition of static conceptualism that Lonergan himself has clearly rejected. Finally, Keefe's own position, in denying the distinction between grace and nature, puts him at odds with the broad tradition of Catholic theology, in ways which he does not seem to have seriously considered.

In these three articles, by Kelly, Reynolds and Keefe, we discern the development of a position which understands Lonergan as basically conceding too much in the spirit of rationalism. Kelly is concerned that Lonergan should not confuse the workings of the Holy Spirit with the natural eros of the mind. Reynolds goes further, taking Lonergan's position on theological method to be the product of pure philosophy. Finally, Keefe sees Lonergan's whole project as a capitulation to a "cosmological consciousness" which displaces Christianity with a philosophy of transcendence. While Keefe's own final position runs into serious difficulties, the fact that a sympathetic and constructive critic such as Kelly raises problems with Lonergan's work on this point does suggest at least a lacuna in Lonergan's stance.

As I have suggested, the way to bridge this gap is to understand Lonergan's work as a contribution to a tradition of rationality. On the basis of this suggestion, Lonergan is not conceding too much to reason at the expense of revelation, but is contributing to a tradition of reasoning precisely as it is initiated, sustained and prolonged by revelation. To the degree that theology grasps this point, it will have a critical stance from which to eliminate an a-historical understanding of rationality which often lies at the heart of the debate between faith and reason. From this critical distance, it can appropriate a critical method of collaborative rationality congruent with, and emergent from, "faith seeking understanding." By developing the understanding of revelation implicit in Lonergan's writings, particularly in *Method*, we are enabled to give due recognition both to the philosophical and religious foundations of a Catholic theology, in a way which avoids the difficulties raised by the authors above.

From the other side of the debate, a question remains: Is it also able to avoid the alternate problem, raised by Pannenberg, of fideism? I shall consider this question in more detail in a little while. However before we take up that issue I shall consider the questions raised by James P. Mackey, who finds Lonergan's work to be simultaneously both rationalistic and dogmatic.

6.2 Is *Method* Rationalist and Dogmatic?[52] - J. P. Mackey: "Divine Revelation and Lonergan's Transcendental Method in Theology"

In an article entitled "Divine Revelation and Lonergan's Tran-scendental Method in Theology"[53], J. P. Mackey attempts what can only be taken as a wholesale demolition of Lonergan's work. Mackey has in his sights, not only Lonergan's work, but the "recently dead God" of Western Stoic and Middle Platonist thought. Because Mackey explicitly raises questions concerning the nature of revelation and its place in Lonergan's project, such questions must now be heard and, if possible, answered.

At the outset Mackey makes clear, even in the language he uses,[54] that he is not at all sympathetic to Lonergan's work. He offers his arti-cle as an apologia for his own preference for "theologians of hope", as opposed to "transcendentalists of the Lonergan kind."[55] Such tran-scendentalist invoke a particular conception of divinity, namely, "the Logos conception of divinity" which Christian theology has "applied to those events it called special revelation."[56]

Mackey begins his analysis with some comments on the meaning of the word, "transcendental", the use of which he finds imprecise in Lonergan's thought. He identifies two meanings of the term, one which he calls classical, the other more contemporary. The classical meaning refers to truth, as in his phrase "transcendental truth refers to propositions the meaning of which does not change in the course of history." The more contemporary meaning of the term refers to "some creative insight" by which I transcend my present state, existentially and historically.[57] A transcendental method, then, would be one "that allows me to transcend myself until I reach a stage of being or of con-tact with being, a goal which can obviously be called transcendent."[58] He is persuaded, then, that Lonergan is transcendentalist in the first of these senses:

... I shall simply try to document my suspicion that Lonergan is a transcendentalist of the classical type, that his transcendental method could work only during the reign of the classical transcendent God of the West, the self-revealing Logos, and that both method and divinity are now either obsolete or obsolescent.[59]

The first evidence that Mackey produces for this claim is Lonergan's proof for the existence of God, given in *Insight*. This proof rests on the complete intelligibility of reality. Mackey considers that the source of such an argument is a Platonic concept of divinity in whose mind lies an "immutable exemplar plan for this universe."[60] This Mackey rejects, not only on the basis of the irreducible statistical element in the world, but also because of human freedom. In place of the completely intelligibility of being, he argues that it is only "partially intelligible now and will be intelligible, presumably, in the future, because it will be made different."[61] Such a partial intelligibility seems to extend even to God for "God belongs at least as much to the future as he does to the past or present, and the future does not exist; at least not yet."[62] For Mackey, the only option is hope in the face of the radically indeterminacy of the future.

Mackey concedes that Lonergan has made a contribution, especially the ways in which *Insight* "revised our too common notion that knowing is a matter of having ideas and images of object." He singles out Lonergan's emphasis on judgment and decision, on interiorization and self-appropriation, as "of lasting value." However, in the end, Lonergan is dismissed as "too rationalist, too platonic", too much in the mould of classical transcendentalism.[63] Such an approach only works, Mackey claims, if "there is a transcendental truth, in the classical sense, which is partially or in principle available now to man."[64]

At this point, Mackey raises the issue of Lonergan's understanding of revelation, since "special divine revelation is often tacitly assumed to be a source of truth which is transcendental in the classical sense of the term." Mackey accurately observes that there are few explicit references to revelation in Lonergan's writings; hence it is difficult "to decide how Lonergan now thinks about revelation."[65] Yet he proceeds to find clues within *Method* as to how Lonergan conceives it.

Mackey identifies two strands in Lonergan's thought. The first is a propositional understanding of revelation. This is based mainly on a reading of what Lonergan has to say about the functional specialty of doctrine. There, Mackey detects an "implied conviction that special divine revelation resulted in a deposit of truths already complete and inalterable in meaning content."[66] He finds this confirmed in Lonergan's notion that there can be progress in understanding the meaning of defined dogma but not real change in the meaning itself.

However, there is a second strand. Mackey argues that Lonergan identifies a further means of access to the divine, apart from such special revelation:

> When he writes about a prior word of God which pertains to the unmediated experience of the mystery of love and awe, he is clearly not thinking of a propositional revelation at all ... In such contexts he seems perfectly satisfied that this prior act or 'word' of God is the fundamental source of man's religious faith.[67]

Further, Lonergan distinguishes between faith and belief. Beliefs are historically conditioned, and their meaning depends on varying circumstances. Thus Mackey discerns two settings, one of doctrines or truths from God with a final formulated meaning, and another where God acts interiorly resulting in beliefs whose meaning changes "in accord with the changing conditions of place and time." Mackey asks whether these are complementary or contradictory settings, only to conclude that Lonergan "is not clear on this."[68] The problem, as Mackey understands it, lies mainly in Lonergan's adherence to the first of these settings:

> It is a simple and inescapable fact of theology that people who use revelation as a primary category, people who start with, or live with, the conviction that God revealed former mysteries, must sooner of later admit that they deal in truth or truths which are the gift of God rather than the discovery of man ... Once that is the case, we late-comers are dealing with truth or meaning which can be quarried in history but not changed by history; we are dealing with transcendental truth in the classical sense.[69]

Once this is admitted then the expression of such truth must be both authoritarian and dogmatic. Mackey's solution to this problem is to demote revelation from its status as a primary theological category. He writes:

> The only way to solve this problem is to remove revelation from its role as the fundamental category of theology; to make it instead a secondary category to the category of faith, which is the basic datum

of theology ... Faith, not revelation is the fundamental category for theology, and it allows full scope to human freedom and creativity in this radically historical existence.[70]

Mackey concludes his analysis with the assertion that it is "impossible to have a critically established transcendental method unless there is a transcendental truth after the classical manner", and he clearly reject this as an option.[71] He finds Lonergan's attempt to do so as "brazen naiveté", and his method little more than "hearty advice" to "use your head and do the best you can with what you have."[72]

In response, we can concede that Lonergan, at least in his later writings, might well have agreed with the final conclusion that Mackey draws. For faith, defined as a "knowledge born of religious love", is a more fundamental category than revelation in Lonergan's later writings. For that reason, he says far more about faith, religious experience and conversion than he does about revelation. Even though Mackey draws attention to the comparative meagre references to revelation in Lonergan's work, he still places him amongst theologians for whom revelation is a primary category.

I have already traced the shift in Lonergan's uses of the category of revelation in Chapter 2 and 3 of this thesis. Given such an analysis, some of Mackey's comments may hold for Lonergan's earlier writings, but not for his later writings, *Method* included. As McDermott has noted, the whole tone of Lonergan's work, involving as it does an increasing "turn to the subject", makes it more difficult to give an account of historical revelation.[73]

On the other hand, Lonergan would certainly be of one mind with Mackey inasmuch as both assert that the key issues facing contemporary theology is that of the "radical historicity" of human existence. Because of the challenge posed by historical studies, Lonergan saw his whole methodological enterprise as one of integrating those studies into the theological project. Now Mackey could claim that Lonergan's approach fails, but he could hardly say that Lonergan has ignored the problems in question. Lonergan's failure, according to Mackey, is that he has attempted to maintain a normativity to revelation in his notion of dogma. Yet the rejection of any such normativity would require a radical, if not revolutionary, shift in Christianity's self-understanding. Could the Church continue, for example, to maintain the unique and universal saving significance of Jesus Christ?

Regrettably, Mackey's comments are not based on a careful reading of Lonergan's writing. The absence of any sympathetic, or
systematic, references to the text under consideration is brought home
by the fact that his first reference to *Method*, the book Mackey is analysing, is not given until the seventh page of his article.

Mackey's handling of the term "transcendental" is unfortunately
typical of the unsympathetic treatment he accords his adversary. He
claims that Lonergan's use of the term reveals a "lack of precision in
the man's thought." He goes on to give two meanings for the term, the
"classical", and the "contemporary" we noted above. Yet neither of
the meanings Mackey gives corresponds to standard philosophical
definitions of the terms, either the "classical" Scholastic usage, or the
more "contemporary" Kantian usage. This is especially unusual since
Lonergan explicitly refers to both in the text of *Method*.[74] Lonergan is
well aware of both these meanings of the terms, and he uses the term
"transcendental" in relation to them both. The "lack of precision" in
question here is not entirely a problem with Lonergan. It appears as
much to be a question of Mackey's own lack of awareness of the
philosophical tradition of transcendental Thomism within which Lonergan is writing.

But beyond these issues of philosophical terminology, a more
precise analysis of Mackey's own position might draw attention to a
tension present in his appraisal of Lonergan's work. Mackey has
found that Lonergan's "emphasis on judgment" is of "lasting value",
while at the same time he rejects Lonergan's stance on doctrine. This
must cause problems for Mackey: for these two aspects of Lonergan's
work, on judgments and on doctrines, stand in direct correlation. For
Lonergan, judgments involve a grasp of the "virtually unconditioned";
they seek to assert what is, what is true, what is real. With this
Mackey seems to agree. Yet, for Lonergan, a doctrine is a *judgment* of
religious fact or value. It is a knowledge born of religious love. However, Mackey can find no place for such judgments.

The problem is compounded when Mackey himself makes an
implicit claim to such a "knowledge." He singles out the importance
of Jesus – "I am the inheritor of Jesus' kind of faith and of his kind of
life-style." What is the significance of such a claim if not a judgment
on the religious value of the person of Jesus? Mackey is apparently
allowed to make such a judgment, yet the Christian community, as a
whole, is not allowed to make it, for fear of being authoritarian or
dogmatic. Thus, while Mackey sees Lonergan's contribution on judg-

ment as of "lasting value", it is not clear that he fully grasps what its value is when the act of judgment refers to religious meanings and values. Mackey's failure to grasp the significance of Lonergan's position on judgment is further illustrated by Mackey's treatment of being and reality. While Mackey does not seem to object to Lonergan's identification of reality with being, he does object to Lonergan's demand for the complete intelligibility of being:

> So we cannot say that being is completely intelligible. It is partially intelligible now and will be intelligible, presumably in the future, because it will be made different.[75]

For Lonergan such a stance is counter-positional, that is, intrinsically contradictory. It makes of being and reality a subdivision of the 'already-out-there-now'. It seeks to contain being and reality within space and time, ignoring the fact that both space and time exist and are real. Given such a stance, it is little wonder that Mackey is drawn to compromise divine transcendence when he claims that,

> ... one might say that God belongs at least as much to the future as he does to the past or the present, and the future does not exist; at least not yet.[76]

In adopting this position, Mackey is seeking to keep a place for human freedom and creativity. We are not totally subjected to some "pre-determined" plan. Otherwise history "can only be conformity, not real creativity."[77] Yet his equating God's truth, or "transcendent truth", with some type of "plan", which would squash real human freedom, leads him to reject the possibility of such truth, and hence leads him to compromise divine transcendence.

Admittedly, as with any attempt to give a coherent account of divine transcendence and human freedom, theology faces a most profound problem. It has surfaced in a particularly daunting form in the Banezian and Molonist debates initiated at the end of the sixteenth century. Lonergan addressed the issue in his doctoral work on *gratia operans* in the writings of Thomas Aquinas, published as *Grace and Freedom*. He went on to explore the question systematically in Chapter 19 of *Insight*. There he develops his own distinctive position in order to coherently maintain both divine transcendence and the reality of human freedom.[78] Mackey, on the other hand, because of his position on being and reality, compromises the claims of divine transcendence, in order to maintain the reality of human freedom. One is set against the other.

At its root, Mackey's stance is a denial of the complete intelligibility of reality. Some may judge that this is a high price to pay in the name of human freedom. To retreat from the complete intelligibility of reality is to entertain the possibility that reality is partially unintelligible. To open such a doorway to the unintelligible is to invite the entrance of every gnostic New Age belief, however irrational. Quickly one can find oneself in a situation where Christianity is seen as simply another irrational choice in a market place of irrational choices. Though Mackey may choose to be "the inheritor of Jesus' kind of faith", another may equally choose faith in, say, New Age crystals. When there is no demand for "complete intelligibility", what is to prevent a progressive capitulation to irrationality? It is difficult to find in Mackey any answer to such a question.

Nonetheless, the special value of Mackey's investigation lies in the way he explicates a range of questions on the manner in which Lonergan holds together the inner and outer words of God's love. It is this interaction between the inner world of grace and the outer word of God's entry into history which constitutes the historical process of revelation. That Lonergan is holding a taut balance between these two poles is evidenced by the diverse ways in which his position can be interpreted in diametrically opposed manners. Thus while Kelly, Reynolds and Keefe understand Lonergan's project as tending towards the rationalistic, Mackey claims to have found not only rationalistic but also dogmatic tendencies. I hope the above analysis has highlighted the inadequacy of Mackey's argument on this point. I shall now consider the criticism which judges Lonergan's work to be overly dogmatic or fideistic.

6.3 Is *Method* affectively fideist?

Not only Pannenberg, but a number of critics have suggested that Lonergan's reliance on conversion, as the keystone of his theological method, is ultimately a capitulation to a kind of subjectivism that is necessarily dogmatic and fideist in character. Doran refers to "some of Lonergan's most devoted students" who "were not prepared for his talk of conversion" and saw *Method* as a "capitulation of a rigorous critical intellectualism to the softheadedness of religious piety."[79] Further, Michael Dummett characterises Lonergan's two phases of theology, one positive, the other normative as: "first reason with no acknowledgment of faith, then faith, with no appeal to reason."[80] These concerns raise a serious challenge to Lonergan's whole project and one that needs to be faced head on. Conversion is central to that project. It involves a movement from one horizon to another, dialectically opposed, horizon. The challenge that must be faced is: How can such a movement be justified? Surely not on the basis on the initial horizon, for it is precisely this horizon which is being negated in the conversion? Does not such an account of conversion mean that each horizon has its own self-enclosed rationality, from which position other horizons appear irrational? Pannenberg pinpoints the problem, as I noted before:

> One wonders how people who are imprisoned in such different horizons could communicate at all. It is certainly true that in many cases communication is extremely difficult. But Lonergan's theory of horizons would confine individuals to separate worlds except for some decision of conversion, which could scarcely be called rational any longer, because it lacks the possibility of motivation within a coherent horizon.[81]

Hence the question must be posed: Does not such subjectivism result in the total relativism that Lonergan so strongly rejects? In response to such a question, there are a number of points to be emphasised.

First, we must consider the process of conversion. Conversion is basically an apprehension of values which previous to conversion were not apprehended or were even resented. Such an apprehension is a falling-in-love, as both a receptive apprehension of, and active commitment to, values beyond my present grasp. In religious conversion, there is an other-worldly falling in love, a love without restriction. According to Lonergan, no extrinsic justification for such an unrestricted love is needed. It is self-justifying: ."..there is no need to justify critically the charity described by St Paul in the thirteenth chapter of his first epistle to the Corinthians."[82]

On the other hand:

> there is always a great need to eye very critically any religious individual or group and to discern beyond the real charity which may

well be granted the various types of bias that may distort or block
their exercise of it.[83]

To this end Lonergan has catalogued the different forms of dramatic, individual, group and general bias. Given such a hermeneutical
suspicion of distorted subjectivity, his position cannot be accused of a
naive subjectivism.

Still, it must be acknowledged that for Lonergan objectivity cannot be separated from subjectivity: "Genuine objectivity is the fruit of
authentic subjectivity." Any other meaning of the term "objectivity" is
merely illusion.[84] Conversion is ultimately conversion to authenticity;
and only authentic subjects, in the final analysis, can judge objectively
the genuineness of their own conversion. Just as Aristotle's account of
virtue requires the existence of a virtuous person as a reference point,
so too Lonergan's account presupposes the existence of authentic subjects as a reference point.

Secondly, Lonergan's account of values includes reference to an
objective and hierarchical scale of values. He distinguishes, in
ascending order, vital, social, cultural, personal and religious values.
He claims that this scale is both transcultural and normative. Such a
claim is based on the structural isomorphism between the scale of
values and the different levels of intentional consciousness. For
example, vital values correlate with empirical consciousness, social
values correlate with intellectual consciousness, and so on. Because
he has identified invariant structures in human consciousness which
are normative and transcultural, he can carry his analysis further into
moral consciousness, and so account for an objective scale of values
which likewise transcends any one culture.[85]

Now, the scale of values is important to the question of objectivity
because it specifies the relative relationship between different types of
values, the normativity of these relationships and the importance of the
overall integrity of the scale. True, such a scale is merely heuristic. It
does not specify, for example, what cultural values one should hold.
However, the objective structure can be a framework of reference in
discerning the genuineness of any conversion. On the other hand, for
there to be anything more than a notional apprehension of the scale of
values, a converted subjectivity must come into play as the touchstone
of discernment. Because, radically, authenticity is self-critical and
self-validating, there is no Archimedean point outside authenticity
itself by which to judge and discern.

Thirdly, a distinction must be made between the implicit rationality of the subject and the explicitly formulated horizon of the subject. To arrive at the stage of dialectically opposed horizons, of the type which concern Pannenberg, requires a degree of explicit formulation which goes beyond the undifferentiated horizon of a common sense world view. It requires some degree of explicit formulation on questions of knowing, objectivity and reality, on values and transcendent being. Yet, as Lonergan has repeatedly argued, such explicit formulation can be at marked variance with the implicit rationality of the subject propounding a position. For example, in the case of David Hume, Lonergan notes:

> The intelligence and reasonableness of Hume's criticizing were obviously quite different from the knowledge he so successfully criticized.[86]

Employing the technique of retortion, typical of transcendental philosophy, Lonergan contrasts the performance of the subject's own normative operations with the theoretical account of those operations.[87]

Now, while the new converted horizon may not be justifiable from within the old horizon, it is not as if the experiences which are being interpreted are located beyond the subject involved. As a subject, I experience myself asking and answering questions, coming to judgments of truth and falsehood, and making commitments for or against certain values. Inasmuch as I am present to myself in such experiences, the rationality of the new horizon can be drawn from my own experiences. To that extent, both the pre-conversion and the post-conversion horizons share a common field of data which require intelligent interpretation, reasonable judgment and existential commitment.

Perhaps, then, the movement from one horizon to the new horizon can be justified by "appeal to the facts of the matter"? Yet, what are the "facts"? Are they found simply by appealing to such common experiences? Or are they to be found in the meaning of those experiences as can be reasonably judged to be the case on the basis of evidence. For these latter to be "the facts", one must already be within the horizon of an intellectually converted subject. Without intellectual conversion, the term "facts" denotes quite different things to different subjects. As Lonergan comments:

Empiricism, idealism, and realism name three totally different horizons with no common identical objects. An idealist never means
what an empiricist means, and a realist never means what either of
them means.[88]

"Fact" is certainly one of those terms whose meaning differs
within different horizons, as we saw in the case of Pannenberg and his
treatment of the "facts" of history.[89] Once again we see that, outside of
authenticity, there is no point from which authenticity can be judged.

When an account, such as Lonergan's, takes its stand on conversion and authenticity, the question is inevitable: "Who is the authentic
subject?" As McDermott has pointed out, we can no longer "point,
like Aristotle, to the good man as the norm of virtue without identifying him."[90] As I have argued in Chapter 4, Lonergan's position on
authenticity has the structure of what Rahner would call a "searching
Christology." Once the discussion of authenticity is moved out of an
abstract a-historical context, it takes on an historical urgency. The
possibility arises that true rationality can only be sustained in historical
relationship to genuinely authentic subjects, who incarnate divine
meaning's entry into human history. Thus, the discussion inevitably
centres on the issue of revelation and a tradition of rationality which it
establishes.

Finally, the question of fideism and the problems associated with
it cannot be addressed outside of a context which takes into account
the tradition of rational inquiry to which Lonergan belongs. Our
argument to this point is that revelation establishes its own tradition of
rationality. I would contend that, historically speaking, revelation has
inspired the emergence of critical realism and the transcendental
method serving it. Further, we can appreciate the emergence of critical realism, and its associated method, as part of the redemptive action
of God in human history. Though this tradition has emerged under the
influence of revelation, it can be rationally justified.

6.4 Rational superiority – Alasdair MacIntyre and the "turn to the subject"

However, there are problems associated with such a claim. Now,
the connections between faith, tradition and rationality have been a
constant concern of Alasdair MacIntyre, and his writings have done
much to clarify the claims to rationality of the Christian faith tradi-

tion.[91] Yet, a claim regarding the rational justifiability of this tradition is necessary if Lonergan's work is to address the problem of fideism. The way in which revelation elicits the emergence of something like Lonergan's transcendental method will be more fully illustrated in the next chapter. For the moment, I shall simply indicate how Lonergan's work marks a further stage in a process of a developing tradition of rationality which takes revelation as its starting point. Such a point of view relies not on an abstract notion of rationality. For it depends on an historical notion, wherein a tradition must establish its own rational integrity against contending claims and traditions.

In large measure, MacIntyre is an ally in this contention. He has argued for the rational superiority of the Thomistic synthesis of Augustinian theology, based on revelation, and Aristotelian philosophy over these two component parts. What, then, does MacIntyre mean by "rational superiority"? He answers as follows:

> Just as a later stage within [a] tradition is held to be superior to an earlier stage only if and insofar as it is able to transcend the limitations and failures of that earlier stage, limitations and failures by the standards of rationality of that earlier stage itself, so the rational superiority of [a] tradition to rival traditions is held to reside in its capacity not only for identifying and characterizing the limitations and failures of that rival tradition as judged by that rival tradition's own standards, limitations and failures which that rival tradition itself lacks the resources to explain or understand, but also for the explaining and understanding of those limitations and failures in some tolerably precise way.[92]

Thus, MacIntyre would see Aquinas' synthesis of Augustine and Aristotle as a high point in the emerging tradition of rationality initiated by revelation.[93]

MacIntyre identifies problems in both Augustinianism and Aristotelianism which Aquinas overcomes with his own synthesis of the two. The problem for Augustine, as I noted above, is his account of divine illumination as necessary for any cognitional event. Aristotle had overcome this difficulty with his account of the immanent operations of the human intellect. On the other hand, Aristotle's failure consists in his inability to give an account of the human experience of moral impotence, as for example, Paul's Letter to the Romans describes it. Augustine overcomes this difficulty with the concept of will, a concept not part of Aristotle's account of moral action.[94]

Aquinas' new synthesis of these two competing tradition is then rationally superior to either in that it can recognise, explain and overcome the limitations and failures of these two rival traditions.

MacIntyre goes further. He argues that a genuine Thomistic tradition is still rationally superior to the main rival versions of moral enquiry which dominate moral discourse at present. These he identifies as "encyclopedia", grounded in Enlightenment rationalism, and "genealogy", grounded in Nietzschian suspicion.

I cannot offer here a wholesale rehearsal of MacIntyre's arguments, as found in his works, *Whose Justice? Which Rationality?* and *Three Rival Versions of Moral Enquiry*. Still, we can identify limitations in his own stance which can be overcome only by a turn to the subject, a turn to that interiority which lies at the foundation of Lonergan's transcendental method.

Ostensibly, MacIntyre is quite hostile to the modern "turn to the subject." As he puts it, with characteristic incisiveness:

> Suppose, then, that someone aspired to adjudicate between Augustinian and Aristotelian claims by appealing away from their theoretical conceptualization to how things *in fact* are in the human *psyche*. Any such appeal would have to present empirical data. Yet at the level at which such data are characterizable in a way that makes them independent of and neutral between schemes as conceptually rich and organized as the Aristotelian and the Augustinian ... the data are too meagre and underdetermine any characterization at the required level. They are no more than matter still to be given form by characterization at a higher, more theoretical level. And if the data are themselves presented as more fully and richly characterized, in a way which makes them relevant to the disputes between Augustinians and Aristotelians, then some conclusion as to where the truth lies in those disputes will already have been presupposed by the way in which the data have been conceptualized.[95]

It would seem, then, that for MacIntyre human consciousness is to remain an unknown quantity, a kind of black box which cannot be understood in terms of our own experience. Any understanding of consciousness must always be subject to a conceptualisation which arises independent of that experience. But such a stance creates problems which MacIntyre is unable to solve within the tradition he seeks to develop.

In Chapter IX of *Whose Justice? Which Rationality?*, MacIntyre dwells on one of the main contributions of Augustine to our understanding of the moral life and moral enquiry. It is the concept of "will." He refers to this as "Augustine's – invention? Or discovery?"[96] How, then, is one to determine whether Augustine's concept of will is a discovery, or an invention? On MacIntyre's own argument it is not possible to appeal to the data of consciousness: "the data are too meagre." One possible response is to minimise the significance of the issue by answering, "It doesn't really matter, as long as it produces a richer conceptualisation which is rationally superior to what went before." However, MacIntyre himself closes off such an option when he adopts a Thomistic account of truth based on correspondence. He writes:

> Hence in judging of truth and falsity there is always some ineliminable reference beyond the scheme within which those judgments are made and beyond the criteria which provide the warrants for assertibility within that scheme. Truth cannot be identified with, or collapsed into warranted assertibility. And a conception of *what is* which is more or other than a conception of *what appears to be the case in the light of the most fundamental criteria governing assertibility within any particular scheme* is correspondingly required, that is, a metaphysics of being, of *esse*, over and above whatever can be said about particular *entia* in the light of particular concepts.[97]

If Augustine's concept of will is nothing more than a clever invention, then we have nothing more than an assertion warranted simply within the scheme he creates. It has its meaning within the scheme but it cannot demand our assent apart from it. If, however, his concept of will is to be ranked as a discovery, then it has a point of "reference beyond the scheme ... and beyond the criteria which provide the warrants for assertibility within that scheme." It must survive on its own evidence whatever the fate of the Augustinian scheme. Yet how can we move beyond warranted assertibility to the question of truth without attending to the data of consciousness?

The only way through such a dilemma, I would argue, is to follow Lonergan with the "turn to the subject." For Lonergan, consciousness is a reality which is intelligible, and intelligible on its own terms, not simply in terms of a conceptual scheme developed in a manner extrinsic to it. Such an understanding is not immediate, after the manner of some Cartesian inspection of consciousness. Rather, it is a slow and painstaking enquiry operating on particular data – the polymorphism of human consciousness – and seeking to clarify such. Lonergan understands his own achievement as the outcome of generations of thinkers who have sought to clarify this one polymorphic fact. Here, Lonergan claims continuity with the work of Aquinas. He develops a metaphysics which is largely congruent with that of his mentor. What is more, he claims to find evidence that Aquinas himself appealed to the data of consciousness.[98] In terms of historical development, Lonergan's scheme can be thought of as rationally superior to that of Aquinas in this respect: it not only encompasses the gains of Aquinas over Augustine and Aristotle, but includes a systematic account of interiority which grounds Thomistic metaphysics. It also accounts for the emergence of modern science in a way which classical Thomism was not called to do; and, most of all, it has integrated the demands of historical studies into theological method. Finally, it allows us to address problems which MacIntyre's approach to the Thomistic tradition would seem to rule out of court.

From this perspective the "turn to the subject" is not a retreat into subjectivism and fideism, as feared by Pannenberg. Nor is it a problem with no solution, as proposed by MacIntyre. Rather, it may be seen as a new development in a continuing tradition of rationality initiated, sustained and prolonged by Christian revelation. In the terminology of *Method*, it represents the emergence and consolidation of a new, third stage of meaning.

6.5 Conclusion

The purpose of this chapter has been to examine the variety of questions that a number of critics have expressed regarding Lonergan's achievement. Lonergan has been criticised from both extremes: on the one hand, the charge of rationalism, on the other, fideism. In addressing these criticisms, I have attempted to show how revelation establishes a tradition of rationality, within which Lonergan's own work could located. This was the key to addressing both forms of criticism.

Certainly, this argument has structural features similar to that given by MacIntyre criticism of the tradition of "encyclopedia" and "genealogy" in the field of moral enquiry.[99] Those who see in Lonergan's position as excessively rationalistic are suspicious of the claims of an autonomous reason. Hence, they seek to deconstruct the hubris of the mind, in favour of the startling and unexpected demands of divine revelation. Conversely, those who judge his position as excessively fideist are suspicious of the claims of a dogmatic and authoritarian religious tradition. They appeal to a universal reason, an ahistorical conception of reason born of Enlightenment prejudice against tradition. In both cases, the solution proposed is to grasp Lonergan's method as part of a tradition of rationality initiated, sustained and prolonged by revelation itself. Inasmuch as it is initiated, sustained and prolonged by *revelation*, it is not rationalist. Inasmuch as it is a tradition of *rationality*, it is not fideist, so long as it continues to grow and develop, proving itself rationally superior to its alternatives. While MacIntyre argues that the Thomistic tradition of enquiry is superior to its main alternatives, I have attempted to give a brief outline as to why Lonergan's stance, based on a turn to the subject, may be considered a development of, and indeed rationally superior to, that same Thomistic tradition, at least as MacIntyre grasps it.

The final issue then is to what extent the tradition of rationality initiated by revelation demands the turn to the subject. This is the issue which I shall seek to illustrate in the next chapter.

---

1. A. Kelly, "Is Lonergan's *Method* Adequate to Christian Mystery", *The Thomist*, 39/3 (1975), 437-470.
2. A. Kelly, "Is *Method* Adequate", 447.
3. Kelly, "Is *Method* Adequate?", 440.
4. Kelly, "Is *Method* Adequate?", 444.
5. Kelly, "Is *Method* Adequate?", 466, n.42, quoting from Hans Urs von Balthasar, *Love Alone: The Way of Revelation* (London: Burns & Oates, 1968), 43.
6. Lonergan, *Method*, 119.
7. Kelly, "Is *Method* Adequate?", 451.
8. Kelly, "Is *Method* Adequate?", 452.
9. Kelly, "Is *Method* Adequate?", 455.
10. Kelly, "Is *Method* Adequate?", 463.
11. Kelly, "Is *Method* Adequate?", 464.
12. Kelly, "Is *Method* Adequate?", 465.
13. Kelly, "Is *Method* Adequate?", 467.
14. Kelly, "Is *Method* Adequate?", 468.
15. Kelly, "Is *Method* Adequate?", 469.

16. T. Reynolds, "Method Divorced from Content in Theology: An Assessment of Lonergan's *Method in Theology*", *The Thomist*, 55/2 (1991), 245-269.

17. Reynolds, "Method Divorced from Content", 264.

18. Reynolds, "Method Divorced from Content", 264-5.

19. Reynolds, "Method Divorced from Content", 267.

20. Reynolds, "Method Divorced from Content", 268.

21. Doran's major studies are *Subject and Psyche: Ricoeur, Jung, and the Search for Foundations* (Lanham: University Press of America, 1980), *Psychic Conversion and Theological Foundations: Towards a Reorientation of the Human Sciences* (Chico; Scholars Press, 1981) and *Theology and the Dialectics of History* (Toronto: University of Toronto Press, 1990).

22. See, for example, *Theology*, where Doran refers to the "disclosive significance and transformative function of the soteriological differentiation of consciousness that is coincident with Christian conversion", 175.

23. See, for example, Doran, *Psychic Conversion*, especially Chapter 5, Section 4, "Toward a Transcendental Aesthetic", and *Theology*, Chapter 6, Section 6, "Depth Psychology and the Beautiful".

24. See, for example, *Theology*, Chapter 4, where Doran exploits the two-fold movement of healing and creating with regard to the scale of values.

25. Reynolds, "Method Divorced from Content", 267.

26. Reynolds, "Method Divorced from Content", 265.

27. Indeed it would be asking too much to find the answers in the restricted format allowed in journal articles of this type.

28. Lonergan, *Method*, 243.

29. Lonergan, *Method*, 298ff.

30. The paper was delivered as the 17th Annual Robert Cardinal Bellarmine Lecture at St Louis University School of Divinity, Sept. 27, 1972 and appeared in print in *Theology Digest*, 20 (1972), 292-305.

31. Doran, *Theology*, 165.

32. Doran, *Theology*, 166.

33. Lonergan, *Method*, 243.

34. D. Keefe, "A Methodological Critique of Lonergan's Theological Method", *The Thomist*, 50/1 (1986), 28-65.

35. Keefe, "A Methodological Critique", 44.

36. Keefe, "A Methodological Critique", 45.

37. Keefe, "A Methodological Critique", 55.

38. Keefe, "A Methodological Critique", 35.

39. Keefe, "A Methodological Critique", 39.

40. Keefe, "A Methodological Critique", 42.

41. See, for example, Lonergan, "The Natural Desire to See God", *Collection*, 84-95.

42. I have argued this position more fully in Chapter 4 of this thesis. You could say that Rahner's position on grace is halfway between Lonergan's and Keefe's.

43. T. Tekippe, "A Response to Donald Keefe on Lonergan", *The Thomist*, 52/1 (1988), 94.

44. What Keefe refers to as "cosmological consciousness" is quite different from the way in which the same term is used in the writings of Robert Doran. Keefe's cosmological consciousness corresponds more to Doran's notion of anthropological consciousness, cf. Doran, *Theology*, 502.

45. Keefe, "A Methodological Critique", 41.

46. Such an accusation has been levelled, for example, at Rahner, and Keefe seems to be implying the same of Lonergan. I can agree, however, that there are not as many references to the problems of moral impotence and bias in *Method* as in *Insight*.

47. Cf. Lonergan, *Insight*, 692.

48. A. MacIntyre, *Whose Justice? Which Rationality*, (Notre Dame; Univ. of Notre Dame, 1988), 156.

49. A. MacIntyre, *Three Rival Versions: Encyclopedia, Genealogy and Tradition* (Notre Dame: Univ. of Notre Dame Press, 1990), 100-101.

50. Tekippe, "A Response to Donald Keefe", 94.

51. Tekippe, "A Response to Donald Keefe", 92.

52. See also J. O'Leary, "The Hermeneutics of Dogmatism", *Irish Theological Quarterly*, 47/2 (1980), 96-118, who sees Lonergan as both rationalist and dogmatic.

53. J.P. Mackey, "Divine Revelation and Lonergan's Transcendental Method", *Irish Theological Quarterly*, January, 40/1 (1973), 3-19, also in *Looking at Lonergan's Method*, Corcoran (ed), 144-163. I shall refer to the version in the *Irish Theological Quarterly*.

54. Mackey speaks of Lonergan's "disciples" and "catechumens", of prestigious congresses, and of the "apocalyptic tone of the expectation" surrounding the publication of *Method*. This is not the language of detached scholarship.

55. Mackey, "Divine Revelation", 3.

56. Mackey, "Divine Revelation", 4.

57. Mackey, "Divine Revelation", 4.

58. Mackey, "Divine Revelation", 5.

59. Mackey, "Divine Revelation", 6.

60. Mackey, "Divine Revelation", 6.

61. Mackey, "Divine Revelation", 7.

62. Mackey, "Divine Revelation", 8.

63. Mackey, "Divine Revelation", 8.

64. Mackey, "Divine Revelation", 9.

65. Mackey, "Divine Revelation", 10.

66. Mackey, "Divine Revelation", 11.
67. Mackey, "Divine Revelation", 12.
68. Mackey, "Divine Revelation", 13.
69. Mackey, "Divine Revelation", 15.
70. Mackey, "Divine Revelation", 17-18.
71. Mackey, "Divine Revelation", 18.
72. Mackey, "Divine Revelation", 19.
73. McDermott, "Tensions", 121ff.
74. Cf. Lonergan, *Method*, 13-4, n.4.
75. Mackey, "Divine Revelation", 7.
76. Mackey, "Divine Revelation", 8.
77. Mackey, "Divine Revelation", 16.
78. For a full and detailed account of Lonergan's work on these questions, see, J.M. Stebbins, *The Divine Initiative: Grace, World Order, and Human Freedom in the Early Writings of Bernard Lonergan* (Toronto: University of Toronto Press, 1995).
79. Doran, *Theology*, 166. Doran does not identify anyone by name, but internal evidence suggests one person he has in mind is David Tracy.
80. M. Dummett, "Theology and Reason", *New Blackfriars*, 69/816, 242.
81. W. Pannenberg, "History and Meaning in Bernard Lonergan's Approach to Theological Method", in *Looking at Lonergan's Method*, Corcoran (ed), 97.
82. Lonergan, *Method*, 284.
83. Lonergan, *Method*, 284.
84. Lonegan, *Method*, 292.
85. The work of Robert Doran has done much to explicate the significance of the scale of values, particularly in his work, *Theology* , 93ff.
86. Lonergan, *Insight*, 389.
87. On the method of retortion, see J. Donceel, *The Searching Mind* (Notre Dame: Univ. of Notre Dame Press, 1979), 11-12, and B. Meyer, *Reality and Illusion in New Testament Scholarship* (Collegeville: Glazier, 1994), 40ff.
88. Lonergan, *Method*, 239. There is a tension even in this quote since empiricist, idealist and realist all mean something different by the term "object". For example, for the empiricist an object is intended in the act of pointing, an already-out-there-now body of extroverted consciousness, while for the realist it is something intended in questions and known in correct answers.
89. Cf. Chapter 4, Section 2, of this thesis.
90. McDermott, "Tensions", 129, n.81.
91. See, in particular, A. MacIntyre, *Whose Justice? Which Rationality?* (Notre Dame: University of Notre Dame Press, 1988), though the same themes are developed in *After Virtue, a Study in Moral Theory*, 2nd Edition (Notre Dame: University of Notre Dame Press, 1984) and *Three Rival Version of*

Moral Enquiry: Encyclopedia, Genealogy and Tradition (Notre Dame: University of Notre Dame Press, 1990).

92. MacIntyre, *Three Rival Versions*, 180-1.

93. I should note that MacIntyre, being concerned primarily with moral consciousness, sees Augustinianism as representative of a moral tradition influenced by revelation. By way of contrast, Lonergan's work, because he focuses on cognitional issues, understands the emergent realism of Aristotle as also something sustained and developed by revelation.

94. On Aristotle's position, see MacIntyre, *Whose Justice? Which Rationality?*, 140: "It follows that when the premises have been affirmed, if they are true and the inference is valid and the agent is fully rational, then the premises must afford sufficient reasons for the immediate performance of the action. There is no logical space for something else to intervene: a decision, for example".

95. MacIntyre, *Three Rival Versions*, 111-2.

96. MacIntyre, *Whose Justice? Which Rationality?*, 156. He states: "the authors of classical antiquity prior to Augustine lacked any vocabulary and for the most part any conception of the will". Note, however, MacIntyre's own latent conceptualism. Does Augustine discover a "concept" of the will, or does he discover "the will" itself?

97. MacIntyre, *Three Rival Versions*, 122.

98. Cf. Lonergan, *Verbum*, 76-7, where Lonergan argues that the "Aristotelian and Thomist programme ... is a process of introspection that discovers the act of insight into phantasm and the definition as an expression of the insight, that almost catches intellect in its forward movement towards defining and its backward reference to sense for the concrete realization of the defined". What is significant for this thesis is that *Verbum* is a study of Aquinas' Trinitarian psychological analogy. Thus revelation is eliciting profound philosophical considerations.

99. Cf. MacIntyre's argument as expounded in *Three Rival Versions*, particularly in Chapter 8 and 9.

CHAPTER SEVEN: REVELATION AND CULTURE

In Chapter 4, I raised the question of the relationship between revelation, history and culture. In Chapter 5, I clarified the nature of the relationship by contrasting Lonergan's position with that of Pannenberg (on history) and Lindbeck (on culture). In Chapter 6, the question was further explored by considering Lonergan's work as a contribution to an ongoing tradition of rationality, which allowed me to respond to criticisms of his project. The question is particularly significant for this thesis because the relationship between revelation, history and culture is a key distinguishing feature of Lonergan's account of revelation. It arises from the constitutive role he gives to judgment in the cognitional process. The role of judgment leads to a focus on the relationship between history, culture and doctrines, which are all elements of his method corresponding to the cognitional activity of judgment. In this chapter I would like to explore this relationship more fully with specific reference to key areas of Trinitarian and Christological doctrine.

These areas are, of course, not chosen at random. Most of Lonergan's direct theological work, as opposed to his methodological interests, was concerned with Christological and Trinitarian questions. Here I shall be drawing on some of this material to explore the relationship between revelation and human culture. Indeed, the argument is that there is an intrinsic connection between these theological topics with their doctrinal basis and the relationship of revelation to Lonergan's transcendental method.

As I have already concluded in Chapter 4, one function of revelation is to establish a "tradition of rationality." In this chapter I illustrate the suggestion that this tradition of rationality, as established by revelation, demands the emergence of a "turn to the subject." It demands the emergence of something like Lonergan's transcendental method for its own intellectual integrity, and to bring about the reversal of the longer cycle of decline operative in human history. I am intending to illustrate three points:

i) the historical involvement of Christian doctrine in the turn to the subject;

ii) the open-ended and developing nature of the tradition of rationality initiated by revelation;

and

iii) the significance of the issues raised by this ongoing tradition in reversing the longer cycle of decline.

By attempting to link the development of transcendental method to an unfolding "tradition of rationality" initiated by the very events of revelation, I will further demonstrate that criticisms of Lonergan's method as lacking a basis in revelation are ill-founded, given the larger context of his methodological project.

To illustrate these points I propose three examples in which revelation has influenced Lonergan's methodological project to make it part of a larger "tradition of rationality."

7.1 Revelation and Critical Realism

The first deals with the relationship between the Trinitarian notion of substance and the emergence of critical realism.

Lonergan has written extensively on the relationship between the doctrinal development leading up to the Council of Nicea and the emergence of critical realism as a philosophical position. By critical realism Lonergan means the philosophical position, grounded in an analysis of interiority, that reality is known in objective judgments. He distinguishes critical realism from various forms of naive realism where reality is considered to be grasped in some prior act of extroverted consciousness, such as looking. In Part One of *De Deo Trino*, published in English as *The Way to Nicea*, he establishes at length a relationship between doctrinal development and critical realism, and develops this theme further in the essay, "The Origins of Christian

Realism." This latter essay is the most convenient reference for our present purposes.

The revelation of the Trinity is the central event of Christian history, and is acknowledged as a central doctrine of Christian faith. It encompasses the mystery of the Father sending his Son and the Spirit into our human world of meaning, so as to draw us to Him through the outer Word, incarnate in Jesus Christ, and the inner movement of the Spirit. It is not surprising that the earliest controversies within the Christian community revolved around the Trinity and the divine nature, particularly in regard to the relationship between Father and Son. Lonergan draws attention to questions of a philosophical nature which are usually ignored by the many historians and theologians who have explored the emergence of this doctrine. For Lonergan, these philosophical issues are crucial to the understanding of what is happening, of "what is moving forward", in the Christian community as it progresses towards the doctrinal definition of Nicea.

To this end, he discusses the relationship between Christianity and realism by distinguishing the infant's world of immediacy from the adult's world mediated by meaning. The confusion between these two worlds lies at the heart of the philosophical differences between naive realism, empiricism, idealism and critical realism. Inevitably Christianity is drawn into such philosophical issues. Christianity is involved, at least remotely, in the world mediated by meaning through the communicative, cognitive, constitutive and effective functions of meaning. It is also involved in the world of immediacy through the inner transformation of persons through grace. Still, there is a more "proximate involvement in which the problems of realism gradually manifest themselves and meet with an implicit solution."[1] It is in this context of proximate involvement that Lonergan begins his discussion of doctrinal development up to Nicea.

Lonergan focuses on Tertullian, Origen and Athanasius. To his mind, they each represent a different philosophical approach to the problem posed by the revelation of the Trinity. Each seeks to maintain an orthodoxy which sees Father and Son as somehow together in the realm of the divine. Yet the philosophical differences between these thinkers mean that the manner in which they conceive the "togetherness" of Father and Son is radically different, even though each may see Father and Son as being "of the same substance." The problem lies in the meaning of the word "substance." In Lonergan's words,

Empiricism, idealism, and realism name three totally different horizons with no common identical objects. An idealist never means
what an empiricist means, and a realist never means what either of
them means.[2]

And "substance" is one of those word over which these three do
not agree.

Thus Tertullian is considered to represent an empiricist, material-
ist or naive realist understanding of the word, substance. When he
asserts that the Father and Son are of one substance, he means that
they are made from the same "stuff" in a materialistic sense. Consequently, the Son is somehow extruded from the substance of the
Father. In *Way to Nicea*, Lonergan cites Tertullian to illustrate that
this early Latin theologian even thought of God as corporeal: for every
spirit, even God, is a specific body in some way.[3] Tertullian's
involvement with Stoic materialism is considered to be at the core of
his difficulty. Tertullian holds to the "Stoic fancy that all reality was
corporeal."[4] While Lonergan acknowledges the contribution to Trinitarian theology that Tertullian made, particularly his knack for finding
"very happy formulae for expressing Christian belief",[5] it is clear that
he is entrapped in problems arising from his Stoic assumptions:

> If the Father is God and the Son is God, then all that is true of the
> Father must also be true of the Son, except that the Son is not the
> Father. For Tertullian there were things true of the Father but not of
> the Son. He could write, "There was a time when there was neither
> sin to make God a judge nor a Son to make God a Father" ... In a
> later theology such expressions were regarded as subordinating the
> Son to the Father.[6]

As long as Tertullian was held by an already-out-there-now reality
of extroverted empirical consciousness, he could not do justice to the
fundamental equality of Father and Son.

Origen, on the other hand, elaborates his vast system, not in terms
of Stoic materialism, but in a variant of Platonic idealism:

> ... for Origen the real was ideal, as in middle Platonism. Moreover,
> because the Father and the Son were distinct, theirs had to be the
> reality of distinct ideas. The Father was divinity itself, but the Son
> was divine only by participation ... The distinction between Father
> and Son is sharp and subordinationist. Their unity is what today

would be called moral ... They are two realities in respect of hypostasis, but a single one by consent, concord, and identity of will.[7]

As with Tertullian, Origen concludes to a subordinationist position which was subsequently rejected by the Church as unorthodox. Yet it would be anachronistic to use the word "heresy" in either case. For what is at stake is not a question of orthodoxy of faith, but a question of the proximate involvement of Christian faith in the problems of realism. These problems "gradually manifest themselves and meet with an implicit solution."[8] The positions of Tertullian and Origen, respectively, mark steps along the path towards a dialectic clarification of these problems. This process of clarification reflects not so much on the faith of these early thinkers as upon the inadequacy of the philosophical positions they adopted. Faith demands more than their respective philosophies can deliver.

In contrast to the materialism of Tertullian and the Platonism of Origen is the implicit realism of Athanasius and the early Church councils:

> But it was the Council of Nicea and the ensuing controversies that provoked from Athanasius, along with his other clarifications, the fundamental little rule that all that is said of the Father also is said of the Son except that the Son is Son and not Father.[9]

For Lonergan, this rule is the clue to the meaning of *homoousios*. To say that the Father and Son are of one substance means that what is true of one is true of the other, except the Father is not the Son. Such a stance demands that we move beyond the "umbilical cord" of our imagination; beyond also the exciting world of insight and ideas alone. We must move into the decisive world of judgment, of what is true, of what is real. If I may quote Lonergan at length:

> Now it would seem that Tertullian's Christology and, specifically, his identification of the incorporeal with the non-existent, are connected with an apprehension of reality in terms of the world of immediacy. Again, it would seem that Origen's Christology pertains to the world mediated by meaning, where the meanings in question are ideas, that is, answers to questions for intelligence. But there is a third possibility, in which one's apprehension of reality is in the world mediated by meaning, where the meanings in question are

affirmations and negations, that is, answers to questions for reflection ... It is this third view that we find in Christian preaching and teaching and more generally, in Christianity as a reality mediated by meaning. Finally it is this third view that is implicit in conciliar pronouncements and particularly in the canons to the effect, If anyone says so and so, let him be anathema. What is said is all-important to a group whose reality, in part, is mediated by meaning.[10]

Lonergan thus differentiates between three levels of consciousness – empirical, intellectual and reasonable. The elaboration of these differing but related levels of consciousness was Lonergan's major achievement in *Insight* and related writings. By exploiting this differentiation, he is able to delineate the differences between the three patristic writers in question.

Of course, Lonergan is not claiming that Athanasius would have seen the matter in these terms. In fact, he considers that "in most cases, contemporaries do not know what is going forward."[11] It would be as anachronistic to hail Athanasius as a critical realist as it would be to dismiss Tertullian and Origen as heretics. For that reason, Lonergan refers to Athanasius' position simply as "dogmatic realism": it merely asserts that reality is known in true judgments. But a truly critical realism must do more than make such an assertion. It must argue its position and relate it dialectically to other competing positions, as Lonergan does in *Insight*. However, he is claiming that Athanasius and Nicea have arrived at an implicit solution to the problems raised by Christianity's proximate involvement with the world mediated by meaning.

The significance of this point for our thesis lies in the fact that an implicit solution of this kind comes about precisely because the Church was dealing with a fundamental aspect of revelation, that is, the doctrine of the Trinity. Revelation moves the intellectual culture of faith to develop a dogmatic realism congruent with the revealed reality involved. The historical process of an unfolding dialectic from Tertullian, through Origen to Athanasius is not merely an accidental by-product of revelation. It is part of the salvific transformation of culture which revelation initiates. A tradition of rationality is elicited which culminates in the kind of critical realism which Lonergan's method so impressively exhibits.

This position is far removed from the popular, if misconceived, notion that the early Councils of the Church are nothing more than an instance of Christian faith capitulating to Hellenism. Such a view was originally propounded by Harnack, and, more recently, was a feature of the writings of Leslie Dewart.[12] Far from capitulating to Hellenism, the pronouncements of the early Councils are in fact resisting the dominant philosophy. Even while using its terms and techniques, the Councils are carrying forward a movement to transcend the limited horizon of the Platonic Hellenism of the day. No early Christian thinker was more influenced by Platonism than Origen. Yet, because his position was so evidently subordinationist, it was subsequently rejected by the Church.

The positions of Lonergan and Harnack represent two dialectically opposed readings of "what is going forward" in the dogmatic development of the early Church. Lonergan understands the movement as one of a progressive dialectic clarification, as the Church struggles with its "proximate involvement" in the problems of realism. Harnack, on the other hand, understands the movement as a capitulation of the spirit of the Gospel to Greek philosophy.

These diverse readings are perhaps illustrative of a point Lonergan makes on the implementation of dialectic to history. He contrast the conclusions of a historian who knows "just what intellectual, moral and religious conversion is" with those of a historian who lacks conversion in one or other area:

> While the implementation of dialectic in the first case led to an idealised version of the past, its implementation in the second case does just the opposite; it presents the past as worse than it really was.[13]

While Lonergan may be willing to concede that his version of the history of events culminating in the Council of Nicea seems "idealised", still, Harnack's version is "worse than it really was." Further, Lonergan's version is illustrative of the claim of this thesis, that revelation initiates, sustains and extends a tradition of rationality.

Doran, in reflecting on Lonergan's analysis, surmises: "perhaps only a Christian theologian could have articulated critical realism."[14] Is this supposing too much? Doran does not assume that critical realism could not have emerged outside a Christian context. After all, the work of Aristotle is a classic example of the tradition of "critical realism" that both Lonergan and Doran applaud. However, there is still the question of the probability of sustaining such a philosophical position so that it can generate a tradition of rationality, that is, a tradition of philosophical argument, debate, controversy and genuine achievement. This probability is greatly increased when critical realism is coupled with a Christian revelation which demands such a realism to explicate the reality of what has been revealed. It is further increased by a flourishing Christian community with its own social and cultural forms which can sustain such a tradition. In Lonergan's terms, revelation shifts both the probability of emergence and the probability of survival of the scheme of recurrence of the objective meanings we have identified as "critical realism."[15]

The potential of such a collaboration between faith and reason was classically realised in the theological achievement of Aquinas. Still, as Lonergan regularly pointed out, there would have been no Aquinas without the painstaking work of others, such as Peter Lombard, who gathered the texts from Scripture and from other sources to pose the problems that needed resolving if theology was to advance in a systematic fashion.[16] Nor would there have been an Aquinas without the emergence of new social and cultural institutions such as universities which took theology out of the monasteries and put it into dialogue with Greek classical philosophies (not to mention the Islamic and Jewish commentaries on them), newly accessible through translation into Latin.[17]

However, this medieval achievement appears now in history to be a phase of a larger development. Lonergan identifies it as belonging to a second stage of meaning, in which theory differentiates itself from commonsense.[18] Granting Aquinas' achievement, the tension between commonsense and theory remained unresolved; and, indeed, unresolvable, at the level of theory alone. The underlying tension eventually led to the collapse of Scholasticism into a decadent nominalism.[19] Only a further development into a third stage of meaning, grounded in interiority, can resolve the tensions between theory and commonsense. While Lonergan has shown that Aquinas did in fact use the data of consciousness in his work, it remains that Thomas stated his results in the realm of theory, that is, in terms of Aristotelian metaphysics. The culture of the day simply did not demand, nor could it sustain, a systematic turn to the subject with the exigence characteristic of this later era.[20] In Lonergan's *Method*, this exigence has been notably met, to produce a tradition of rationality deeply influenced by revealed truth.

7.2 "Person" and the emergence of personal value

The dialectic clarification of the term *substance* is one part of the history of early Trinitarian and Christological doctrine. Still, there is another element in this history: the meaning of *person*.

Both Trinitarian and Christological doctrine make use of the term. *Persona* was first introduced into the theological discourse by Tertullian. As Lonergan repeatedly points out, the initial doctrinal and theological uses of the term are little more than heuristic. Later, when Augustine asks what is meant by the term *person* in a Trinitarian setting, he answers that is it what there are three of in the Trinity. The term is a heuristic device; it names an unknown. It is better to have such a name than to remain silent.[21] Lonergan, therefore, considers that, when the Council of Chalcedon uses the term *person*, it means that of which there is one in the Incarnation, namely, the one and the same Jesus Christ. There is no hint of "Hellenization" at this point. The process is simply an instance of logical clarification.

The difficulty emerges when one wants to move beyond logical clarification and towards some type of metaphysical explanation of both Trinitarian belief in three distinct persons in one nature, and of Christological belief in one person with two distinct natures. Such a movement requires more than logical clarification. It demands an exploration of the ontology of personhood. When such a move is made we begin to see two patterns emerge, one dealing with the Christological problem, the other dealing with the Trinitarian problem. Jean Galot has recently drawn attention to these patterns in an article in *Gregorianum*:

> La difficulté de déterminer en quoi consiste la réalité fondamentale de la personne apparaît dans les vois diverse suivies en doctrine trinitaire et en christologie. Dans la théologie de la Trinité, la personne a été définée par la relation; pour expliquer que les trois personnes ont la même perfection, on reconnaît qu'elles sont constituées par les relations. Ce qui leur est propre, c'est relation subsistante; elles ont en commun une essence absolue. En christologie les théologiens ont cherché dans une autre direction le constitutif formel de la personne: certains ont caractérisé la personne par l'indépendance ou la totalité de la nature, d'autres l'ont définée comme un mode substantiel, ou même comme l'être ou l'existence. Au lieu d'y discerner un élément relationel, ils l'ont donc caractérisée par un élément absolu.[22]

Galot seeks a mediating path between these two elements, seeing the two concepts of relationship and subjecthood as indispensable in the definition of person.

On the other hand, Lonergan, at least in his Latin theological works, seems to deny that a relational, interpersonal aspect is constitutive of finite personhood. After considering Aquinas' definition of person as *subsistens distinctum in natura intellectuali*, he raises the objection that perhaps the definition should contain reference to persons being essentially constituted by interpersonal relations. He responds:

> Omnem personna intra systema quoddam relationum interpersonalium ita versari ut personae infinitae per tales relationes constituantur et personae finitae tales relationes per modem proprietatis consequentis habeant, conceditur; personam finitam per tales relationes constitui, negatur.[23]

Thus while Lonergan admits the essential interpersonal nature of the Trinitarian persons, he denies it of finite persons at this stage of his writings.

It is significant that this quotation comes from Lonergan's writings in Christology. His Christological writings consistently employ what Galot would refer to as the absolute element of personhood, in order to address the Christological problem of the distinction between *person* and *nature*. Lonergan raises the problem of the notion of *person* in the context of the dogmatic declaration of Chalcedon. He focuses our attention on the phrase of Chalcedon, "one and the same." *Person* is then what is "one and the same", that is, the basis of identity. William Loewe puts it succinctly:

> At the level of experience one encounters the oneness of a datum, of an instance of something, but what that something is remains to be grasped by understanding. Understanding in turn yields the oneness of an intelligible unity, but again there is a further step. Only critical reflection grasps the correlation of that understanding with the datum of experience, issuing in the judgment which posits the intelligible unity as real, as in fact itself and nothing else. It is, in Chalcedon's phrase, "one and the same", and to be such is its identity. Identity, then, designates the concrete existence of an actual individual, distinct from all others.[24]

We find a similar pattern emerging here as was the case in the discussion of the notion of substance. Just as reality is correlated with the term of the third level of intentional consciousness, namely judgment, so too is identity. In arguing thus, Lonergan goes no further than Scholasticism which employed the distinction between essence and existence to ground the distinction between nature and person.[25] A person is, then, a distinct substance of a rational nature, *naturae rationalis individua substantia*. One finds this same pattern in Lonergan's Latin writings, in his essay, "The Origins of Christian Realism" and his more recent essay, "Christology Today: Methodological Reflections." While this is certainly adequate to ground the necessary Christological distinctions, one could argue that the ontological status of personhood remains incomplete.

Here we pose a question: Does not an ontology of personhood require a distinction which goes beyond one drawn from the first three levels of intentional consciousness? Does it not require a distinction which draws upon on the fourth, existential level of consciousness, where, as Lonergan himself, at a later stage, states, the full person emerges? His words are as follows:

> There is a still further dimension to being human, and there we emerge as persons, meet one another in a common concern for values, seek to abolish the organization of human living on the basis of competing egoisms and to replace it by an organization on the basis of man's perceptiveness and intelligence, his reasonableness, and his responsible exercise of freedom.[26]

The "further dimension to being human" occasions a consideration of the cultural significance of the term *person*, in both Christological and Trinitarian theology. Lonergan has argued that the use of the term *substance* necessitated the emergence of a realism grounded in the constitutive role of judgment in the knowledge of reality. His argument at this juncture could be extended: What is the cultural significance of the use of the term *person*? Does it necessitate the emergence of the recognition of the existential dimension of consciousness as distinct from the first three level of intentional consciousness? Further, is it at this fourth level of intentional consciousness that the interpersonal constitution of the person become clear?

The reason for raising these questions is to illustrate the contention that revelation has an ongoing role in helping clarify the transcendental constitution of the subject. The tradition of rationality, to which Lonergan has contributed, remains open to further development in light of the demands of revelation. In addressing these questions I shall seek to exploit suggestions already found in Lonergan's writings but not fully developed by him, while acknowledging that a whole thesis could be devoted to this subject.

7.2.1 From *quid sit?* to *quis sit?*

A more adequate understanding of the ontology of person requires more than the distinction between the second and third levels of intentional consciousness. It looks to the grounding of personhood in relationship to the fourth, existential level of consciousness. As we noted above, in the early Lonergan the notion of person arises from distinguishing the questions *quid sit?* (what is it?), and *an sit?* (is it so?). However, I would suggest that the notion of person should arise from a consideration of the question *quis sit?* (who is it?). Further, this question cannot be reduced to an instance of the previous questions, and is irreducible to any other form of question. I would argue that its proper context is not to be found in the first three levels of intentional consciousness, but in the fourth level where spontaneous intersubjectivity is sublated into existential consciousness. The contention is then that personhood, even finite personhood, is inherently interpersonal.

There are a number of hints to these suggestions in Lonergan's writings as revealed doctrines are more fully attended to:

i) The essay "Christ as Subject: A Reply" defends his Christological studies from misinterpretation by a certain Fr. A. Perego. Much of the defence has to do with clarifying the differentiation between consciousness as experience and consciousness as knowledge or perception. As we have seen above, Lonergan's Christological distinction between nature and person is based on distinguishing between the questions *quid sit?* and *an sit?*, between essence and existence. Yet, when Lonergan wants to put things in their simplest, in a way that "were they not so elementary and so obvious they might be included in a catechism"[27], he begins with the question: "*Who* suffered under Pontius Pilate?" [emphasis added]. It is the "who?" question which Lonergan spontaneously raises in reference to the question of the person of Jesus. However, at this stage the answer to the "who?" question can be reduced to one of identity, to the question *an sit*?

It would seem, even at this stage, that Lonergan does allow for the correlation of the question *quis sit?* with the notion of person. But it is a spontaneous correlation arising from the dynamism of questioning itself. It does not arise from any intrusion of a prior theory or explanation.

ii) The second hint is found in his later Christological essay, "Christology Today: Methodological Reflections." Here, a more explicit tension is present regarding the same issue. Once again, Lonergan addresses the problem of the distinction between nature and person by reference to identity:

> By *identity* I understand the third of the three meanings of *one*. There is *one* in the sense of an instance ... There next is *one* in the sense of intelligible unity ... Thirdly, there is *one* in the sense of one and the same. It is the one which presupposes the intelligible unity already mentioned but adds to it an application of the principles of identity and contradiction ... Such is the "one and the same" of the Chalcedonian decree.[28]

However, prior to this statement there are other remarks pointing in the direction that I am suggesting, that of correlation the "who?" question with existential consciousness. In considering the New Testament writings under the categories of research, interpretation, history and dialectics, he concludes by referring to the "critical issue" of the New Testament writings:

> The third step placed the New Testament in the genre of salvation history, and it placed our response to it on the *existential level* of confrontation, deliberation, evaluation, decision, deed. But the New Testament not only is a religious document calling for religious living; it is also a personal invitation and the appropriate response to it is *personal commitment*. So ineluctably there arises the question, *Who* is this Jesus? [emphasis added][29]

Here, Lonergan clearly begins to correlate the question, Who is it?, with the fourth level of consciousness, with deliberation, evaluation, decision, deed and commitment.

Whereas in the first hint we saw the "who?" question correlated with the term "person", here we see the "who?" question correlated

with the fourth, existential level of intentional consciousness. This
tends to indicate a more ample notion of person emerging in Lonergan's thought, and illustrates the way in which revelation elicits further
reflection on the nature of personhood.

iii) Finally, there is another range of references indicating the
interpersonal nature of existential consciousness.

Firstly, Lonergan's *Philosophy of God, and Theology* argues for a
greater unity between the traditional subjects of the philosophy of God
and systematic theology. Among the many issues dealt with is the
nature of personhood. The words of a "final consideration" refer to,

> ... the contemporary notion of person. The traditional view was the
> product of trinitarian and christological problems as these were con-
> ceived with the systematic differentiation of consciousness as
> originated by Aristotle and transposed to Christian soil by Thomas
> Aquinas. The contemporary view comes out of genetic biology and
> psychology. From the "we" of the parents comes the symbiosis of
> mother and child. From the "we" of the parents and the symbiosis
> of mother and child come the "we" of the family. Within the "we"
> of the family emerges the "I" of the child. In other words the person
> is not the primordial fact. What is primordial is the community. It
> is within community through the intersubjective relations that are
> the life of community that there arises the differentiation of the indi-
> vidual person.
>
> It follows that "person" is never a general term. It always de-
> notes this or that person with all of his or her individual
> characteristics resulting from the communities in which he has lived
> and through which he has been formed and has formed himself. *The
> person is the resultant of the relationships he has had with others
> and of the capacities that have developed in him to relate to others.*[30]
> [emphasis added]

These brief two paragraphs reveal a rich potentiality for development which, as far as I can see, is nowhere exploited in a systematic
fashion in Lonergan's writings.[31] For example, the implications of the
above notion of person for trinitarian theology are obvious, especially
with the emphasis on relationship as defining personhood. Further,
personhood is not grounded in the judgment of a static identity.
Rather, the person is a dynamic resultant of relationships and capaci-
ties, whose proper setting is not simply cognitional, but existential and
interpersonal.

Lonergan further explicates the interpersonal elements of the fourth level of consciousness in the essay "Aquinas Today: Tradition and Innovation":

> The key position now pertains to the deliberating subject, and his deliberation are existential, for they determine what he is to be; *they are interpersonal, for they determine his relations with others*; they are practical, for they make this earth a better or a worse place ...[32] [emphasis added]

Here, the fourth level of consciousness is seen as interpersonal and determinative of relationality to others.

Then, there are number of complementary remarks on the subject of the "passionateness of being" in the essay "Mission and Spirit." This passionateness "underpins and accompanies and reaches beyond the subject as experientially, intelligently, rationally, morally conscious." As underpinning the subject, it is "the quasi-operator that presides over the transition from the neural to the psychic." It accompanies the subject's conscious and intentional operations as "the mass and momentum of our lives." As it "overarches" conscious intentionality:

> There it is the topmost quasi-operator that by intersubjectivity prepares, by solidarity entices, by falling in love establishes us as members of community.[33]

Significantly, spontaneous intersubjectivity is here related to the "topmost quasi-operator" within consciousness. While Lonergan continually speaks of intersubjectivity as a principle of limitation at the cognitional levels of consciousness, here he gives it a role in the self-transcendence of the subject at the existential level of consciousness.

Finally, in the recently published paper, "Philosophy and the Religious Phenomenon", Lonergan refers not to four, but six levels of consciousness. One new level is added by making a distinction within the previously identified empirical level.[34] A further new level arises from locating a realm distinct from the previously identified existential level, where the "realm of interpersonal relations" is raised to a level beyond the "moral operator":

> Again, beyond the moral operator that promotes us from judgments of fact to judgments of value with their retinue of decisions and

actions, there is a further realm of interpersonal relations and total commitment in which human beings tend to find the immanent goal of their being and with it their fullest joy and deepest peace.[35]

While the significance of Lonergan's talking of a fifth or sixth level of consciousness may be debated,[36] the *extra* significance Lonergan is giving to the interpersonal by referring it to a *higher* level is quite clear. At this stage of his development, the interpersonal dimension of consciousness is viewed as constitutive of even finite subjects, in contrast to Lonergan's earlier position in his Latin works, where this was denied.

7.2.2 *Quis Sit?*

Some insight into the status of the interpersonal constitution of the subject can be gained by a reflection on the question, "Who is it?" in contrast to the question, "What is it?".

The "what?" question arises as an articulation of our spontaneous desire to know. It initiates the movement from a purely empirical consciousness towards intellectual consciousness. In Lonergan's terms, it is an operator. It introduces a tension in consciousness which is released only by an act of insight. This involves a conscious act of the subject, which grasps the unity-identity-whole in that which is addressed by the question. Intellectual consciousness must itself be sublated by rational consciousness with its further question of judgment. This leads to a "yes" or "no" concerning the correctness of the initial insight.

The "who?" question, on the other hand, arises as an articulation of our spontaneous intersubjectivity. It is a factor in initiating a movement from a purely cognitional consciousness to an existential consciousness. It was, to repeat Lonergan words in "Christology Today" on this point,

> The third step [which] placed the New Testament in the genre of salvation history, and it placed our response to it on the *existential level* of confrontation, deliberation, evaluation, decision, deed. But the New Testament not only is a religious document calling for religious living; it is also a personal invitation and the appropriate response to it is *personal commitment*. So ineluctably there arises the question, *Who* is this Jesus? [emphasis added][37]

As noted previously, Lonergan also refers to our spontaneous intersubjective feelings as elements in the "topmost quasi-operator." These feelings move us from cognitional to moral consciousness. While they are spoken of as "quasi-operators", the "who?" question should rather be spoken of as an operator. It is a question demanding an answer. And here we see a key difference between the "who?" question and the "what?" question. While the "what?" question is answered by an insight within the subject, the most natural and spontaneous response to the "who?" question comes from another person. The "who?" question is inherently interpersonal. It seeks to establish relationship with another subject who, like myself, can ask and answer questions.

At this stage, we may ask ourselves how we answer such a "who?" question. When someone asks us, "Who are you?", how do we answer? A name may be a ready identifier, but basically it is a heuristic device, a convenient handle, but nothing else. In many pre-modern societies the "who?" question produces a litany of relationship, father, mother, brothers, sisters, forebears for two, three or four generations.[38] Such societies identify who I am in terms of my many relationships with others. As Lonergan notes,

> The person is the resultant of the relationships he has had with others and of the capacities that have developed in him to relate to others.[39]

We can see the same dynamic illustrated in Scripture when Jesus asks his disciples, "Who do you say that I am?" Peter replies, "You are the Christ, the Son of the living God" (Matthew 16:16ff). The title, Christ identifies a role, while the remainder of the answer refers to Jesus' relationship to his Father. Indeed, much of modern Christology has seen Jesus' relationship to his Father as the central issue of his identity.[40]

To conclude this discussion of the "who?" question, we may note that it has a finality of its own. It does not lead to some further question, for persons are never means, only ends. It is perhaps for this reason that Lonergan was moved to speak of a sixth level of consciousness as again I quote:

a further realm of interpersonal relations and total commitment in which human beings tend to find the immanent goal of their being and with it their fullest joy and deepest peace.[41]

It is the interpersonal which represents the peak, the *apex animae* of the soul, the level of communion with another being like ourselves.

Once more we have a striking instance of how revelation affects the techniques and terms of theological method, by eliciting further clarification of human interiority. We shall now move to our third example, that of the trinitarian psychological analogy, wherein revelation elicits an even more radical "turn to the subject."

7.3 Trinitarian analogies and the move to interiority[42]

While the doctrine of the Trinity is universally acknowledged as central to Christian faith, the status of the psychological analogy as a way of understanding the Trinity has not met with universal approval. Protestant authors, in particular, are very critical of it. Karl Barth sees it as an offensive intrusion of natural theology into Christian faith.[43] More recently, Colin Gunton has been scathing in his evaluation of the analogies of Augustine:

> ... I want to suggest that the problem with the trinitarian analogies as Augustine presents them is that they impose upon the doctrine of the Trinity a conception of the divine threeness which owes more to neoplatonic philosophy than to the triune economy, and that the outcome is, again, a view of an unknown substance *supporting* the three persons rather than *being constituted* by their relatedness. The true ontological foundations of the doctrine of the Trinity, that is to say, are to be found in the conception of a threefold mind and not in the economy of salvation.[44]

Gunton understands Augustine's "problem" as a precipitating factor in what he calls the theological crisis of the West.

However, even Catholic theologians are not completely at home with the psychological analogy. Rahner, for example, expresses serious reservations about its utility:

> ... it postulates *from* the doctrine of the Trinity a model of human knowledge and love, which either remains questionable, or about which it is not clear that it can be more than a *model* of human

knowledge as *finite*. And this model it applies again to God ... it becomes clear too that such a psychological theory of the Trinity has
the character of what the other sciences call an "hypothesis."[45]

For Rahner, the analogy is an hypothesis drawn from a model of
human knowledge, where the model itself is drawn from belief about
the Trinity. There is a circularity to this procedure which renders it
questionable. Moreover, Catholic theologian Walter Kasper, in his
magisterial work *The God of Jesus Christ,*[46] shows scant interest in the
psychological analogy, referring briefly to Thomas Aquinas as
"showing very great courage" in describing the procession of the Word
as an "intellectual emanation."[47]

Lonergan, on the other hand, has been an outstanding proponent
of the approach initiated by Augustine and systematised by Aquinas.
His early work on Aquinas, the *Verbum* articles, and his Latin works
on the Trinity analyse and extend the approach of Aquinas. Lonergan
uses his own critical metaphysics to overcome the deficiencies of the
conceptualist tradition that neo-Scholasticism had adopted. More
recently he has spoken of the need for a new psychological analogy
and has made tentative suggestions in that direction.[48]

Given such contradictory testimony, we are forced to ask whether
or not the psychological analogy is a huge theological distraction,
blighting Western thinking since the time of Augustine. Is it, in fact,
an unwanted intrusion of neo-Platonic thinking into the pure stream of
Christianity? On the other hand, is it a move elicited, or even necessitated, by revelation? Does revelation, in fact, demand a move to
interiority as exemplified by the interior searching which the psychological analogy typifies?

7.3.1 The Classical Analogies

Historically, the classical Trinitarian psychological analogies have
been a paradigmatic example of the Anselmian adage, "theology is
faith seeking understanding." They were an attempt to understand the
divine, not primarily in relation to us (the economic Trinity), but as
God is in God's own being (the immanent Trinity). They attempt to
add an understanding to what we know through faith and the data of
revelation. They support the contention that Christian faith in a triune
God is not unreasonable. Against Rahner, Lonergan defends the
hypothetical character of the psychological analogy.[49] He sees the

demand for certainty as a residual element of a decadent conceptualism in theology. The appeal to human psychology is an attempt to render the doctrine intelligible, if only analogously. It is not an attempt to prove the doctrine in a rationalistic manner, nor is the psychological analogy a proof from natural theology existing apart from revelation. Any serious proponent of the analogies is aware of the limited nature of the project being undertaken. The analogies are explicated simply out of a desire to understand, even though the object exceeds the limits of that understanding.

It may be observed that the underlying assumptions of the psychological analogy seem unremarkable in themselves. God is fully conscious being – not unconscious. God knows and loves Godself and creation. To these "philosophical" assumptions are added the historical experience of the missions of the Son and Spirit which grounds the belief in the processions of the Son and Spirit within the Trinity. We may then ask whether there is a connection between these divine processions and the conscious acts of knowing and loving within the divine consciousness. In these assumptions and questions lie the starting point for the psychological analogy.

Yet we have to ask ourselves where the "tension" in this process resides. To make sense of any proposed connection between the processions and divine conscious acts we must move beyond general statements about "knowledge and love." The only way to do so is on the basis of an analogous comparison with human consciousness and conscious acts. What then is the real unknown? Is it our revealed knowledge concerning the divine processions? Or is it human consciousness, that polymorphic fact which thousands of philosophers have struggled to clarify since the beginning of philosophising? Surely this is the point of greatest tension. As with our previous considerations of the terms *person* and *nature*, we see the doctrine of the Trinity pushing us to a greater clarity concerning interiority. It is not simply God who is known more fully in this process, but also our own conscious selves.[50]

We can agree with Rahner that, to some extent, the psychological analogy arises in response to the doctrine of Trinity: "it postulates *from* the doctrine of the Trinity a model of human knowledge and love".[51] Yet one may ask, why should this cause a problem? The doctrine of Trinity is revelatory, not just of divine being but of human being. Why should it not enlighten our understanding of our own conscious acts? Where we might disagree with Rahner is in his second contention. It is not at all clear that the ensuing model must necessarily be "questionable" or simply hypothetical. Lonergan has consistently argued that the basic lines of his account of interiority are irrevisable. Further, its grounding in Trinitarian thought is evident from his *Verbum* articles. Simply because *historically* the account of human interiority given in the psychological analogy is inspired by the doctrine of the Trinity does not mean that it cannot be independently derived and critically grounded.

Though an account of human interiority is not the direct object of revelation, the possibility that revelation has implications for philosophical development should not be surprising, given what I have presented above in 7.1 and 7.2.

As I have argued in Chapter 5 of this thesis, Rahner's stance incorporates an incomplete turn to the subject. His account of subjectivity remains basically metaphysical. Further, that metaphysics is not critically grounded. Lonergan, on the other hand, argues that his psychological account of the subject is self-grounding, and this account can then critically ground his metaphysics. By attaining only an incomplete "turn to the subject" Rahner misses the essential historical and cultural point of the psychological analogy. The doctrine of the Trinity demands a greater understanding of human interiority.

It lies beyond the scope of this thesis to enter into a nuanced account of the classical psychological analogy, particularly as it is presented in Lonergan's Latin writings.[52] In the briefest terms, we can say the following. Lonergan conceives of the procession of the Word in terms of the intelligible emanation of the concept from an act of understanding, or, at times, in terms of the procession of a judgment from the grasp of sufficent evidence. McDermott, in particular, notes the way Lonergan subtly shifts between the essential and the existential orders, between concept and judgment, in his account of the first procession.[53] The procession of the Holy Spirit is then conceived as Love which issues from the truth expressed in the Word. "The Son is proceeding Truth, not cold, abstract truth, but such truth as issues in love."[54] Lonergan himself speaks of the Holy Spirit as "the dynamic presence of God in God."[55] Such a conception of the Holy Spirit clearly models the *filioque*. Lonergan, as with Aquinas and Augustine, quotes the adage, "nothing is loved which is not first known", to explain the relationship between the first and second procession, and hence to illustrate the *filioque*. Such in broad outline is the psychological analogy.

Two philosophical assumptions are deeply embedded in this account of the psychological analogy. The first is a rejection of any form of conceptualism. In the above account of interiority, under-stand-ing does not arise from juggling concepts. Rather the concept (the Logos) is itself the product, the intelligible emanation, of expressive understanding (the Father). This position of dynamic intellectualism implies a rejection of conceptualism, nominalism, the modern "linguistic turn" in philosophy,[56] and various forms of the "method of correlation" found in contemporary theology.[57] The second assumption concerns the relationship between reason and value. Proceeding love (the Holy Spirit) flows from expressive (the Father) and expressed (the Logos) understanding and judgment. Put simply, such an assumption implies the rationality of value, against forms of emotivism and moral relativism.[58] Value is not the result of pure feeling or arbitrary choice. Rather, it is grasped through reasoned discourse and reflective consideration (through the proceeding Logos). The significance of these two philosophical assumptions can hardly be underestimated, yet here they find expression in what some would call a piece of esoteric theology.

7.3.2 Difficulties with the classical analogy

Though the psychological analogy and the philosophical assump-tions embedded within it represent a triumph of the analysis of interiority, it is not without its difficulties. The difficulties I shall now refer to arise from within this tradition of theologising rather than from a rejection of it (as represented above by Gunton and Barth).

The first difficulty is that the conscious operations on which the analogy are based are those of a single conscious human subject. Yet what the analogy refers to, at least on Lonergan's understanding, is three conscious subjects within a single divine consciousness.[59] While we clearly have no experience of this in ourselves, the focus on the operations of a single conscious subject undermines the important in-terpersonal aspects of consciousness relevant to a theology of the tri-personal God. Put simply, the psychological analogy can reinforce the impression of a modalist God. It could lead us to conceive of God as a single subject of conscious acts, and, by extension, reinforce the present climate of individualism arising from the Enlightenment.

The second difficulty reinforces the first. The focus of the anal-ogy for the first procession lies in the cognitional acts of the human subject. It considers the operations of understanding, conceiving, weighing evidence and judging. In our discussion of personhood, we saw that a focus on these levels of human consciousness has obscured the interpersonal dimensions of consciousness. These dimensions only become really apparent through a consideration of existential consciousness, where the notion of person fully emerges.

The third difficulty lies in the repeated use of the axiom, "nothing is loved which is not first known." As Lonergan's later writings make clear, this axiom is appropriate for the upward, creative vector within human consciousness. On the other hand, it does not account for the downward healing vector, whereby "nothing is known that is not first loved." This downward vector most closely corresponds to the operation of the divine presence within human consciousness. It is experienced in God's love flooding our hearts. This love gives us reasons of the heart which reason does not know. Significantly Lonergan sees the "reasons of the heart" as "feelings which are intentional response to values."[60] Now it seems incongruous that an analogy for the divine consciousness should be found in the upward creative vector of human consciousness but not in the downward healing vector. For this latter vector is so closely linked to the divine presence in that consciousness.

Finally, there is a difficulty which arises from the very shift in culture that the move to interiority initiates. The repeated use of the axiom, "nothing is loved unless known", reflects the context of an age concerned with the "rationality of value." It was an age in which "to be is to be good." However, I would argue that the key issue facing the modern age is not the "rationality of value" but the "value of rationality." Its concerns are about foundational issues of personal commitment, self-constitution and self-affirmation, as a cognitional, existential and religious subject. Moreover, the equating of being and value looks more and more like the underlying assumptions of a classicist culture.[61] Philosophical assumptions about the rationality of value and the identity of being and goodness are not the foundational concerns of the present era. Nor do they necessarily identify the healing impetus revelation now seeks to evoke. The shift to interiority has identified the priority of existential consciousness over cognitional consciousness, and of the downward, healing vector within consciousness over the upward, creative vector. Perhaps it is for these reasons that Lonergan could concede that what is most needed in Trinitarian theology is an updated, relevant psychological analogy.[62]

7.3.3 A New Psychological Analogy

In his essay, "Christology Today: Methodological Reflections", Lonergan presents a new and, in some ways, startlingly different version of the psychological analogy. While this new version contains elements which are continuous with the Augustinian-Thomistic tradition, it also has elements which represent a radical departure from it. Lonergan expresses the analogy in the following terms:

> The psychological analogy, then, has its starting point in that higher synthesis of intellectual, rational and moral consciousness that is the dynamic state of being in love. Such love manifests itself in its judgments of value. And the judgments of value are carried out in the decisions that are acts of loving. Such is the analogy found in the creature.
>
> Now in God the origin is the Father, in the New Testament named *ho theos*, who is identified with *agape* (*I John 4:8,16*). Such love expresses itself in its word, its Logos, its *verbum spirans amorem*, which is a judgment of value. The judgment of value is sincere, and so it grounds the Proceeding Love that is identified with the Holy Spirit.[63]

The first and most obvious contrast between this analogy and the traditional one is the shift from cognitional to existential concerns. Instead of beginning with an unlimited act of understanding, as in traditional theology, Lonergan now finds his starting point in "that higher synthesis of intellectual, rational and moral consciousness that is the dynamic state of being in love." This is clearly a reference to Lonergan's account of "being in love with God." "Being in love with God" is a conscious state which dismantles our old horizon. It establishes a new horizon which transvalues our values and transforms our knowing. It brings peace and joy, kindness and self-control. It remains ever an experience of mystery. Finally, it occupies the ground and root of our existential consciousness, the *apex animae*.[64]

Instead of beginning with the creative upward dynamism in human consciousness, Lonergan now locates his starting point at the peak of the soul, namely, at the highest level of consciousness. In some of his later writings Lonergan will refer to this as a fifth (or even sixth) level of consciousness, distinct from moral consciousness. This is evidence of a shift from the locus of the traditional analogy (on the creative vector in human consciousness) to a concentration on the healing vector, which transforms consciousness from above down-wards.

The second contrast may not be as obvious as the first. Both the traditional analogy and Lonergan's new version can refer to the Word as a judgment of value. Yet the context in each case is very different. In the traditional analogy there is a tension between seeing the procession of the Word in terms of the formation of a concept and a judgment of truth. In fact, as Lonergan argues, the two coincide. In forming the concept, unlimited understanding grasps that there are no further questions to answer. Thus, unlimited understanding also grounds a judgment of truth. However, a judgment of truth is also a judgment of value, since being and goodness are identified. Thus the traditional analogy can see the procession of the Word as a judgment of value.

Nevertheless, this constellation of connections is not the context of Lonergan's new analogy. The basis of the new analogy is now not unlimited understanding, but the dynamic state of being in love. A different constellation of connections arises in the new analogy. While the first constellation arises out of the creative vector, the second arises from the healing vector in human consciousness. *Method* provides clues to the new context. Firstly, in *Method* Lonergan clearly distinguishes between judgments of fact and judgment of value, locating judgments of value in the fourth, moral level of consciousness. Secondly, Lonergan speaks in a new way about how such judgments may occur. He relates these judgments to the dictum of Blaise Pascal that "the heart has reasons which reason does not know." He explains it in the following terms:

> Here by reason I would understand the compound of the activities of the first three levels of cognitional activity, namely, of experiencing, of understanding, and of judging. By the heart's reasons I would understand feelings that are intentional responses to value ... by the heart I understand the subject on the fourth, existential level of intentional consciousness and *in the dynamic state of being in love* ... besides the factual knowledge reached by experiencing, understanding, and verifying, there is another kind of knowledge reached through the discernment of value and *the judgments of value of a person in love*.[65] [emphasis added]

Here Lonergan is contrasting what he later refers to as the upward creative vector (which moves from experiencing, understanding, and judgments of fact to judgments of value and decisions), to the down-ward, healing vector (which moves from the dynamic state of being in love to judgments of value and decisions). The similarity between this language and Lonergan's new analogy is clear; and I would suggest that it puts the new analogy in the best interpretative framework.

These two shifts do much to meet the objections raised in the previous section. The shift from cognitional to existential conscious-ness as the focus of the analogy addresses the second of the four difficulties I raised in Section 7.3.2. The shift from the creative vector to the healing vector as the basis of the analogy does much to address the third and fourth difficulties. However, what is not brought out explic-itly in the analogy is the interpersonal nature of existential consciousness. This is the first difficulty I raised above. As I have argued in 7.2.2, this was a theme which was only slowly emerging in Lonergan's writings and something which could have profound significance for Trinitarian theology.

Fred Crowe has analysed this development in Lonergan's analogy. In particular he draws attention to the shift from unlimited under-standing to the dynamic state of being in love. He concludes his analysis with the suggestion that a further development may be neces-sary:

> Would Lonergan have followed through in this way? ... I have not found an answer to that historical question in the record he left us. As for the objective question in itself, on use of the downward movement for a trinitarian analogy, I think it likely that we will get Lonergan's answer only by carrying his idea beyond the point he himself had reached in 1975.[66]

To carry his idea beyond this point would require a new explora-tion of human interiority. Such an exploration may have a cultural significance similar to that played by the exploration which led to the traditional analogies. In particular, it may need to bring out the inter-personal constitution of existential consciousness.[67]

7.4 Culture and revelation

So far I have illustrated how the revealed Christological and Trinitarian doctrines lead to a reflection on the nature of personhood and that this reflection can in turn lead to a recognition of the interpersonal nature of existential consciousness. I shall now explore the manner in which this developing reflection has an important, indeed salvific, cultural significance. In this way we can see that revelation remains culturally effective in the present era.

In his discussion of the Council of Nicea, Lonergan has already shown the significance of differentiating the three levels of cognitional consciousness. Indeed, Lonergan sees the whole history of Western thought as a process of clarifying the polymorphism of human consciousness. This process involves learning to distinguish differing levels of consciousness, to identify their functions, to clarify their interrelations and intentionalities. The last of these levels to be distinguished is existential consciousness. I have argued above that this is implicit in the classical distinction between *person* and *nature*. I would now like to reflect upon the cultural significance of this distinction and how revelation thus inspires a genuine tradition of rationality with salvific value. For the sake of clarity and simplicity of expression I shall speak of the scale of values, rather than levels of consciousness in what follows. After all, there is an isomorphism between the two. For example, I shall speak of the emergence of personal value, as distinct from other values, rather than of existential consciousness, as distinct from cognitional levels of consciousness.

Lonergan reflects on an "axial period" (so described by Karl Jaspers) in ancient Greece, in terms of the "Greek discovery of mind." This discovery initiates a movement from a first stage of meaning where "conscious and intentional operations follow the mode of common sense" to a second stage of meaning where "besides the mode of common sense there is also the mode of theory, where the theory is controlled by logic."[68] Key figures in this discovery are Socrates, Plato and Aristotle. Yet it would be a mistake to focus solely on the cognitional issues raised by these great thinkers. MacIntyre, for example, reminds us of their overwhelming moral concerns. The discovery of mind is the discovery of order, in particular, of social order, and of human history as a form of that order. Not only does this era begin to distinguish between empirical and higher cognitional levels of consciousness; it begins also to distinguish vital values from social and cultural values. It begins to ask questions about the relationship between them. Indeed, for Plato, moral discourse is impossible outside the *polis*. Outside the *polis* one cannot be formed in the social and cultural values which are the basis of such discourse.[69]

Now Lonergan has contended that, with the *homoousios* of Nicea, Christian revelation has played its own role in the emergence of mind in Western culture. Neither the Stoic materialism of Tertullian, nor the middle Platonism of Origen can deal with the *homoousios*, but only the dogmatic realism of Athanasius which understands reality as mediated by true propositions. In its own way, Christian revelation reinforces and sustains the Greek discovery of mind. Christianity develops its own tradition of rationality, merging Biblical and Greek traditions into a new cultural identity.

Here too, the issues raised by revelation are not only cognitional. Revelation does not simply occasion a conflict between competing epistemologies. Moral issues are more centrally at stake. The first Christian communities found it necessary to distinguish religious and moral concerns from cultural and social concerns (for example, in facing the question, "Must a Christian be a Jew?", Cf. Acts 15) as they struggled to establish their own identity distinct from Judaism. Nevertheless, the Christians of the Roman empire tended to collapse the distinction between socio-cultural and religious values, as an emerging Christendom sought to establish a Christian culture and a Christian social order. In this historical process a key figure was Augustine, whose theological and political writings provide a basis for the Christian Middle Ages.

Medieval Christendom was a stunning intellectual, social, cultural and religious achievement. As an intellectual achievement, it was the apex of the second stage of meaning. In this stage, common sense is distinguished from theory, and theology achieves a fully theoretic stance, as evidenced in Scholasticism. The social, cultural and religious achievements of Christendom were legion. Yet it did not last. Lonergan identifies a key issue in the collapse of Christendom's scholastic culture to be the tension between theoretic and common sense horizons. This tension was heightened, as Lonergan points out, by the emergence of the theoretic horizon of modern empirical science.[70] I would suggest a further issue which helped undermine that culture. It was the failure of the era to distinguish, in the scale of values, personal value from social and cultural values below, and from religious value above. Here an added tension emerged at the Reformation with its emphasis on personal conversion and its revival of personal categories in religious experience.[71]

The result of these cultural forces is that complex, multifaceted and variously evaluated phenomenon we call the Enlightenment. Lonergan has emphasised the positive impact that modern science, philosophy and historical scholarship, all born of the Enlightenment, have had on modern theology. Others, for example, Alasdair MacIntyre, have emphasised the negative features of the Enlightenment, particularly its rejection of traditional forms of reasoning and its adoption of an a-historical and abstract approach to moral rationality. What light does the issue of the emergence of personal value shed on the complex phenomenon of the Enlightenment?

Lonergan identifies the key issue of the modern era as the "turn to the subject." This turn allows for the emergence of a third stage of meaning grounded in interiority. In keeping with the above discussion, I would prefer to talk of the disengagement of personal value from social and cultural value, below, and from religious value, above, in the scale of value. (Alternatively, I could speak of the differentiation of existential consciousness from cognitional consciousness below and religious consciousness above.) This emergence is marked by a shift from questions about the "rationality of value", which can be settled within a stable social and cultural tradition of reasoning, to questions about the "value of rationality." These questions are about foundational issues of personal commitment, self-constitution and self-affirmation, as a cognitional, existential and religious subject. While the answers to such questions may be sustained by culture (from below) and illuminated by religious experience (from above), they are really distinct from both and require their own distinct approach. They require a move to interiority, the turn to the subject, the existential leap of the modern era.

The emergence of personal value, as distinct from religious, social and cultural value, has three important consequences. Firstly, it allows us to distinguish moral from religious issues. Thus, we are prevented from collapsing religion into morality or from subsuming morality completely into religion. Secondly, it allows us to recognise the relative transcendence of morality from cultural and social conditions. Thirdly, if personal value is distinguished from cultural and religious value, we can raise important questions about how we then relate personal value to religious and cultural values.

On the religious side there are profound issues relating to the connection between religious value (grace) and personal value (nature, freedom, morality). One failed solution is an extrinsicism which was unable to establish any real relationship between the two, while asserting the overwhelming importance of religious value. As one commentator puts it, extrinsicism views grace as like a lump of gold in the stomach: it is clearly of value, but it is not doing me much good.[72] The other failed solution is a secularism which rejects religious values as irrelevant to life and seeks to establish morality without reference to the divine.[73]

There are also failed solutions to the problem of the relationship between personal and cultural values. One such failure consists in subsuming personal values within cultural values, thus denying the distinction. The consequence is an overall cultural relativism which recognises no personal vantage point from which to transcend cultural limitations. While rejecting the old classicism, where one culture is normative, it substitutes a plurality of incommensurable cultural norms.[74] Another kind of failure results when personal value is cut off from its cultural, interpersonal context and the person is reduced to an individualistic monad. MacIntyre sees this individualistic, abstract conception of the person as the source of the failure of the Enlightenment moral project to establish morality without reference to a cultural tradition.

The individualism flowing from the Enlightenment is a central component of contemporary Western culture. An emerging theological response to it can be found in contemporary reflections on the Trinity which emphasise the relational, interpersonal aspects as constitutive of personhood.[75] This relational understanding of personhood is applied to finite persons, a move originally denied by Lonergan. Yet it is a move congruent with the development of Lonergan's thought as I have attempted to show above. Moreover, it is a move with salvific import. The consequences of rampant individualism have become increasingly evident in a social order and cultural superstructure torn apart by it. The turn to the subject, the value of rationality and the emergence of personal value, are all issues which must be addressed by the move to interiority. Such a move can initiate a third stage of meaning, and hence reverse the long cycle of decline which threatens an end to human history as a form of order.[76]

This account of the emergence of personal value illustrates the two-fold dynamics of what Lonergan calls "the healing and creative vectors" in human history. The creative vector is the upward dynamic of intentional consciousness. It unfolds through asking questions, meeting problems, and seeking solutions. Given time, and persistence, this dynamic will learn to distinguish between vital values and the social order which supplies a steady stream of vital values; between the good of social order and critical reflection on social orders, on life and its meaning; between such critical reflection on these questions and questions about the questioner, the meaning and value of the human person; between issues of personal value and the source of all that was, is and forever will be, transcendent value. Nonetheless, in this arduous process, many false trails and many errors in understanding can and do occur.

As I have maintained above, the modern era has produced the answers of extrinsicism, secularism, relativism, and individualism. To meet these errors, to heal the damage done to human history, revelation introduces a healing vector into history. Revelation yields truths which go beyond the mix of truth and error attained by the fumbling attempts of the creative vector. It introduces a new cultural dynamic into human history. It demands distinctions, for example, between person and nature, which can only be met by a slow and painful turn to the subject, by a move to interiority and the development of transcendental method.

7.5 Conclusion

In this chapter I have attempted to illustrate the connection between revelation and culture. A signpost has been Robert Doran's surmise that "perhaps only a Christian theologian could have articulated critical realism." One claim of this thesis has been that Christian revelation demands a turn to interiority, as exemplified in Lonergan's *Method*, for its coherent explication. I have attempted to illustrate this claim by reference to the contribution of Lonergan in the areas of Christology and Trinity.[77] Following Lonergan, I have argued that the shift to interiority has major cultural significance: not only can it heal the rift between theory and commonsense, but also it explicates the interpersonal nature of existential consciousness, and its correlate of personal value. Such an explication becomes necessary if a culture dominated by an individualistic conception of personhood is to be healed. In conclusion, I would say that the turn to interiority is the major achievement of a tradition of rationality initiated by Christian revelation. If such is the case, Lonergan's *Method* is not simply an accidental and purely extrinsic element of Christian intellectual history but a culmination of a process with lies at the heart of the cultural significance of revelation itself.

1. Lonergan, "Origins of Christian Realism", *Second Collection*, 244.
2. Lonergan, *Method*, 239.
3. According to Tertullian: "for who will deny that God is a body, although God is a spirit? For a spirit is a body *sui generis*, in its own form. And if those things which are invisible have in God's presence, their own bodies and shapes, by which they are know to God alone, how much more shall that which was emitted from his own substance [i.e. the Son] be not without substance." *Against Praxis*, Chapter 7, quoted in *Way to Nicea*, 44.
4. Lonergan, "Origins of Christian Realism", 246. Lonergan is referring to a remark by Ernest Evans who edited and wrote an significant translation and commentary on *Against Praxis*.
5. Lonergan, "Origins of Christian Realism", 247.
6. Lonergan, "Origins of Christian Realism", 247-8.
7. Lonergan, "Origins of Christian Realism", 248-9.
8. Lonergan, "Origins of Christian Realism", 244.
9. Lonergan, "Origins of Christian Realism", 250.
10. Lonergan, "Origins of Christian Realism", 250.
11. Lonergan, *Method*, 179.
12. See, for example, L. Dewart's works *The Future of Belief: Theism in a World Come of Age* (New York: Herder & Herder, 1966), and *The Foundations of Belief* (New York: Herder & Herder, 1969) and Lonergan's response in the essay, "The Dehellenization of Dogma", in *Second Collection* 11-32. Dewart describes Harnack's position in the following terms: "The early development of Christian doctrine is to be understood as the gradual *substitution* of Hellenic elements for the corresponding original elements of the Apostolic Church, and the accumulation of these changes amounts ... to a substantial change in Christian truth" (*Foundations of Belief*, 106). The essay of Keefe, considered in the previous chapter, takes a similar stance to that of Dewart.
13. Lonergan, *Method*, 251.
14. Doran, *Theology*, 165.
15. These comments about the probability of emergence and survival of the schemes of recurrence of acts of meaning relate to the difficult issued raised in Chapter 19 of Doran's *Theology and the Dialectics of History* on the "ontology of meaning".
16. Cf. Lonergan, *Grace and Freedom*, 9ff.
17. Cf. A. MacIntyre, *Three Rival Versions*, 107ff on the role of the University of Paris in bringing Aristotelian and Augustinian traditions into fruitful dialogue.
18. Lonergan, *Method*, 85ff.
19. MacIntyre identifies Duns Scotus as a leading figure in the decline of Scholasticism: "The progenitor of, as well as the most distinguished contributor to, this late medieval anti-Thomistic mode was Duns Scotus",

Three Rival Versions, 152. He notes also that "Scotus thus not only made possible but provoked a good deal of later moral philosophy ... from Occam all the way to Kant", ibid, 155.

20. One should note that the Reformation initially produced a turn to the subject in the experiential theology of Luther, cf. S. Pfurtner, "The Paradigms of Thomas Aquinas and martin Luther: Did Luther's Message of Justification mean a paradigm Change?", *Paradigm Change in Theology*, H. Kung & D. Tracy (eds) (NY: Crossroad, 1989), 130-160. However, this was short lived as Lutheranism developed its own version of scholasticism, cf. para.65, "Justification by Faith (Common Statement)", in *Justification by Faith: Lutherans and Catholics in Dialogue VII*, H.G. Anderson et al. (eds) (Minneapolis: Augsburg, 1985), 39.

21. Augustine answers the question, "Three what?" as follows: "The answer, however, is given, three 'persons', not that it might be spoken, but that it might not be left unspoken", *De Trinitate*, (trans. A. Hadden), Book 5, Chap.9, in *Nicene and Post-Nicene Fathers.*, Vol.3 (Michigan: Eerdmans, 1978).

22. J Galot, "La définition de la person, relation et sujet", *Gregorianum*, 75/2 (1994), 281-2.

23. Cf. B. Lonergan, *De constitutione Christi ontologica et psychologica* (Rome: Gregorian University, 1964), 25.

24. W. Loewe, "Jesus, the Son of God", in *Desires of the Heart: An Introduction to the Theology of Bernard Lonergan*, V. Gregson (ed.) (Mahwah: Paulist Press, 1988) 189. A fuller exposition is in B. Lonergan, "Christology Today", *Third Collection.*

25. See Liddy, *Transforming Light*, 114ff, for the significance of the real distinction between essence and existence in Lonergan's own emerging intellectual conversion.

26. Cf. Lonergan, *Method*, 10.

27. Lonergan, "Christ as Subject: A Reply", *Collection*, 192.

28. Lonergan, "Christology Today", *Third Collection*, 91.

29. Lonergan, "Christology Today", 84.

30. B. Lonergan, *Philosophy of God, and Theology* (Philadelphia: The Westminster Press, 1973), 58.

31. For example, at the conclusion of the above quotation (ibid. 59), Lonergan footnotes a work by M. Nédoncelle, *La réciprocité des consciences, Essai sur la nature de la personne* (Paris: Aubier, 1942), a reference not found in any other Lonergan work, to my knowledge. He does however refer to personalists who "have urged that the notions of 'I' and 'You' emerge as differentiations of a prior 'we' or 'us'", cf. "Emerging Religious Consciousness in Our Time", *Third Collection*, 56.

32. Lonergan, "Emerging Religious Consciousness" 46. See also 29, "... to become moral interpersonally, for our decisions affect other persons".

33. Lonergan, "Mission and the Spirit", *Third Collection*, 30.

34. This new distinction within empirical consciousness is perhaps relevant to the work of Robert Doran on the psyche.

35. Lonergan, "Philosophy and the Religious Phenomenon", *Method: Journal of Lonergan Studies*, 12/2 (1994), 134.

36. Cf. the article by M. Vertin, "Lonergan on Consciousness: Is There a Fifth Level?", *Method : Journal of Lonergan Studies*, Spring 12/1 (1994), 1-36, for a discussion on the significance on the language of "levels of consciousness".

37. Lonergan, "Christology Today", *Third Collection*, 84.

38. Cf. A. MacIntyre, *After Virtue* 33, where he notes: "In many pre-modern, traditional societies it is through his or her membership in a variety of social groups that the individual identifies himself or herself and is identified by others. I am brother, cousin and grandson, member of this household, that village, this tribe. These are not characteristics that belong to human beings accidentally, to be stripped away in order to discover 'the real me'."

39. Lonergan, *Philosophy of God and Religion*, 58.

40. See, for example, E. Schillebeeckx, *Jesus, an experiment in Christology*, 256ff, where Schillebeeckx focuses on Jesus' "Abba" experience.

41. Lonergan, "Philosophy and the Religious Phenomenon", 134.

42. The inspiration for the position adopted in this section comes from an unpublished manuscript by Sebastian Moore.

43. Cf. K. Barth, *Church Dogmatics*, Vol.1 Part 1, 399: "The Lord who is visible in the *vestigia* we can only regard as a different Lord from the one so called in the Bible".

44. C. Gunton, *The Promise of Trinitarian Theology* (London: T. & T. Clarke, 1991), 42-3.

45. K. Rahner, *Trinity*, 117-8. Also, in more muted form, see Rahner's *Foundations*, 135-6.

46. W. Kasper, *The God of Jesus Christ* (London: SCM, 1983).

47. Kasper, *The God of Jesus Christ*, 187.

48. Cf. Lonergan, *Caring for Meaning*, 61-2, and "Christology Today", *Third Collection*, 93ff.

49. Cf. Lonergan, *Method*, 336.

50. Crowe has noted that "Trinitarian theology ... was considerably in advance of other theology, using categories of intentionality analysis, meaning and value, long before they became general in theology", cf. "Son and Spirit: Tension in the Divine Mission", *Lonergan Workshop*, Vol.5, 11.

51. Rahner, *Trinity*, 117.

52. For a particularly clear account see, Peter Beer, "The Holy Spirit and Lonergan's Psychological Analogy", *Australian Lonergan Workshop*, 169-198. Also John McDermott, "Person and nature in Lonergan's De Deo Trino", *Angelicum*, 71/2 (1994), 153-185.

53. Cf. J. McDermott, "Person and Nature".

54. F. Crowe, "Rethinking God-with-us: Categories from Lonergan", *Science et Esprit*, XLI/2 (1989), 179.

55. Lonergan, *Verbum*, 203.

56. See Lonergan's comments in *Method*, 254ff, on one proponent of the "linguistic turn", E. MacKinnon, cf. "Linguistic Analysis and the Transcendence of God", *Proceeding of the Catholic Theological Society of America*, Vol.23 (1968).

57. On the conceptualism of the "method of correlation", see Doran, *Theology*, 453-455.

58. The term "emotivism" is used by MacIntyre in *After Virtue*, 11ff, to describe moral theories in which "all evaluative judgments and more specifically all moral judgments are *nothing but* expressions of preference, expressions of attitude or feeling, insofar as they are moral or evaluative in character". It would seem to correspond to the term, "the psychology of passional motivation" used by Doran, cf. *Theology*, 212.

59. Cf. B. Lonergan, *De Deo Trino II: Pars Systematica* (Rome: Gregorian University, 1964), 186ff. Also W. Kasper, *The God of Jesus Christ*, 289.

60. Cf. Lonergan, *Method*, 115.

61. Cf. Doran, *Psychic Conversion and Theological Foundations*, 80. Doran clearly sees the distinction between being and goodness as grounded in the distinction between cognitional and existential consciousness.

62. Cf. Lonergan's response to a question asked by T.A. Dunne in *Caring About Meaning*, 63.

63. Lonergan, "Christology Today", *Third Collection*, 93. Also, see *Caring About Meaning*, 61.

64. Cf. Lonergan, *Method*, 105-107.

65. Lonergan, *Method*, 115.

66. Crowe, "Rethinking God-with-us", 180.

67. I have attempted, with mixed success, to study this question in my master's thesis, *The Holy Spirit: The Feeling of God* (Melbourne: MCD, 1987), unpublished.

68. Lonergan, *Method*, 85.

69. Cf. MacIntyre, *After Virtue*, 126-7.

70. Cf. Lonergan, "Theology in its New Context", *Second Collection*, 55-67.

71. Cf. S. Pfurtner, "The Paradigms of Thomas Aquinas and Martin Luther", 130-160.

72. Cf. J. Donceel, *The Searching Mind* (Notre Dame: Univ. of Notre Dame Press, 1979), 110.

73. Cf. Johann Baptist Metz, *Faith in History and Society: Towards a Practical Fundamental Theology* (London: Burns & Oates, 1980), 14ff, for a critic of Enlightenment secularism.

74. We have seen this stance in the approach of Lindbeck, for example.

75. See various works on Trinity, for example W. Kasper, *The God of Jesus Christ*, C. La Cugna, *God for Us: The Trinity and Christian Life*, (San Francisco: Harper Collins, 1991), C. Gunton, *The One, the Three and the Many: God, Creation and the Culture of Modernity* (Cambridge: CUP, 1993), and L. Boff, *Trinity and Society* (Maryknoll: Orbis, 1988).

76. Something like a full response to these issues can be found in the writings of Robert Doran, in particular his work, *Theology and the Dialectics of History*. Doran investigates the integrity of the scale of values, the dialectic nature of social, cultural and personal values and the normative relationships between the different levels in the scale of values. While Doran draws heavily upon Lonergan, his filling out of Lonergan's account of existential consciousness, particularly by reference to the psychic component of existential consciousness, has been pivotal in the breakthrough he has achieved. His work represents, at least in the opinion of the present author, a more complete turn to the subject, and hence a fuller account of interiority, than that achieved by Lonergan. It also represents a massive assault on an extrinsicism which has dominated Catholic theology from Cajetan until the *novélle theologie* of the twentieth century.

77. One could add of course the significance of the doctrine and theology of grace in Christian culture. The Doctor of Grace, Augustine, is an acknowledged master of interiority and any worthwhile theology of grace must be sensitive to the inner movements of the Spirit. I could have included references to Lonergan's contributions to the theology of grace, but these are generally less accessible than his work on Trinity and Christology. For a detailed account see M. Stebbins, *The Divine Initiative: Grace, World-Order, and Human Freedom in the Early Writings of Bernard Lonergan* (Toronto: University of Toronto Press, 1995). Again the importance of these would be the shift to interiority that revelation demands.

CHAPTER EIGHT: CONCLUSION

The starting point of this thesis was the observation that, while Lonergan has had much to say about theological method, he has had relatively little to say about the topic of revelation. On the other hand, as a number of theologians have commented, there must be some relationship, some correlation, between the two. This thesis has set out to establish just such a correlation between Lonergan's understanding of theological method, as propounded in *Method in Theology*, and the basic structures of revelation.

Having established that Lonergan conceived of revelation as the entry of divine meaning into human history, we applied his notions of carrier and functions of meaning, as found in *Method*, to an analysis of revelation. A consideration of the carriers of divine meaning allowed us to establish a correlation between these carriers and the eight functional specialties, elaborated in *Method*. This basic structure enabled us to develop of framework for understanding revelation which encompassed a number of current approaches to the topic. For example, the various models of revelations developed by Avery Dulles can be seen within a systematic perspective, rather than as a coincidental manifold of competing positions.

The two categories which stood out in this process were the incarnate and historical carriers of revelation. Consideration of incarnate meanings led us to develop a "searching Christology", a heuristic anticipation of the Christ-event. Consideration of historical carriers of meaning led to a more profound understanding of the various functions of revelation in human history, particularly with regard to culture. Revelation could then be understood as initiating, sustaining and prolonging a tradition of rationality. Further, it became evident that Lonergan's own project, as exemplified in *Method*, is itself a significant contribution to this same tradition of rationality. Indeed revelation demands, and in some sense initiates, the modern turn to the subject, for its very well-being and the well-being of human history.

The initial goal of this thesis, as envisaged by its author, was to establish that Lonergan's *Method* could elucidate the theology of revelation. This, I believe, has been demonstrated. However, perhaps surprisingly, this thesis has also shown that the theology of revelation as elucidated the meaning and purpose of *Method in Theology*, by placing it within a larger tradition of rationality. This larger perspective is needed if we are to do justice to the remarkable life and achievement of Bernard Lonergan.

BIBLIOGRAPHY

WORKS BY BERNARD LONERGAN:

Books and Collections:

Insight: A Study of Human Understanding, London: Darton, Longman and Todd, 1958.

De intellectu et methodo, *Reportatio* of course at Gregorian University, 1958.

De Verbo Incarnato, Rome: Gregorian University, 1960.

De methodo theologiae, notes for lectures at Gregorian University, 1962.

De Deo Trino, Pars Dogmatica, Pars Systematica, Rome: Gregorian University, 1964.

De Constitutione Christi Ontologica et Psychologica, Rome: Gregorian University, 1964.

Collection, F. Crowe (ed.), NY: Herder and Herder, 1967.

Verbum: Word & Idea in Aquinas, D. Burrell (ed.), London: Darton, Longman & Todd, 1968.

Grace and Freedom: Operative Grace in the Thought of St. Thomas Aquinas, J.P. Burns (ed.) London: Darton, Longman and Todd, 1970.

Doctrinal Pluralism, Milwaukee: Marquette Unviersityt Press, 1971.

Method in Theology, London: Darton, Longman and Todd, 1972.

Philosophy of God, and Theology, Philadelphia: The Westminster Press, 1973.

Second Collection, W. Ryan and B. Tyrell (eds), Philadelphia: Westminster Press, 1974.

The Way to Nicea: The Dialectical Development of Trinitarian Theology, London: Darton, Longman and Todd, 1976 (trans. Conn O'Donovan).

Caring About Meaning: Patterns in the life of Bernard Lonergan, Montreal: Thomas More Institute, 1982.

A Third Collection, F. Crowe (ed.), New York: Paulist Press, 1985.

Articles and essays:

"Introduction to dissertation *Gratia Operans*" edited by F. Crowe, published in *Method: Journal of Lonergan Studies*, Vol.3, No.2, October, 1985, p.10.

"The Assumption and Theology", *Collection*, F. Crowe (ed), NY: Herder and Herder, 1967, pp.68-83.

"The Natural Desire to See God", *Collection*, pp.84-95.

"Theology and Understanding", *Collection*, pp.121-141.

"Christ as Subject: A Reply", *Collection*, pp.164-197.

"Dimensions of Meaning", *Collection*, pp.252-267.

"The Transition from a Classisist World-View to Historical Mindedness", *Second Collection*, W. Ryan and B. Tyrell (eds), Philadelphia: Westminster Press, 1974, pp.1-9.

"The Dehellenization of Dogma", *Second Collection*, pp.11-32.

"Theories of Inquiry: Responses to a Symposium", *Second Collection*, pp.33-42.

"Theology in its New Context", *Second Collection*, pp.55-67.

"The Subject", *Second Collection*, pp.69-86.

"The Future of Christianity", *Second Collection*, pp.149-163.

"The Response of the Jesuit as Priest and Apostle in the Modern World", *Second Collection*, pp.165-188.

"An Interview with Fr. Bernard Lonergan s.j.", *Second Collection*, pp.209-230.

"The Origins of Christian Realism", *Second Collection*, pp.239-262.

"*Insight* Revisited", *Second Collection*, pp.263-278.

"Functional specialties in theology", *Gregorianum*, Vol.50, fasc.3-4, 1969, pp.485-505.

"Mission and Spirit", in *A Third Collection*, F. Crowe (ed.), New York: Paulist Press, 1985, pp.23-34.

"Christology Today: Methodological Reflections", in *A Third Collection*, pp.74-99.

"Healing and Creating in History", in *A Third Collection*, pp.100-109.

"Religious Knowledge", in F. Lawrence (ed.), *Lonergan Workshop*, Vol.1, pp.309-27, 1978; also published in *A Third Collection*, pp.129-145

"A Post-Hegelian Philosophy of Religion", in F. Lawrence (ed.), *Lonergan Workshop*, Vol.3, pp.179-199, 1982; also published in *A Third Collection*, pp.202-223.

"A Response to Fr. Dych", in *Theology and Discovery: Essays in Honor of Karl Rahner, S.J.*, William J. Kelly (ed.), pp.54-57.

"Philosophy and the Religious Phenomenon", *Method: Journal of Lonergan Studies*, Vol.12, no.2, 1994, pp.121-146, with editorial notes by F. Crowe.

ADDITIONAL BIBLIOGRAPHY:

Augustine, *De Trinitate*, in *Nicene and Post-Nicene Fathers.*, Vol.3, Michigan: Eerdmans, 1978, pp.1-228 (trans. A. Haddan).

Baum, Gregory, *Man Becoming: God in Secular Experience*, New York: Herder & Herder, 1971.

Faith and Doctrine, New York: Newman, 1969.

Barth, Karl, *Epistle to the Romans*, London: OUP, 1933.

Church Dogmatics Vol.1 Part 1, Edinburgh: T. & T. Clarke, 1976 (trans. G.T. Thomson).

Beer, Peter, "The Holy Spirit and Lonergan's Psychological Analogy", in Danaher, W. (ed.), *Australian Lonergan Workshop*, pp.169-198.

Boff, Leonardo, *Trinity and Society*, Maryknoll: Orbis, 1988 (trans. P. Burns).

Boly, Craig, *The Road to Lonergan's Method in Theologt: The Ordering of Theological Ideas*, Lanham: University Press of America, 1991.

Braxton, Edward K., "Bernard Lonergan's Hermeneutic of the Symbol", *Irish Theological Quarterly*, Vol.XLIII, no.3, 1976, pp.186-197.

Brown, Raymond, et al. (eds), *The New Jerome Biblical Commentary*, Englewood, NJ: Prentice Hall, 1990.

Carmody, Brendan, "A Note of the Transcultural Nature of Lonergan's Religious Experience", *Irish Theological Quarterly*, Vol.49, no.1, 1982, pp.59-64.

Coffey, David, *Grace: The Gift of the Holy Spirit*, Sydney: Catholic Institute of Sydney, 1979.

"The Incarnation of the Holy Spirit in Christ", *Theological Studies*, Vol.45, no.3, 1984, pp.466-480.

"A Proper Mission for the Holy Spirit", *Theological Studies*, Vol.47, no.2, 1986, pp.227-250.

Cook, Michael L.,"Revelation as Metaphoric Process", *Theological Studies*, Vol.47, no.3, 1986, pp.388-411.

Corcoran, Patrick, (ed.), *Looking at Lonergan's Method*, Dublin: Talbot Press, 1975.

Crowe, Frederick (ed.), *Collection*, NY: Herder and Herder, 1967.

A Third Collection, New York: Paulist Press, 1985.

Crowe, Fredrick, "Editor's Introduction", *Collection*, NY: Herder and Herder, 1967, pp.vii-xxxv.

Theology of the Christian Word, NY: Paulist Press, 1978.

"Doctrines and Historicity in the Context of Lonergan's *Method*", *Theological Studies*, Vol.38, no.1, 1977, pp.115-124.

The Lonergan Enterprise, Cambridge, Mass.: Cowley Publications, 1980.

"An Exploration of Lonergan's New Notion of Value", Fred Lawrence (ed.), *Lonergan Workshop*, Vol.3, pp.1-24, 1982.

"Rethinking God-with-us: Categories from Lonergan", *Science et Esprit*, XLI, no.2, 1989, pp.167-188.

Lonergan, London: Geoffrey Chapman, 1992.

Cullman, Oscar, *Christ and Time*, Philadelphia: Westminster Press, 1950, rev. ed., 1964.

Salvation in History, New York: Harper & Row, 1967.

Danaher, William (ed.), *Australian Lonergan Workshop*, Lanham: University Press of America, 1993.

Daneliou, Jean, *The Lord of History*, Chicago: Regency, 1958.

Davies, Brian, "Why Should We Believe It?", *New Blackfriars*, Vol.69, no.819, 1988, pp.360-368.

Dewart, Leslie, *The Future of Belief: Theism in a World Come of Age*, New York: Herder & Herder, 1966.

The Foundations of Belief, New York: Herder & Herder, 1969.

Donceel, Joseph, *The Searching Mind: An Introduction to a Philosophy of God*, Notre Dame: University of Notre Dame Press, 1979.

Doran, Robert, "The Theologian's Psyche: Notes Towards a Reconstruction of Depth Psychology", in F. Lawrence (ed.), *Lonergan Workshop*, Vol.1, pp.93-141, 1978.

Subject and Psyche: Ricoeur, Jung and the Search for Foundations, Lanham: University of America Press, 1980.

"Dramatic Artistry in the Third Stage of Meaning", in F. Lawrence (ed.), *Lonergan Workshop*, Vol.2, pp.147-199, 1981.

Psychic Conversion and Theological Foundations: Towards a Reorientation of the Human Sciences, Chico: Scholars Press, 1981.

"Suffering Servanthood and the Scale of Values", in F. Lawrence (ed.), *Lonergan Workshop*, Vol.IV, pp.41-67.

Theology and the Dialectics of History, Toronto: University of Toronto Press, 1990.

"Consciousness and Grace", *Method: Journal of Lonergan Studies*, Vol.11, no.1, 1993, pp.51-75.

Duffy, Eamon, "The Philosophers and the China Shop: a reply to Brian Davies", *New Blackfriars*, Vol.69, no.820, 1988, pp.447-452.

Duffy, Stephen, *The Graced Horizon: Nature and Grace in Modern Catholic Thought*, Collegeville: Michael Glazier, 1992.

The Dynamics of Grace, Collegeville: Michael Glazier, 1993.

Dulles, Avery, "The Symbolic Structure of Revelation", *Theological Studies*, Vol.41, no.1, 1980, pp.51-73.

Models of Revelation, Dublin: Gill & McMillan, 1983.

book review of *Method in Theology*, *Theological Studies*, Vol.33, no.3, 1972, pp.553-555.

"From Images to Truth: Newman on Revelation and Faith", *Theological Studies*, Vol.50, no.2, 1990, pp.252-267.

Dummett, Michael, "A Remarkable Consensus", *New Blackfriars*, Vol.68, no.809, 1987, pp.424-431.

"Unsafe Premises: a Reply to Nicholas Lash", *New Blackfriars*, Vol.68, no.811, 1987, pp.558-566.

"Theology and Reason", *New Blackfriars*, Vol.69, no.816, 1988, pp.237-245.

Dunne, Tad, "Trinity and History", *Theological Studies*, Vol.45, no.1, 1984, pp.139-152.

Dunne, Thomas & Laporte, Jean-Marc (eds), *Trinification of the World: A Festschrift in Honour of Frederick E. Crowe in Celebration of his 60th Birthday*, Toronto: Regis College Press, 1978.

Dupre, Louis, "Experience and Interpretation: A Philosophical Reflection on Schillebeeckx's *Jesus and Christ*", *Theological Studies*, Vol.43, no.1, 1982, pp.30-51.

Dych, William V., "Method in Theology According to Karl Rahner", in *Theology and Discovery: Essays in Honor of Karl Rahner, S.J.*, William J Kelly (ed.), pp.39-53.

Karl Rahner, London: Geoffrey Chapman, 1992.

Eliade, Mircea, *Patterns in Comparative Religion*, New York: Sheed & Ward, 1958.

Fallon, Timothy & Riley, Philip Boo (eds), *Religion and Culture: Essays in Honor of Bernard Lonergan*, Albany: State University of NY Press, 1987.

Religion In Context: Recent Studies in Lonergan, Lanham: University of America Press, 1988.

Fiorenza, Elisabeth Schussler, *Bread not Stone*, Boston: Beacon Press, 1984.

Fiorenza, Francis Schussler, *Foundational Theology: Jesus and the Church*, NY: Crossroad, 1985.

Fitzpatrick, Joseph, "Lonergan's Method and the Dummett-Lash Debate", *New Balckfriars*, Vol.69, no.814, 1988, pp.126-138.
Response: "Michael Dummett's 'Theology and Reason'", *New Blackfriars*, Vol.69, no.817, 1988, pp.295-296.

Flannery, *Vatican Council II: The Conciliar and Post Conciliar Document*, Northport: Costello Publishing Co., 1984.

Fletcher, Frank, *Exploring Christian Theology's Foundations in Religious Experience*, doctoral dissertation, Melbourne College of Divinity, 1982.

Galloway, Allan, *Wolfhart Pannenberg, Contemporary Religious Thinker Series*, London: George Allen and Unwin, 1973.

Galot, Jean, "La Définition de la personne, relation et sujet", *Gregorianum*, Vol.75, fasc.2, 1994, pp.281-299.

Gascoigne, Robert, "The Relation between Text and Experience in Narrative Theology of Revelation", *Pacifica*, Vol.5, no.1, 1992, pp.43-58.

Gifford, Paul J., "The certainty of Change: Questioning Brown's answer to Dummett's problem", *New Blackfriars*, Vol.69, no.818, 1988, pp.330-339.

Gilkey, Langdon, "Symbols, Meaning and the Divine Presence", *Theological Studies*, Vol.35, no.2, 1974, pp.249-267.

Gregson, Vernon (ed.), *The Desires of the Human Heart: An Introduction to the Theology of Bernard Lonergan*, Mahwah: Paulist Press, 1988.

Griffiths, Bede, "A Symbolic Theology", *New Blackfriars*, Vol.69, no.817, 1988, pp.289-294.

Gunton, Colin, *The Promise of Trinitarian Theology*, London: T. & T. Clarke, 1991.
The One, the Three and the Many: God, Creation and the Culture of Modernity, Cambridge: CUP, 1993.

Haight, Roger, *Dynamics of Theology*, NY: Paulist Press, 1990.

Hefling, Charles, "Turning Liberalism Inside-Out: A Review of *The Nature of Doctrine: Religion and Theology in a Post-Liberal Age*" by George A, Lindbeck", *Method, Journal of Lonergan Studies*, Vol.3, no.2, 1985, pp.51-69.

"On Reading *The Way to Nicea*", in *Religion and Culture*, T. Fallon & P. Riley (eds), pp.149-166.

Hellwig, Monika, "Foundations for Theology: A Historical Sketch", in O'Donovan and Sanks (eds), *Faithful Witness*, pp.1-13.

Helminiak, Daniel, *The Same Jesus: A Contemporary Christology* Chicago: Loyola University Press, 1986.

Hibbs, Thomas, "MacIntyre's Postmodern Thomism", *The Thomist*, Vol.57, no.2, 1993, pp.277-297.

Hughson, Thomas, "Dulles and Aquinas on Revelation", *The Thomist*, Vol.52, no.3, 1988, pp.445-471.

Kasper, Walter, *The God of Jesus Christ*, London: SCM, 1983 (trans. M. O'Connell).

Keefe, Donald, "A Methodological Critique of Lonergan's Theological Method", *The Thomist*, Vol.50, No.1, 1986, pp.28-65.

Kelly, Anthony J., "To know the Mystery: The Theologian in the Presence of the Revealed God", Part I, *The Thomist*, Vol.32, no.1, 1968, pp.1-66.

"To know the Mystery: The Theologian in the Presence of the Revealed God", Part II, *The Thomist*, Vol.32, no.2, 1968, pp.171-200.

"Is Lonergan's *Method* Adequate to Christian Mystery", *The Thomist*, Vol.39, No.3, 1975, pp.437-470.

Kelly, William J. (ed.), *Theology and Discovery: Essays in Honor of Karl Rahner, S.J.*, Milwaukee: Marquette University Press, 1980.

Kung, Hans and Tracy, David (eds), *Paradigm Change in Theology*, NY: Crossroad, 1989 (trans. M. Kohl).

LaCugna, Catherine, *God for Us: The Trinity and Christian Life*, San Francisco: Harper Collins, 1991.

Lamb, Matthew, *History, Method and Theology: A Dialectical Comparison of Wilhelm Dilthey's Critique of Historical Reason and Bernard Lonergan's Meta-Methodology*, Missoula: Scholars Press, 1978.

Solidarity with Victims, NY: Crossroad, 1982.

"Inculturation and Western culture: The dialogical experience between gospel and culture", *Communio*, Vol.XXI, no.1, 1994, pp.124-144.

Lamb, Matthew (ed.), *Creativity and Method: Essays in Honor of Bernard Lonergan*, Milwaukee: Marquette University Press, 1981.

Lambert, Pierrot, et al. (eds), *Caring About Meaning: Patterns in the life of Bernard Lonergan*, Montreal: Thomas More Institute, 1982.

Lamont, John, "The Nature of Revelation", *New Blackfriars*, Vol.72, no.851, 1991, pp.335-345.

Lawrence, Fred, (ed.), *Lonergan Workshop*, Vol.1-10, Chico: Scholars Press, 1978-1994.

Lawrence, Fred, "Method and Theology as Hermeneutical", *Creativity and Method*, M. Lamb (ed), pp.79-104.

Lash, Nicholas, "A Leaky Sort of Thing? The Divisiveness of Michael Dummett", *New Blackfriars*, Vol.68, no.811, 1987, pp.552-557.
"Method and Cultural Discontinuity", in *Looking at Lonergan's Method*, P. Corcoran (ed), pp.127-143.

Liddy, Richard, *Transforming Light: Intellectual Conversion in the Early Lonergan*, Collegeville: Michael Glazier, 1993.

Lindbeck, George, *The Nature of Doctrine: Religion and Theology in a Postliberal Age*, Philadelphia: The Westminster Press, 1984.

Loewe, William, "Jesus, the Son of God", in *Desires of the Heart: An Introduction to the Theology of Bernard Lonergan*, V. Gregson (ed.) (Mahwah: Paulist Press, 1988), p.182-200.

MacIntyre, Alasdair, *After Virtue, a Study in Moral Theory*, 2nd Edition, Notre Dame: University of Notre Dame Press, 1984.
Whose Justice? Which Rationality?, Notre Dame: University of Notre Dame Press, 1988.
Three Rival Version of Moral Enquiry: Encyclopedia, Genealogy and Tradition, Notre Dame: University of Notre Dame Press, 1990.

Mackey, J. P., "Divine Revelation and Lonergan's Transcendental Method", *The Irish Theological Quarterly*, January, Vol.XL, no.1, 1973, pp.3-19, also in *Looking at Lonergan's Method*, P. Corcoran (ed), pp.144-163.

MacKinnon, Edward, "Linguistic Analysis and the Transcendence of God", *Proceeding of the Catholic Theological Society of America*, Vol.23, 1968.

McDermott, John, "Tensions in Lonergan's Theory of Conversion", *Gregorianum*, Vol.74, fasc.1, 1997, pp.101-140.
"Person and Nature in Lonergan's *De Deo Trino*", *Angelicum*, Vol.71, fasc.2, 1994, pp.153-185.

McShane, Philip (ed.), *Language, Truth and Meaning: Papers from the International Lonergan Conference 1970*, Dublin: Gill & Macmillan, 1972.

Mansini, Guy, "Quasi-Formal Causality an `Change in the Other': A Note on Karl Rahner's Christology", *The Thomist*, Vol.52, no.2, 1988, pp.293-306.

"Understanding St Thomas on Christ's Immediate Knowledge of God", *The Thomist*, Vol.59, no.1, 1995, pp.91-124.

Mascall, E.L., *The Openness of Being*, London: Darton, Longman and Todd, 1971.

Maxwell, Michael, "A Dialectical Encounter Between MacIntyre and Lonergan on the Thomistic Understanding of Rationality", *International Philosophical Quarterly*, Vol.33, no.4, 1993, pp.385-399.

Metz, Johann B., "An identity Crisis in Christianity? Transcendental and Political Responses", in *Theology and Discovery: Essays in Honor of Karl Rahner, S.J.*, W. Kelly (ed.), pp.169-178.

Faith in History and Society: Towards a Practical Fundamental Theology, London: Burns & Oates, 1980 (trans. David Smith).

Meyer, Ben, *Reality and Illusion in New Testament Scholarship: A Primer in Critical Realist Hermeneutics*, Collegeville: Glazier, 1994.

Moloney, Raymond, "The Mind of Christ in Transcendental Theology: Rahner, Lonergan and Crowe", *The Heythrop Journal*, Vol.XXV, no.3, 1984, pp.288-300.

Moran, Gabriel, *Theology of Revelation*, NY: Herder & Herder, 1966.

The Present Revelation, New York: Herder & Herder, 1972.

O'Callaghan, Michael, *Unity in Theology: Lonergan's Framework for Theology in Its New Context*, Washington: University Press of America, 1980.

"Rahner and Lonergan on Foundational Theology", in M. Lamb (ed.), *Creativity and Method: Essays in Honor of Bernard Lonergan S.J.*, pp.123-140.

O'Collins, Gerald, *Foundations of Theology*, Chicago: Loyola University Press, 1970.

Fundamental Theology, NY: Paulist Press, 1981.

"The Pope's theology", *The Tablet*, 27 June, 1992, p.801.

O'Donnell, John, *The Mystery of the Triune God*, London: Sheed and Ward, 1988.

Hans Urs von Balthasar, London: Geoffrey Chapmamn, 1992.

O'Donovan, Conn, "Translator's Introduction", *Way to Nicea*, London: Darton, Longman and Todd, 1976, pp.ix-xxix.

O'Donovan, Leo and Sanks, T. Howland (eds), *Faithful Witness: Foundations of Theology for Today's Church*, NY: Crossroad, 1989.

O'Leary, Joseph, "The Hermeneutics of Dogmatism", *Irish Theological Quarterly*, Vol.47, no.2, 1980, pp.96-118.

Ormerod, Neil, *The Holy Spirit: The Feeling of God* Melbourne: MCD, 1987, unpublished thesis.

"Schillebeeckx's Theological Prologomenon: A Dialectic Analysis", in W. Danaher (ed), *Australian Lonergan Workshop*, pp.69-78.

"The Transcultural Significance of the Council of Chalcedon", *Australasian Catholic Record*, Vol.LXX, no.3, 1993, pp.322-332.

Pannenberg, Wolfhart, et al., *Revelation as History*, London: Macmillan, 1968 (trans. David Granskou).

History and Hermeneutic, NY: Harper and Row, 1967.

Pannenberg, Wolfhart, "Dogmatic Theses on the Doctrine of Revelation", *Revelation as History*, Pannenberg, W., et al., London: Macmillan, 1968, pp.123-158.

Basic Questions in Theology, Vol.1-3, (trans. George Kehm), London: SCM Press, 1970,71,73.

"Hermeneutic and Universal History", in *History and Hermeneutic*, Pannenberg et al., pp.122-152.

"History and Meaning in Bernard Lonergan's Approach to Theological Method", in *Looking at Lonergan's Method*, P. Corcoran (ed), pp.88-100.

Polanyi, Michael, and Prosch, H., *Meaning*, Chicago: University of Chicago Press, 1975.

Polkinghorne, John, *Reason and Reality*, London: SPCK, 1991.

Quesnell, Quinten, "Beliefs and Authenticity", *Creativity and Method*, M. Lamb (ed.), Marquette University press, Milwaukee, 1981, pp.173-183.

Radcliffe, Timothy, "Interrogating the Consensus: a response to Michael Dummett", *New Blackfriars*, Vol.69, no.814, 1988, pp.116-126.

Rahner, Karl, "The Development of Dogma", *Theological Investigations*, Vol.1, London: Darton, Longman and Todd, 1961 (trans. C. Ernst), pp.39-78.

"Theos in the New Testament", *Theological Investigations*, Vol.1, pp.79-148.

"Considerations on the Development of Dogma", *Theological Investigations*, Vol.4, London: Darton, Longman and Todd, 1966 (trans. K. Smith), pp.3-35
"The Theology of Symbol", *Theological Investigations*, Vol.4, pp.221-252.
Spirit in the World, London: Sheed and Word, 1968.
Hearers of the Word, London: Sheed and Ward, 1969.
The Trinity, London: Burns & Oates, 1970 (trans. J Donceel).
"Kritische Bemerkungen zu B.J.F. Lonergan's Aufsatz: 'Functional Specialties in Theology'", *Gregorianum*, Vol.51, fasc.3, 1970, pp.537-540.
Foundations of Christian Faith: An Introduction to the Idea of Christianity, NY: Crossroad, 1982 (trans. W. Dych).
Ratzinger, Joseph, "Foundations and Approaches of Biblical Exgesis", *Origins NC Documentary Service*, Vol.17, no.35, February 11 1988, pp.593, 595-602.
Reiser, William, "The Primacy of Religious Experience in Theological Reflection", in F. Lawrence (ed.), *Lonergan Workshop*, Vol.IV, 1983, pp.99-113.
Reuther, Rosemary Radford, *Sexism and God-Talk: Toward a Feminist Theology*, Boston: Beacon Press, 1993, 10th anniverary edition.
Reynolds, Terrance, "Method Divorced from Content in Theology: An Assessment of Lonergan's *Method in Theology*", *The Thomist*, Vol.55, no.2, 1991, pp.245-269.
Ricoeur, Paul, *The Symbolism of Evil*, Boston: Beacon Press, 1969.
Rush, Ormond, "Reception Hermeneutics and the 'Development' of Doctrine", *Pacifica*, Vol.6, no.2, 1993, pp.125-140.
Russell, John, "The Theology of Revelation: Avery Dulles, S.J. and Gabriel Moran", *Irish Theological Quarterly*, Vol.54, no.1, 1988, pp.21-40.
Ryan, William, and Tyrell, Bernard, (eds), *Second Collection*, Philadelphia: Westminster Press, 1974.
Schner, George, "The Appeal to Experience", *Theological Studies*, Vol.53, no.1, 1992, pp.40-59.
Schillebeeckx, Edward, *Jesus, an Experiment in Christology*, London: Collins, 1979 (trans. H. Hoskins).
Christ, the Christian Experience in the Modern World, London: SCM Press, 1980 (trans. J. Bowden).

Interim Report on the Books Jesus & Christ, London: SCM Press, 1980 (trans. J. Bowden).

Church, the Human Story of God, NY: Crossroad, 1990 (trans. J. Bowden).

Schleiermacher, Friedrich, *The Christian Faith*, Edinburgh: T. & T. Clarke, 1928.

Stebbins, J. Michael, *The Divine Initiative: Grace, World-Order, and Human Freedom in the Early Writings of Bernard Lonergan*, Toronto: University of Toronto Press, 1995.

Stinnett, T.R., "Lonergan's Critical Realism and Religious Pluralism", *The Thomist*, Vol.56, no.1, 1992, pp.97-115.

Tekippe, Terry, "The Shape of Lonergan's Argument in Insight", *The Thomist*, Vol.36, no.4, 1972, pp.671-689.

"A Response to Donald Keefe on Lonergan", *The Thomist*, Vol.52, no.1, 1988, pp.88-95.

Tillich, Paul, *Systematic Theology*, Vol.1, Chicago: University of Chicago Press, 1951.

Tracy, David, *The Achievement of Bernard Lonergan*, NY: Herder and Herder, 1970.

The Analogical Imagination: Christian Theology and the Culture of Pluralism, London: SCM Press, 1981.

Torrance, T.F., "The Function of Inner and Outer Word in Lonergan's Theological Method", in *Looking at Lonergan's Method*, P. Corcoran (ed), pp.101-126.

Tupper, E. Frank, *The Theology of Wolfhart Pannenberg*, London: SCM Press, 1974.

Vass, George, *A Theologian in Search of a Philosophy, Understanding Karl Rahner*, Vol.1, London: Sheed & Ward, 1985.

The Mystery of Man and the Foundations of a Theological System, Understanding Karl Rahner, Vol.2, London: Sheed & Ward, 1985.

Vertin, Michael, "Philosophy of God, Theology and the Problems of Evil", in F. Lawrence (ed.), *Lonergan Workshop*, Vol.3, pp.149-178, 1982.

"Lonergan on Consciousness: Is There a Fifth Level?", *Method : Journal of Lonergan Studies*, Vol.12, no.1, 1994, pp.1-36.

Von Balthasar, Hans Urs, *The Glory of the Lord, A Theological Aesthetics*, Vol.1, *Seeing the Form*, (trans. E. Leiva Merikakis) Edinburgh: T. & T. Clark, 1982.

Love Alone: The Way of Revelation, London: Burns & Oates, 1968.

Word and Revelation, Herder and Herder, New York, 1964 (trans. A. V. Littledale).

H. Vorgrimler, *Understanding Karl Rahner: An Introduction to his Life and Thought*, NY: Crossroad, 1985.

INDEX

Note: Entries for Lonergan, which appears throughout the book, have not been listed.